A FAIR GLOBALIZATION:
CREATING OPPORTUNITIES FOR ALL

A FAIR GLOBALIZATION:
CREATING OPPORTUNITIES FOR ALL

World Commission on the Social
Dimension of Globalization

ISBN 92-2-115426-2

Created as an independent body, the World Commission on the Social Dimension of Globalization takes full and independent responsibility for this Report. A Secretariat established by the ILO supported the work of the Commission and provided substantive and administrative assistance, including printing facilities.

Photocomposed by the International Labour Office   DTP
Printed in Switzerland   ATA

The World Commission on the Social Dimension of Globalization

Co-Chairs:	H.E. Ms. Tarja Halonen, President of the Republic of Finland
	H.E. Mr. Benjamin William Mkapa, President of the United Republic of Tanzania
Members:	Giuliano Amato
	Ruth Cardoso
	Heba Handoussa
	Eveline Herfkens
	Ann McLaughlin Korologos
	Lu Mai
	Valentina Matvienko
	Deepak Nayyar
	Taizo Nishimuro
	François Perigot
	Surin Pitsuwan
	Julio Maria Sanguinetti
	Hernando de Soto
	Joseph Stiglitz
	John J. Sweeney
	Victoria Tauli-Corpuz
	Aminata D. Traoré
	Zwelinzima Vavi
	Ernst Ulrich von Weizsaecker
Ex officio members:	Bill Brett
	Eui-yong Chung
	Daniel Funes de Rioja
	Juan Somavia
	Alain Ludovic Tou

PREFACE

In his address to the United Nations General Assembly on 23 September 2003, the United Nations Secretary-General, Kofi Annan, succinctly warned the world body that it had "come to a fork in the road." We, the Co-Chairs of the World Commission on the Social Dimension of Globalization, believe the world stands at a historic moment of decision.

The Commission was established to address some of the challenges facing the world as it stands at this fork. As human beings, it is in our power to take a correct turn, which would make the world safer, fair, ethical, inclusive and prosperous for the majority, not just for a few, within countries and between countries. It is also in our power to prevaricate, to ignore the road signs, and let the world we all share slide into further spirals of political turbulence, conflicts and wars.

We believe we have in these following pages enough of the case for political leaders, nationally and internationally, to be persuaded to take the correct turn.

Currently, globalization is a divisive subject. It verges on a dialogue of the deaf, both nationally and internationally. Yet the future of our countries, and the destiny of our globe, demands that we all rethink globalization. This report is timely. The debate is changing. Old convictions and ideologies have been tested by experience, and changed by example. People are open to a fresh start. Now is the time for leadership, to move from sterile debate to positive action.

We believe that, in this report, we have looked at globalization through the eyes of the people, rising above our constituencies and capturing faithfully the hopes and fears of our shared humanity. Many recognize the opportunities for a better life that globalization presents. We believe their hopes are realizable, but only if globalization is subjected to better governance at all levels. More people than ever before do not want to be left behind by the globalization train; but they want to be sure where it is heading, and that it is travelling at survivable speed.

Our driving spirit has been to make globalization a positive force for all people and countries. We propose no panaceas or simple solutions; instead we suggest a new perspective.

We believe the dominant perspective on globalization must shift more from a narrow preoccupation with markets to a broader preoccupation with people. Globalization must be brought from the high pedestal of corporate board rooms and cabinet meetings to meet the needs of people in the communities in which they live. The social dimension of globalization is about jobs, health and education – but it goes far beyond these. It is the dimension of globalization which people experience in their daily life and work: the totality of their aspirations for democratic participation and material prosperity. A better globalization is the key to a better and secure life for people everywhere in the 21st century.

We also propose a process by which such a perspective can be realized at all levels, beginning with empowered local communities and improved and more accountable national governance; fair global rules applied fairly; and global institutions that are more pro-people.

We propose a series of actions – each small in themselves. Yet taken together they will set in train a process to achieve this goal by stimulating and energizing the networks of people and ideas and the economic and social interactions of globalization itself.

Our experience working in the Commission makes us confident of the future. The Commission is a microcosm of the very wide diversity of opinion, concerns and perspectives of the real world. We come from some of the wealthiest and poorest countries. We comprise trade unionists and corporate leaders, parliamentarians and presidents, leaders of indigenous peoples and women's activists, scholars and government advisors. We have seen, in the course of our work, how divergent positions can be spanned and how common interests can lead to common action through dialogue.

The Commission was established by the ILO. It had full and independent responsibility for its Report, and members of the Commission served in their individual capacity. The members of the Commission do not each subscribe to every statement in the text, but they endorse the Report as a whole to stimulate a wider process of public dialogue and common endeavour which will promote a fair and inclusive globalization.

It was a great pleasure and a uniquely enriching experience for us, the Co-Chairs, to work with a Commission composed of such a distinguished, thoroughly committed and energetic group of global citizens. We thank them wholeheartedly for their dedication, contribution and cooperation. We thank the very capable Secretariat that served us so well. And we are grateful to the ILO for the decision to constitute such a Commission and to honour us with the historic responsibility to chair it.

To the world, and especially to political and corporate leaders everywhere, we present these pointers to a better globalization, a better future for people – all people.

Tarja Halonen
President of the Republic of Finland;
Co-Chair

Benjamin William Mkapa
President of the United Republic
of Tanzania; Co-Chair

SYNOPSIS

Introduction

Our remit, the Social Dimension of Globalization, is a vast and complex one. As a Commission we were broadly representative of the diverse and contending actors and interests that exist in the real world. Co-chaired by two serving Heads of State, a woman and a man, from North and South, we came from countries in different parts of the world and at all stages of development. Our affiliations were equally diverse: government, politics, parliaments, business and multinational corporations, organized labour, academia and civil society.

Yet, through a spirit of common purpose, we arrived at the shared understandings that are before you. As a collective document it is quite different from alternative reports each one of us would have written individually. But our experience has demonstrated the value and power of dialogue as an instrument for change. Through listening patiently and respectfully to diverse views and interests we found common ground.

We were spurred on by the realization that action to build a fair and inclusive process of globalization was urgent. This could only happen in the future through forging agreements among a broad spectrum of actors on the course for action. We are convinced that our experience can and should be replicated on a larger and wider scale, expanding the space for dialogue aimed at building consensus for action.

A vision for change

Public debate on globalization is at an impasse. Opinion is frozen in the ideological certainties of entrenched positions and fragmented in a variety of special interests. The will for consensus is weak. Key international negotiations are deadlocked and international development commitments go largely unfulfilled.

The report before you offers no miraculous or simple solutions, for there are none. But it is an attempt to help break the current impasse by focusing on the concerns and aspirations of people and on the ways to better harness the potential of globalization itself.

Ours is a critical but positive message for changing the current path of globalization. We believe the benefits of globalization can be extended to more people and better shared between and within countries, with many more voices having an influence on its course. The resources and the means are at hand. Our proposals are ambitious but feasible. We are certain that a better world is possible.

We seek a process of globalization with a strong social dimension based on universally shared values, and respect for human rights and individual dignity; one that is fair, inclusive, democratically governed and provides opportunities and tangible benefits for all countries and people.

To this end we call for:

- *A focus on people.* The cornerstone of a fairer globalization lies in meeting the demands of all people for: respect for their rights, cultural identity and autonomy; decent work; and the empowerment of the local communities they live in. Gender equality is essential.

- *A democratic and effective State.* The State must have the capability to manage integration into the global economy, and provide social and economic opportunity and security.

- *Sustainable development.* The quest for a fair globalization must be underpinned by the interdependent and mutually reinforcing pillars of economic development, social development and environmental protection at the local, national, regional and global levels.

- *Productive and equitable markets.* This requires sound institutions to promote opportunity and enterprise in a well-functioning market economy.

- *Fair rules.* The rules of the global economy must offer equitable opportunity and access for all countries and recognize the diversity in national capacities and developmental needs.

- *Globalization with solidarity.* There is a shared responsibility to assist countries and people excluded from or disadvantaged by globalization. Globalization must help to overcome inequality both within and between countries and contribute to the elimination of poverty.

- *Greater accountability to people.* Public and private actors at all levels with power to influence the outcomes of globalization must be democratically accountable for the policies they pursue and the actions they take. They must deliver on their commitments and use their power with respect for others.

- *Deeper partnerships.* Many actors are engaged in the realization of global social and economic goals – international organizations, governments and parliaments, business, labour, civil society and many others. Dialogue and partnership among them is an essential democratic instrument to create a better world.

- *An effective United Nations.* A stronger and more efficient multilateral system is the key instrument to create a democratic, legitimate and coherent framework for globalization.

Globalization and its impact

Globalization has set in motion a process of far-reaching change that is affecting everyone. New technology, supported by more open policies, has created a world more interconnected than ever before. This spans not only growing interdependence in economic relations – trade, investment, finance and the organization of production globally – but also social and political interaction among organizations and individuals across the world.

The potential for good is immense. The growing interconnectivity among people across the world is nurturing the realization that we are all part of a global community. This nascent sense of interdependence, commitment to shared universal values, and solidarity among peoples across the world can be channelled to build enlightened and democratic global governance in the interests of all. The global market economy has demonstrated great productive capacity. Wisely managed, it can deliver unprecedented material progress, generate more productive and better jobs for all, and contribute significantly to reducing world poverty.

But we also see how far short we still are from realizing this potential. The current process of globalization is generating unbalanced outcomes, both between and within countries. Wealth is being created, but too many countries and people are not sharing in its benefits. They also have little or no voice in shaping the process. Seen through the eyes of the vast majority of women and men, globalization has not met their simple and legitimate aspirations for decent jobs and a better future for their children. Many of them live in the limbo of the informal economy without formal rights and in a swathe of poor countries that subsist precariously on the margins of the global economy. Even in economically successful countries some workers and communities have been adversely affected by globalization. Meanwhile the revolution in global communications heightens awareness of these disparities.

A strategy for change

These global imbalances are morally unacceptable and politically unsustainable. What is required to change this is not the realization of a Utopian blueprint in one swoop. Rather it is a series of coordinated changes across a broad front, ranging from reform of parts of the global economic system to strengthening governance at the local level. All this should and can be achieved in the context of open economies and open societies. Though interests diverge, we believe that there is increasing convergence of opinion throughout the world on the need for a fair and inclusive process of globalization.

We have formulated a wide-ranging set of recommendations to realize this. Given the necessary political will, immediate action is feasible on some trade and financial issues that have been the subject of protracted multilateral negotiations and discussion in policy circles. On these issues, the required course of action is clear but the urgent need for change has not yet dawned on some major players. Here continued advocacy and a stronger public opinion is essential to carry the proposals forward. Advocacy to prepare the ground for the consideration of new issues will also be important. But on these newer issues, such as the development of a multilateral framework for the cross-border movement of people or the accountability of international organizations, the prime lever for the decision to act is broad-based dialogue among State and non-State actors. Through this, consensus and resolve can be forged on what needs to be done, how, and by whom.

The governance of globalization

We judge that the problems we have identified are not due to globalization as such but to deficiencies in its governance. Global markets have grown rapidly without the parallel development of economic and social institutions necessary for their smooth and equitable functioning. At the same time, there is concern about the unfairness of key global rules on trade and finance and their asymmetric effects on rich and poor countries.

An additional concern is the failure of current international policies to respond adequately to the challenges posed by globalization. Market opening measures and financial and economic considerations predominate over social ones. Official Development Assistance (ODA) falls far short of the minimum amounts required even for achieving the Millennium Development Goals (MDGs) and tackling growing global problems. The multilateral system responsible for designing and implementing international policies is also under-performing. It lacks policy coherence as a whole and is not sufficiently democratic, transparent and accountable.

These rules and policies are the outcome of a system of global governance largely shaped by powerful countries and powerful players. There is a serious democratic deficit at the heart of the system. Most developing countries still have very limited influence in global negotiations on rules and in determining the policies of key financial and economic institutions. Similarly, workers and the poor have little or no voice in this governance process.

Beginning at home

There is thus a wide range of issues to be addressed at the global level. But this alone will not suffice. Global governance is not a lofty, disembodied sphere. It is merely the apex of a web of governance that stretches from the local level upwards. The behaviour of nation States as global actors is the essential determinant of the quality of global governance. Their degree of commitment to multilateralism, universal values and common goals, the extent of their sensitivity to the cross-border impact of their policies, and the weight they attach to global solidarity are all vital determinants of the quality of global governance. At the same time, how they manage their internal affairs influences the extent to which people will benefit from globalization and be protected from its negative effects. In this important sense the response to globalization can be said to begin at home. This reflects the simple but crucial fact that people live locally within nations.

We therefore anchor our analysis at the national level. We do not, of course, presume to make specific recommendations for all the greatly diverse countries of the world. Rather, we set out the broad goals and principles that can guide policy to deal more effectively with the social dimension of globalization, fully recognizing that their implementation must respond to the needs and specific conditions of each country. From this perspective it is clear that national governance needs to be improved in all countries, albeit more radically in some than in others. There is wide international agreement on the essentials which we must all urgently strive for:

- good political governance based on a democratic political system, respect for human rights, the rule of law and social equity.

- an effective State that ensures high and stable economic growth, provides public goods and social protection, raises the capabilities of people through universal access to education and other social services, and promotes gender equity.

- a vibrant civil society, empowered by freedom of association and expression, that reflects and voices the full diversity of views and interests. Organizations representing public interests, the poor and other disadvantaged groups are also essential for ensuring participatory and socially just governance.

- strong representative organizations of workers and employers are essential for fruitful social dialogue.

The highest priority must be given to policies to meet the central aspiration of women and men for decent work; to raise the productivity of the informal economy and to integrate it into the economic mainstream; and to enhance the competitiveness of enterprises and economies.

Policy must focus squarely on meeting peoples' needs where they live and work. It is thus essential to nurture local communities through the devolution of power and resources and through strengthening local economic capabilities, cultural identity, and respecting the rights of indigenous and tribal peoples.

Nation States should also strengthen regional and sub-regional cooperation as a major instrument for development and for a stronger voice in the governance of globalization. They should reinforce the social dimension of regional integration.

Reform at the global level

At the global level, we have more specific recommendations to make. Some key ones are highlighted below.

Global rules and policies on trade and finance must allow more space for policy autonomy in developing countries. This is essential for developing policies and institutional arrangements best suited to their level of development and specific circumstances. Existing rules that unduly restrict their policy options for accelerating agricultural growth and industrialization and for maintaining financial and economic stability need to be reviewed. New rules must also respect this requirement. The policies of international organizations and donor countries must also shift more decisively away from external conditionality to national ownership of policies. Affirmative action provisions in favour of countries that do not have the same capabilities as those who developed earlier need to be strengthened.

Fair rules for trade and capital flows need to be complemented by fair rules for the cross-border movement of people. International migratory pressures have increased and problems such as trafficking in people and the exploitation of migrant workers have intensified. Steps have to be taken to build a multilateral framework that provides uniform and transparent rules for the cross-border movement of people and balances the interests of both migrants themselves and of countries of origin and destination. All countries stand to benefit from an orderly and managed process of international migration that can enhance global productivity and eliminate exploitative practices.

Global production systems have proliferated, generating the need for new rules on Foreign Direct Investment (FDI) and on competition. A balanced and development-friendly multilateral framework for FDI, negotiated in a generally accepted forum, will benefit all countries by promoting increased direct investment flows while limiting the problems of incentive competition which reduce the benefits from these flows. Such a framework should balance private, workers' and public interests, as well as their rights and responsibilities. Cooperation on cross-border competition policy will make global markets more transparent and competitive.

Core labour standards as defined by the ILO provide a minimum set of global rules for labour in the global economy and respect for them should be strengthened in all countries. Stronger action is required to ensure respect for core labour standards in Export Processing Zones (EPZs) and, more generally, in global production systems. All relevant international institutions should assume their part in promoting these standards and ensure that no aspect of their policies and programmes impedes implementation of these rights.

The multilateral trading system should substantially reduce unfair barriers to market access for goods in which developing countries have comparative advantage, especially textiles and garments and agricultural products. In doing so, the interests of the Least Developed Countries (LDCs) should be safeguarded through special and differential treatment to nurture their export potential.

A minimum level of social protection for individuals and families needs to be accepted and undisputed as part of the socio-economic 'floor' of the global economy, including adjustment assistance to displaced workers. Donors and financial institutions should contribute to the strengthening of social protection systems in developing countries.

Greater market access is not a panacea. A more balanced strategy for sustainable global growth and full employment, including an equitable sharing among countries of the responsibility for maintaining high levels of effective demand in the global economy, is essential. Enhanced coordination of macroeconomic policies among countries to this end is a key requirement. A successful global growth strategy will ease economic tensions among countries and make market access for developing countries easier to achieve.

Decent Work for all should be made a global goal and be pursued through coherent policies within the multilateral system. This would respond to a major political demand in all countries and demonstrate the capacity of the multilateral system to find creative solutions to this critical problem.

The international financial system should be made more supportive of sustainable global growth. Cross-border financial flows have grown massively but the system is unstable, prone to crises and largely bypasses poor and capital scarce countries. Gains in the spheres of trade and FDI cannot be fully reaped unless the international financial system is reformed to achieve greater stability. In this context developing countries should be permitted to adopt a cautious and gradual approach to capital account liberalization and more socially sensitive sequencing of adjustment measures in response to crises.

A greater effort is required to mobilize more international resources to attain key global goals, particularly the MDGs. The 0.7 per cent target for ODA must be met and new sources for funding over and above this target should be actively explored and developed.

The implementation of reforms in international economic and social policy will require worldwide political support, the commitment of key global actors, and the strengthening of global institutions. The UN multilateral system constitutes the core of global governance and is uniquely equipped to spearhead the process of reform. For it to cope with the current and emerging challenges of globalization it has to enhance its effectiveness and improve the quality of its governance, especially with respect to democratic representation and decision-making, accountability to people, and policy coherence.

We call on developed countries to reconsider their decision to maintain zero nominal growth in their mandated contributions to the UN system. It is essential that the international community agree to increase financial contributions to the multilateral system and reverse the trend towards raising voluntary contributions at the expense of mandatory ones.

Heads of State and Government should ensure that the policies pursued by their countries in international fora are coherent and focus on the well-being of people.

Parliamentary oversight of the multilateral system at the global level should be progressively expanded. We propose the creation of a Parliamentary Group concerned with the coherence and consistency between global economic, social and environmental policies, which should develop an integrated oversight of major international organizations.

A critical requirement for better global governance is that all organizations, including UN agencies, should become more accountable to the public at large for the policies they pursue. National parliaments should contribute to this process by regularly reviewing decisions taken by their countries' representatives to these organizations.

Developing countries should have increased representation in the decision-making bodies of the Bretton Woods Institutions, while the working methods in the World Trade Organization (WTO) should provide for their full and effective participation in its negotiations.

Greater voice should be given to non-State actors, especially representative organizations of the poor.

The contributions of business, organized labour, civil society organizations (CSOs), and of knowledge and advocacy networks to the social dimension of globalization should be strengthened.

Responsible media can play a central role in facilitating a movement towards a fairer and more inclusive globalization. Well-informed public opinion on issues raised in this Report is essential to underpin change. Policies everywhere therefore need to emphasize the importance of diversity in information and communication flows.

Mobilizing action for change

We believe that broad-based dialogue on our recommendations, especially on issues that are not currently being negotiated on the global agenda, is the essential first step in mobilizing action for change. It is of primary importance that such dialogue begins at the national level in order to construct the foundations of the necessary consensus and political will.

At the same time the multilateral system has to play a pivotal role in carrying forward reforms at the global level. We propose a new operational tool for upgrading the quality of policy coordination between international organizations on issues in which the implementation of their mandates intersect and their policies interact. Policy Coherence Initiatives should be launched by the relevant international organizations to develop more balanced policies for achieving a fair and inclusive globalization. The objective would be to progressively develop integrated policy proposals that appropriately balance economic, social, and environmental concerns on specific issues. The first initiative should address the question of global growth, investment, and employment creation and involve relevant UN bodies, the World Bank, the International Monetary Fund (IMF), the WTO, and the ILO. Priority areas for other such initiatives include gender equality and the empowerment of women; education; health; food security; and human settlements.

A series of multi-stakeholder Policy Development Dialogues should also be organized by relevant international organizations to further consider and develop key policy proposals – such as a multilateral framework for the cross-border movement of people, a development framework for FDI, the strengthening of social protection in the global economy, and new forms of accountability of international organizations.

A Globalization Policy Forum should be organized by the UN and its specialized agencies to review on a regular and systematic basis the social impact of globalization. Participating organizations could produce a periodic 'State of Globalization Report'.

Our proposals call for a wider and more democratic participation of people and countries in the making of policies that affect them. And they also require those with the capacity and power to decide – governments, parliaments, business, labour, civil society and international organizations – to assume their common responsibility to promote a free, equitable and productive global community.

ACRONYMS AND ABBREVIATIONS

AIDS	Acquired Immune Deficiency Syndrome
APEC	Asia and Pacific Economic Cooperation
AU	African Union
BIT	Bilateral Investment Treaty
CSO	Civil Society Organization
CSR	Corporate Social Responsibility
ECOSOC	United Nations Economic and Social Council
EPZ	Export Processing Zone
EU	European Union
FAO	Food and Agriculture Organization of the United Nations
FDI	Foreign Direct Investment
FSA	Financial Sector Assessment
G7	Group of 7
G8	Group of 8
G10	Group of 10
G77	Group of 77
GATS	General Agreement on Trade and Services
GATT	General Agreement on Tariffs and Trade
GAVI	Global Alliance for Vaccines and Immunization
GDLN	Global Distance Learning Network
GDP	Gross Domestic Product
GSP	Generalized System of Preferences
HIPC	Debt Initiative for Heavily Indebted Poor Countries
HIV	Human Immunodeficiency Virus
ICC	International Chamber of Commerce
ICFTU	International Confederation of Free Trade Unions
ICT	Information and Communications Technology
IFAD	International Fund for Agricultural Development
IFF	International Financing Facility
IFIs	International Financial Institutions
IMF	International Monetary Fund
ILO	International Labour Organization
IOE	International Organisation of Employers
IOM	International Organization for Migration
IPRs	Intellectual Property Rights
IPU	Inter-Parliamentary Union
IT	Information Technology
ITU	International Telecommunications Union
LDCs	Least Developed Countries
MAI	Multilateral Agreement on Investment

MDGs	Millennium Development Goals
Mercosur	Southern Cone Common Market
MNEs	Multinational Enterprises
NAFTA	North American Free Trade Agreement
NEPAD	New Partnership for African Development
NGO	Non-governmental Organization
NIE	Newly Industrializing Economy
ODA	Official Development Assistance
OECD	Organization for Economic Cooperation and Development
OHCHR	Office of the High Commissioner for Human Rights
PRSP	Poverty Reduction Strategy Papers
R&D	Research and Development
ROSC	Review of Standards and Codes
SADC	Southern African Development Community
SCM	Subsidies and Countervailing Measures
SDRs	Special Drawing Rights
SMEs	Small and Medium-sized Enterprises
SRI	Socially Responsible Investment
TPRM	Trade Policy Review Mechanism
TRIMs	Trade-Related Investment Measures
TRIPS	Trade-Related Aspects of Intellectual Property Rights
UN	United Nations
UNCTAD	United Nations Conference on Trade and Development
UNDP	United Nations Development Programme
UNEP	United Nations Environment Programme
UNESCO	United Nations Educational, Scientific and Cultural Organization
UNHCR	United Nations High Commissioner for Refugees
UNIDO	United Nations Industrial Development Organization
UNIFEM	United Nations Development Fund for Women
UNODC	United Nations Office on Drugs and Crime
WCL	World Confederation of Labour
WHO	World Health Organization
WTO	World Trade Organization

CONTENTS

I. GLOBALIZATION FOR PEOPLE: A VISION FOR CHANGE

Where do we stand today?

Where do we want to go?

How do we get there?

A stronger ethical framework

Towards a global community: Strengthening dialogue and governance

1. The current path of globalization must change. Too few share in its benefits. Too many have no voice in its design and no influence on its course.

2. The results of globalization are what we make of it. They depend on the policies, rules and institutions which govern its course; the values which inspire its actors; and their capacity to influence the process.

3. We, the members of the World Commission represent a very wide diversity of opinion and interests, which are often polarized in the public debates on globalization. But we have come to agreement on a common goal: a fair globalization which creates opportunities for all. We wish to make globalization a means to expand human well-being and freedom, and to bring democracy and development to local communities where people live. Our aim is to build a consensus for common action to realize this vision, and to foster a process of sustained engagement to this end by the actors themselves, including States, international organizations, business, labour and civil society.

4. Ours is a critical but positive message. We believe the benefits of globalization can be expanded; its results better shared; and many of its problems resolved. The resources and the means are at hand. Our proposals are ambitious but feasible. We are certain that a better world is possible.

5. We seek a process which is fair, and which gives all women and men the rights, opportunities and capabilities they need to exercise their own choices for a decent life.

6. We reaffirm the value of values, and the importance of human rights in guiding the governance of globalization, and in defining the responsibilities of its actors.

7. We call for a more cohesive governance of globalization with policies to better link economic growth with social progress and environmental sustainability.

8. We must be realistic. Globalization has many aspects, but our mandate is to focus on its social dimension. We also recognize the many different dialogues and initiatives which are under way and seek to encourage and build on them.

9. Globalization is being judged by what it delivers. Although many of the ills of the world today – poverty, the lack of decent work, the denial of human rights – existed long before the present phase of globalization, there has been growing exclusion and deprivation in certain regions of the world. For many, globalization has dislocated traditional livelihoods and local communities, and threatens environmental sustainability and cultural diversity. As the current process of cross-border interaction and interconnectivity gathers speed, there is increasing debate not only about inequalities between countries but also about inequalities within countries, and its effects on people, families and communities. These concerns lie at the heart of politics. The debate on globalization is fast becoming a debate on democracy and social justice in a global economy.

10. We recognize that globalization has opened the door to many benefits. It has promoted open societies and open economies and encouraged a freer exchange of goods, ideas and knowledge. In many parts of the world, innovation, creativity and entrepreneurship have flourished. In East Asia, growth lifted over 200 million people out of poverty in a single decade. Better communications have enhanced awareness of rights and identities, and enabled social movements to mobilize opinion and strengthen democratic accountability. As a result, a truly global conscience is beginning to emerge, sensitive to the inequities of poverty, gender discrimination, child labour, and environmental degradation, wherever these may occur.

11. Yet there is growing concern about the direction globalization is currently taking. Its advantages are too distant for too many, while its risks are all too real. Its volatility threatens both rich and poor. Immense riches are being generated. But fundamental problems of poverty, exclusion and inequality persist. Corruption is widespread. Open societies are threatened by global terrorism, and the future of open markets is increasingly in question. Global governance is in crisis. We are at a critical juncture, and we need to urgently rethink our current policies and institutions.

Where do we stand today?

12. There are deep-seated and persistent imbalances in the current workings of the global economy, which are ethically unacceptable and politically unsustainable. They arise from a fundamental imbalance between the economy, society and the polity. The economy is becoming increasingly global, while social and political institutions remain largely local, national or regional. None of the existing global institutions provide adequate democratic oversight of global markets, or redress basic inequalities between countries. These imbalances point to the need for better institutional frameworks and policies if the promise of globalization is to be realized.

13. The imbalance between the economy and society is subverting social justice.

- There is a growing divide between a formal global economy and the expansion of an informal local economy in most societies. The majority of the world's people, who live and work in the informal economy, continue to be excluded from directly participating in markets and globalization on a fair and equal basis. They enjoy none of the property and other rights, nor the capabilities and assets they need to enter into productive economic transactions.

- The benefits of globalization have been unequally distributed, both within and between countries. There is growing polarization between winners and losers. The gap between rich and poor countries has widened. In sub-Saharan

Africa and Latin America, more people lived in poverty at the end of the 1990s than at the beginning of that decade.

- There is imbalance in the global rules. Economic rules and institutions prevail over social rules and social institutions, while the effectiveness of existing rules and institutions themselves are being tested by current global realities. Trade in manufactures is liberalized, while agriculture remains protected. Goods and capital move much more freely across borders than people do. In times of crisis, developed countries have wider options for macroeconomic policy, while developing countries are constrained by demands for adjustment. International policies are too often implemented without regard for national specificities. Unbalanced global rules can reinforce initial inequalities. The rules of world trade today often favour the rich and powerful, and can work against the poor and the weak, whether these are countries, companies or communities.

- Structural change, without adequate social and economic provision for adjustment has brought uncertainty and insecurity to workers and businesses everywhere, both in the North and in the South. Women, indigenous peoples, and the working poor without skills and assets, are among the most vulnerable. Unemployment and underemployment remain stubborn realities for the majority of the world's population.

14. The imbalance between the economy and the polity is undermining democratic accountability.

15. Institutions for governance today – whether national or international – do not adequately meet the new demands of people and countries for representation and voice.

- Globalization has made public opinion a potent political power in its own right. It now presses insistently on all established political institutions – ranging from national States and political parties to international organizations – creating new tensions between representative and participative democracy. International organizations, in particular the United Nations, the Bretton Woods institutions and the World Trade Organization (WTO), have come under increasing pressure for fairer decision-making and greater public accountability. There is a lack of public trust in global decision-making.

- Global markets lack institutions for public supervision which, in many countries, provide national markets with legitimacy and stability. The present process of globalization has no means to keep the balance between democracy and markets.

- In many countries, the compulsion of international markets is seen to narrow the options available for national economic policies. Many people feel that this abridges national sovereignty and shifts power from elected governments to transnational corporations and international financial institutions.

16. Everywhere, expectations have run ahead of opportunities, and resentments have clouded hope. At the same time, people recognize the reality of globalization, and few wish to opt out or reverse the process. They are in favour of freer cross-border exchanges of ideas, knowledge, goods and services. What women and men seek is respect for their dignity and cultural identity. They ask for opportunities to earn a decent living. They expect globalization to bring tangible benefits to their daily lives and ensure a better future for their children. And they wish to have a voice in the governance of the process, including the extent and nature of the integration of their economies and communities into the global market, and to participate more fairly in its outcome.

17. We believe it essential to respond to these aspirations. The potential of globalization must be used to create a better world.

Where do we want to go?

18. Our vision is of a process of globalization which puts people first; which respects human dignity and the equal worth of every human being.

19. We seek a more inclusive process which is fair and brings benefit and real opportunities to more people and more countries; and one which is more democratically governed.

20. We seek a globalization with a social dimension which sustains human values and enhances the well-being of people, in terms of their freedom, prosperity and security. Globalization is seen through the eyes of women and men in terms of the opportunity it provides for decent work; for meeting their essential needs for food, water, health, education and shelter and for a liveable environment. Without such a social dimension, many will continue to view globalization as a new version of earlier forms of domination and exploitation.

21. The essentials of this social dimension include:

- A process of globalization based on universally shared values, which require all actors – including States, international organizations, business, labour, civil society and the media – to assume their individual responsibilities. It demands respect for obligations and duties under international law. And it requires economic development to be based on respect for human rights.

- An international commitment to ensure the basic material and other requirements of human dignity for all, enshrined in the Universal Declaration of Human Rights. The eradication of poverty and the attainment of the Millennium Development Goals (MDGs) should be seen as the first steps towards a socio-economic 'floor' for the global economy.

- A sustainable path of development which provides opportunities for all, expands sustainable livelihoods and employment, promotes gender equality, and reduces disparities between countries and people. It calls for greater coherence between economic, social and environmental policies.

- A more democratic governance of globalization, which allows for greater voice and participation, and ensures accountability, while fully respecting the authority of institutions of representative democracy and the rule of law.

22. This is a realizable vision. The resources exist to overcome the most pressing problems of poverty, disease and education. Mahatma Gandhi put it very simply: "There is enough in the world for everybody's need, but there cannot be enough for everybody's greed".

How do we get there?

23. Our greatest asset is the multilateral system of the United Nations, which is essential for global action. Recent events have dramatically highlighted its importance in the changing world in which we live. The events of September 11 and global terrorism have brought home the reality of our common vulnerability and the need for unified action. The erosion of organized society through disease, civil strife and the collapse of governance in various parts of the world have reinforced the need for multilateral cooperation and collective action. There is growing recognition that solutions to these problems cannot be sought independently of the context of a globalizing and interdependent world.

24. Globalization is making multilateralism both indispensable and inevitable. The multilateral system of the United Nations and its related organizations provide the basis for the global policies which are needed in the areas of development, trade, finance and international peace and security, as well as in a variety of social and technical fields. Its declarations and covenants reflect universally shared values, and universal participation gives the multilateral system a global legitimacy which no individual state, however powerful, can match. It provides a time-tested framework to guide the process of globalization in accordance with the international rule of law.

25. There is no durable alternative which can respond to the needs and aspirations of people in an interdependent world. Multilateralism ensures transparency, and provides protection – however inadequate – against the asymmetries of power and influence in the international community. But, globalization is also making multilateralism an increasingly valuable asset for the rich and the powerful. It has become essential to their prosperity and security. In a world with emerging centres of economic power and vast sources of untapped consumer demand, a rule-based multilateral system is the only means of ensuring a fair and sustainable expansion of global markets. In an unstable world, such a system also ensures that bilateral economic conflicts do not automatically translate into bilateral political conflicts. And the proliferating demands of global security make multilateral cooperation essential for all, including the most powerful countries.

26. However, at the very moment when it is most needed, multilateralism has come under challenge. The conflicts in the Middle East, and the persistence of global poverty and inequality, have demonstrated the urgent need to bring together the contemporary realities of state power and public opinion in a durable alliance for peace and development.

27. The United Nations system and its Member States have to adjust to a globalizing world. The current structures and workings of the multilateral system are premised on the post-war balance of power between Member States. But globalization is changing the underlying configurations of economic and political power, and the strains are being felt in the United Nations system. The multilateral system also has to accommodate insistent demands from developing countries for a larger role in decision-making, and from civil society for greater voice and transparency. Many of these tensions have been building over the years. As globalization gains momentum, they have broken out into the open, disrupting international negotiations, leading to anger and frustration for all parties, and diminishing the effectiveness of international organizations.

28. This situation must be redressed. As Kofi Annan said, we need "stronger international solidarity and responsibility, together with greater respect for decisions reached collectively and greater determination to put them into effect. The question that inevitably arises is whether it is sufficient to exhort States and individuals to more enlightened attitudes and greater efforts, or whether a radical reform of our international institutions is also needed. My own view is that Member States need at least to take a hard look at the existing 'architecture' of international institutions and to ask themselves whether it is adequate for the tasks we have set before us".[1] We fully support the view of the Secretary-General.

29. We need to devise better instruments for the governance of globalization, and the functioning of the multilateral system. Specific proposals are made in Parts III and IV of the Report for more coherent international policies and institutional reform.

---

[1] UN: Implementation of the United Nations Millennium Declaration: Report of the Secretary-General (General Assembly, A/58/323, 2003).

30. A fairer globalization has to be built upon a productive and equitable global economic system.

31. An open market economy is today generally recognized as the necessary foundation for development, growth and productivity. No country can today opt out of the global economy. The challenge is to manage interaction with global markets to ensure growth, development and equity. That requires successful and responsible enterprises, which can generate jobs, wealth and innovation and contribute to public resources, as well as strong and representative organizations of employers and workers, to ensure sustainable growth and equitable distribution of its outcomes.

32. Efficient markets require effective States. If countries are to benefit from globalization, they need a State which can develop the institutional capabilities – both social and economic – needed for sound and equitable economic growth. Local action is as important as national and global action. Strong and democratic local authorities and communities are central to effective States.

33. Better governance of globalization must enlarge the space for national policy to stimulate enterprise development, employment creation, poverty reduction and gender equality. It must reinforce social protection and enhance skills and capabilities. It must support action to overcome informality, inequality and exclusion. It must help each country and community to define its own path of growth and development and achieve its own social and economic goals. Better governance of globalization to ensure sustainable development requires greater coherence between economic and social policies.

34. Good governance at all levels of society – in terms of the rule of law, democracy, human rights and social equity – is essential for a fair and productive process of globalization. It ensures the public accountability of both the State and private actors, as well as the efficiency of markets. No country – whether rich or poor, North or South – has a monopoly of good governance, and there is no unique institutional model to achieve it.

35. We do not seek the utopian refuge of world government. We recognize the realities of power and inequality. But we draw our inspiration from the determination of men and women today to exercise greater control over their own destinies, and from the potential of a fairer and more inclusive globalization to deliver on their needs.

36. Where do we begin?

A stronger ethical framework

37. The governance of globalization must be based on universally shared values and respect for human rights. Globalization has developed in an ethical vacuum, where market success and failure have tended to become the ultimate standard of behaviour, and where the attitude of "the winner takes all" weakens the fabric of communities and societies.

38. There is today a deep-seated desire by people to reaffirm basic ethical values in public life, as seen, for example, in calls for a more "ethical globalization". Values are also the driving force behind the many public campaigns for universal causes, ranging from the abolition of child labour to the banning of landmines.

39. Cohesive societies are built around shared values, which create a moral and ethical framework for private and public action. Globalization has not yet created

a global society, but the increased interaction between people and countries throws into sharp relief the urgent need for a common ethical frame of reference.

40. To a large extent, such a framework can already be found in the declarations and treaties of the multilateral system of the United Nations. They are enshrined, for example, in the Charter of the United Nations, the Universal Declaration of Human Rights, the ILO Declaration on Fundamental Principles and Rights at Work and, more recently, in the United Nations Millennium Declaration. These universal values and principles represent the common ground of the world's spiritual and secular beliefs. They must provide the foundation for the process of globalization. They should be reflected in the rules of the global economy, and international organizations should apply their mandates in accordance with them.

41. Certain aspects of these universally shared values and principles are repeatedly echoed in the public debate on globalization. They express the concerns of people at a time of great change and uncertainty:

• Respect for human rights and human dignity, including gender equality. This lies at the heart of commitments already undertaken by the international community.

• Respect for diversity of culture, religion, political and social opinion, while fully respecting universal principles.

• Fairness. Fairness is a notion which is deeply felt and clearly recognized by people in every country. It is a standard of justice which many use to judge globalization and the equitable distribution of its benefits.

• Solidarity is the awareness of a common humanity and global citizenship and the voluntary acceptance of the responsibilities which go with it. It is the conscious commitment to redress inequalities both within and between countries. It is based on recognition that in an interdependent world, poverty or oppression anywhere is a threat to prosperity and stability everywhere.

• Respect for nature requires globalization to be ecologically sustainable, respecting the natural diversity of life on earth and the viability of the planet's ecosystem, as well as ensuring equity between present and future generations.

42. Universally shared values and principles have to be the basis of the democratic governance of globalization. They include those values which are essential for an open and effective market economy - responsibility, initiative, respect for the law, honesty and transparency.

43. A fairer and more prosperous world is the key to a more secure world. Terror often exploits poverty, injustice and desperation to gain public legitimacy. The existence of such conditions is an obstacle in the fight against terrorism.

44. The problems lie in bridging the gap between principles and practice. The international community makes more commitments than it is prepared to implement. Nowhere is the gap between declaration and practice more glaring than in the record of Official Development Assistance (ODA) to the world's poorest countries.

45. Action to realize values in a global economy must come from both individual actors and from institutions.

46. Actors in globalization - States, civil society, business, trade unions, international organizations and individuals - must be inspired by these values to accept their own responsibilities, and be publicly accountable for respecting them in all

their transactions. The rich and the powerful – whether States or corporations – have special responsibilities, as their actions have the widest impact on global welfare.

47. There are a variety of voluntary initiatives which need to be strengthened. They include the social responsibilities of business; movements to mobilize the ethical concerns of consumers and investors; campaigns by unions to promote labour standards, and by civil society to inform and mobilize opinion on a variety of public issues.

48. The multilateral institutions of the United Nations system have a special role to play, as they set and promote international norms and policies. Universally shared values and the rule of law must guide the terms of international engagement and systems of national and global governance.

49. We believe globalization has made it imperative to have a better international dialogue on universally shared values. Values have become central to many political negotiations because of the dynamics of globalization. Structural adjustment often gives rise to domestic tensions and suspicions as to whether other countries are playing by the same ethical rules. This is seen, for example, in international debates on trade, finance, human rights and development assistance. Such tensions impair solidarity between people in rich and poor countries.

50. Culture is a potent symbol of identity and belonging. Globalization should lead to multi-cultural diversity, not homogenization, undesired integration or static preservation. It must be a process of creative redefinition in which global and local traditions and ways of life join to recreate new forms at all levels. There must be recognition of the integrity and autonomy of different national and local cultures as the source of confidence and energy for people to undertake creative endeavours across borders.

51. Ultimately, a common commitment to a fair and inclusive globalization must be based on a common perception of a shared humanity and a shared planet. Such a perception is the basis of stable national communities and States. We have an increasingly global economy, but we are far from being a global community. However, some elements are beginning to emerge, which need to be promoted and supported.

Towards a global community: Strengthening dialogue and governance

52. The post-war order was set up on the basis of an international community of nations. States were then the prime actors, although some non-State actors, such as business and labour, have been represented in the ILO since 1919.

53. Today, a myriad of actors, both State and non-State, play critically important roles in shaping the evolution of globalization. In addition to the organizations of the United Nations system, they include parliamentarians and local authorities, multinational corporations, trade unions, business groups, cooperatives, religious groups, academia, economic and social councils, foundations and charities, community-based organizations and non-governmental organizations (NGOs), and the media. Global networks bring together diverse groups such as youth and consumer associations, farmers, scientists, teachers, lawyers and physicians, women and indigenous peoples.

54. These emerging networks increasingly relate to each other through bonds of common interest or conviction. Many initiatives are already under way to address

common problems. They range from the management of the Internet to issues of gender equality, migration, health and human security.

55. We can already discern some distinguishing features of these processes. They are usually defined in terms of specific issues. They involve many actors, both State and non-State, interacting from the local to the global level. In all cases, they are marked by expanding public dialogue and public participation. The new technologies and the networks they support are creating the conditions for expanding and innovative forms of interaction.

56. It is far too soon to call this assembly of various players a global community. It is far from being a unity. There are great inequalities of power and influence. There is an often explosive diversity of opinions and interests. It is fragmented and incomplete, hardly touching the millions who live on the margin of subsistence.

57. Yet the human interactions are multiplying, and the networks are becoming more dense. It is an evolution driven by globalization itself, by the increasing integration of trade and production, and by the expansion of communication, travel and exchange of ideas.

58. The potential for a more participatory and democratic system of global governance lies today more in the future evolution of these expanding networks of people and institutions, rather than in blueprints for world government or institutional re-engineering. These networks complement – and extend beyond – the existing system of international organizations. They can be the seedbed of a future global community with shared interests and common goals.

59. The way forward is to encourage more systematic dialogues within and between these emerging networks of State and non-State actors in specific domains. Such dialogue widens participation, builds consensus and identifies needs from the perspective of those most directly concerned. It helps mediate the inevitable tensions arising from economic transition and global adjustment and provides a means of translating values into action through setting common objectives and fixing individual responsibilities. These dialogues need to take place at all levels. They are the basis for more coherent action to link economic growth with social progress.

60. This Report is a call for action based on dialogue as the foundation for a genuine global community of the future. Though interests often diverge, we believe that there is an increasing convergence of opinion throughout the world on the need for a more fair and inclusive globalization. This convergence is based on growing awareness of our interdependence, and the danger of inaction. Such awareness is being expanded and heightened by globalization itself. We base our confidence in the future on the power of this reality.

61. We believe that if the recommendations we propose are adopted in a reasonable period of time, globalization as we know it today can significantly change for the better, bringing benefit and stability to more people and countries.

II. GLOBALIZATION AND ITS IMPACT

II.1 Views and perceptions

Common ground

Africa

Arab world

Asia

Latin America and the Caribbean

Transition countries of Europe and Central Asia

Western Europe and North America

Business, labour and civil society

Globalization from a wide range of perspectives

62. A key priority for the Commission was to see globalization from a wide range of perspectives, in regions throughout the world: how it had affected people's lives; what hopes, fears and concerns it had aroused; and what action people believe should be taken to expand its opportunities and reduce its insecurities.

63. To achieve this, we launched a wide-ranging programme of dialogues and consultations at national, regional and global levels. Participants included over 2000 decision-makers and social actors involved in globalization issues, among them government ministers and administrators, local politicians and parliamentarians, national leaders of workers' and employers' associations, representatives of civil society and religious leaders, organizations of women and indigenous peoples, academics and journalists.[2] The dialogues were designed to be interactive and participants exchanged ideas both among themselves and with Commissioners.

64. Although the participants were not intended to be representative of public opinion as a whole, these dialogues have helped us to see globalization through the eyes of people.[3] There was broad recognition of the benefits of globalization, but a clearly critical strand of opinion ran through the dialogues. We present this brief summary, not because we agree with everything that was said – indeed there were divergent or contradictory views among different participants – but because they help us understand the questions that are being posed, the concerns that are being expressed, the interests at stake, and the values and goals to which people sub-

---

[2] Altogether some 26 national and regional dialogues were held. In addition to regional consultations for Africa, the Arab States, Asia, Europe, Latin America and the Caribbean, national dialogues and consultations were held in the following countries: Argentina, Brazil, Chile, China, Costa Rica, Egypt, Finland, Germany, India, Mexico, Philippines, Poland, Russia, Senegal, South Africa, Tanzania, Thailand, Uganda, the United States, and Uruguay. Nine special consultations were organized to hear the views of international business, labour, and civil society groups. More details are given in an annex to the Report. To supplement this information, we have also considered the results of some opinion polls carried out by other organizations.

[3] Full reports of the dialogues are available at: www.ilo.org/wcsdg/consulta/index.htm

scribe. Above all they have underlined the importance of a better process of dialogue among different social actors if a fairer globalization is to be constructed.

Common ground

65. The views and perceptions of people depend on who they are, where they live and what they possess. But in the kaleidoscope of opinions that emerged from the dialogues there was also much common ground.

Kaleidoscope of opinions – but much common ground

66. From almost everywhere came a sense of the power of globalization, whether driven by technology, economics or politics. *"We were sleeping on the shore when a big wave came"*, said a participant in the dialogue in Egypt. Globalization could be frightening, stimulating, overwhelming, destructive or creative, depending on one's point of view.

67. There was a widespread sense of instability and insecurity. In the Costa Rica dialogue a participant said, *"There is a growing feeling that we live in a world highly vulnerable to changes we cannot control; a growing sense of fragility among ordinary people, countries and entire regions"*. Unstable global financial systems had devastating effects. In all parts of the world there were voices calling for stronger systems of social protection and income security.

68. Another common concern was the impact of globalization on culture and identity. Some saw it as *"threatening traditional institutions such as the family and the school"*, or threatening the way of life of whole communities. Others saw benefits in overturning traditional ways and developing modern attitudes. There was frequent reference to the implications for gender equality, both positive and negative.

Impact of globalization on culture and identity

69. The one issue which came to the fore time and time again was employment and livelihoods. While people largely favour more openness and interconnection between societies, they are much less positive when asked about the impact on their jobs and incomes.[4] A participant in the Philippines dialogue said, *"There is no point to a globalization that reduces the price of a child's shoes, but costs the father his job"*. There was frequent reference to the difficulties faced by small enterprises in taking advantage of globalization – and yet that is where most employment is created. The rural and informal economies remain on the margins, and the result is persistent poverty. Others were concerned with the loss of jobs as a result of industrial restructuring in the face of competitive global markets, and the downward pressures on conditions of work and workers' rights – in Europe and North America as well as in middle-income and transition countries.

Employment and livelihoods

70. Since globalization is only one of many factors affecting people's lives, the dialogues sparked broader debate on the role of the market in society and how the needs and aspirations of people can be expressed and met in their own communities. It was widely argued that progress was impeded by the unfair rules of the

Markets and global rules

---

[4] Multi-country opinion polls reach similar conclusions. For example, an average 48% of people polled by Environics International in seven countries thought that globalization was good for quality of life and economic development, but only 38% thought the same about jobs and workers' rights (full survey report in *Global Issues Monitor 2002*, Toronto, Environics International, May 2002). Another multi-country survey found that "people generally view the growth in foreign trade, global communication and international popular culture as good for them and their families" while at the same time finding that "many aspects of their lives – including some affected by globalization – are getting worse", including "the availability of good-paying jobs". (See *Views of a changing world*, Washington DC, the Pew Research Center for the People and the Press, June 2003, p.10.)

global economy. These were biased in favour of the rich and powerful and neglected the social impact of economic policies. The adverse effects were sometimes strikingly similar in different parts of the world. For instance, the damage done by agricultural subsidies was illustrated by identical complaints in the Brazil and Tanzania dialogues: that the import of European powdered milk was crowding out demand for their domestic milk, while at the same time introducing an inferior product.

71. However, fair rules do not automatically lead to a fair result. Efforts were needed to help those in a weaker position to *"jump on the bandwagon of development"*. The current agenda was considered to be too focused on trade and investment, and not enough on human rights and the environment, partly due to a "democratic deficit" at the international level.

72. There was widespread agreement on the need for a renewed role for the State, built on the rule of law and democratic institutions, and working in partnership with other social actors. While the concept of an all-embracing State has been discredited, globalization had weakened the State too much. In order to respond effectively to globalization the State needed to be able to develop national capacities, regulate economic activity, promote equity and fairness, provide essential public services and participate effectively in international negotiations.

Need for investment in education and skills

73. A recurring theme was that to take advantage of the opportunities of globalization, people and countries had to invest in education, skills and technological capabilities across the board. Education systems needed reform and illiteracy had to be tackled.

Migration and regional integration

74. Migration was another widespread concern, for countries of in-migration and out-migration alike. In many low-income countries there was criticism of the barriers to broad-based migration to industrialized countries, and concern about the "brain drain", which undermined efforts to build national capabilities. Migrants from all regions, particularly women, were often driven into an illegal economy in countries of destination, leaving them vulnerable to exploitation. A fairer framework for the movement of people was essential, and in the European regional dialogue it was argued that *"any policy of restriction should be linked to a policy of trade liberalization and development cooperation"*.

75. In all parts of the world regional integration was seen as a route towards a fairer, more inclusive globalization. Countries are better able to manage the social and economic challenges of globalization by working together. That calls for better integration of social and economic policies in the process of regional integration, as has been the aim in the European Union (EU), the Southern African Development Community (SADC) and the Southern Cone Common Market (Mercosur), among others.

76. There were repeated expressions of support for the United Nations and the multilateral system as the best means of responding to the challenges of globalization.

"If globalization is a river, we must build dams to generate power"

77. One final area of common ground: most participants in the dialogues believed that solutions were possible, and many were already actively seeking or promoting them. Whatever the negatives of the present model of globalization, it was recognized that globalization is a reality, that it is necessary to adjust policy priorities to deal with it (*"the outside world can do without us; but we can't do without it"*), and above all that answers can and must be found. A participant in the dialogue in Poland gave an analogy of a force which could be harnessed: *"If globalization is a river, we must build dams to generate power"*.

78. Beyond the common concerns and beliefs, there was much diversity as well. Without pretending to capture the richness of the discussions, we highlight below a range of perspectives from different regions of the world.

Africa

79. No one doubted that over the past 20 years of globalization, Africa has fared far worse than other regions. However, the extent to which globalization was to blame for Africa's problems remained a matter of debate. At best Africa felt bypassed, at worst abused and humiliated.

Africa fared worst

80. At one extreme, a contributor to the Senegal dialogue likened it to *"the re-colonization of our countries"*. Globalization was unwanted, foreign and forced on Africa.

81. Another contributor to the Senegal dialogue said the impact on African business was an *"unequal combat which would lead to certain death"*. According to a leader from civil society, Africa needed to *"develop a culture of resistance"* to globalization in order to avoid being reduced to the status of a *"beggar economy"*.

82. Elsewhere, participants in the dialogue in Uganda recognized that globalization could lead to greater democracy, education and employment. As the regional dialogue made clear, whatever the impact of globalization on the continent, people did not believe that Africa could advance by isolating itself from the process.

83. The strong critical sentiment prevailing at the dialogues was explained by the long list of negatives which participants attributed to the current pattern of globalization. High on the list was rich nations' farm and tariff policies. Mali had no reason to respect the trade rules when one of its few competitive exports, cotton, was being undercut by subsidies. Western tariffs continued to discriminate against local processing of commodities, making producers hostage to the declining price of raw materials. The price of unprocessed coffee was the lowest in history, said a participant in the dialogue in Tanzania, but there had been no drop in the price of a cup of coffee in New York, Tokyo or Geneva.

Unfair rules, foreign debt, HIV/AIDS, poverty and migration major concerns

84. Frustration with the policies of the leading international organizations proved a common theme. African negotiators lacked the resources and information needed to promote their interests at the WTO. The International Monetary Fund (IMF) and the World Bank were described as arrogant, ignorant of local conditions, and applying "one-size-fits-all" policies. They imposed tight fiscal policies which cut down funds for education and social spending. Little of the foreign investment which was promised to follow liberalization had materialized. Above all, the foreign debt overhang was crippling despite the efforts of even the best-run governments.

85. HIV/AIDS, poverty and migration were high on the African agenda. Of special concern were the high costs of patented drugs for HIV/AIDS and other diseases. At the same time, migration and HIV/AIDS were draining Africa's already meagre supply of skilled workers.

86. But Africans did not just blame others for their problems. They too felt responsible for failures to build trade, integrate with other economies and benefit from the positive aspects of globalization. They recognized that economic regression was often caused by poor governance as much as outside influences. Meanwhile, scarce fiscal resources were wasted on armaments and devastating

conflicts. Although many trade and other regional cooperation agreements existed on paper, there was a lack of political will, or of physical infrastructure, to make them work. Nevertheless, regional integration could be an effective vehicle for integrating Africa into the global economy. Much had to be done to create the conditions for reducing poverty. Local initiatives and *"African solutions for African problems"* were best. However, outside help was very important to ensure that Africa was included in global progress.

Arab world

Oil exports and migration colour perceptions

87. In the Arab world, perceptions of globalization were overshadowed by war and the continuing Arab-Israeli conflict. Perceptions were conditioned by two factors: the current pattern of integration with the rest of the world, dominated by oil exports and migration, and the fears for the impact of globalization on cultural identity and local traditions.

88. Oil was seen as a mixed blessing. While it funded infrastructure projects and had permitted a large increase in both public and private consumption, it had also undermined the growth of local industry and agriculture and had increased inequality within and across the countries of the region. The rich states had come to rely on imported workers from both within and beyond the Arab world. The global importance of oil had encouraged political interference from outside forces.

89. Many people in the region associated globalization with the intrusion by foreign powers into their economic and political affairs, which undermined sovereignty and encouraged wasteful military expenditure. Some also felt that Western interests failed to adequately support democratization in the region for fear of the popularity of political Islam or in order to maintain the existing regime in the oil sector. Such feelings were exacerbated by the plight of the Palestinians and by the many worries about the impact of Western media and Western values. There was also widespread concern about the possible loss of jobs that could result from the liberalization of trade and investment and competition from developing countries with lower labour costs.

90. Others argued that economic modernization through globalization was the path to greater strength and the ending of dependence on foreign powers. Opinion surveys show growing support for regional integration, both among Arab countries and with Europe. This could be a conduit for reaping some of globalization's benefits and resisting competition from low-cost producers from Asia.

Asia

Benefits for some but not for all

91. The Asian dialogues underscored the diversity of the continent. Most participants saw globalization working selectively: beneficial for some countries and people, but not for others. The most impressive gain had been in the poverty reduction associated with the opening up of China and India. Yet some 1 billion people in the region had hardly seen any reward. The process had to be managed to make it more inclusive.

92. The dialogue in China emphasized that the opportunities and benefits of globalization outweighed the risks. Globalization had spurred economic growth and industrial productivity, and had helped China come to grips with the country's major challenge: employment. But it had also undermined traditional livelihoods in agriculture, changed the traditional social security system and increased rural-

urban and intra-regional inequalities. Some multinational investment was exacerbating environmental degradation and generated pressures for cheaper and more flexible labour in order to retain competitiveness. As consumers, people in China appreciated low prices and quality goods and services, but as workers they wished for better and more secure job opportunities.

93. In India, the message was more mixed. There had been winners and losers. The lives of the educated and the rich had been enriched by globalization. The information technology (IT) sector was a particular beneficiary. But the benefits had not yet reached the majority, and new risks had cropped up for the losers – the socially deprived and the rural poor. Significant numbers of "non-perennial" poor, who had worked hard to escape poverty, were finding their gains reversed. Participants at the dialogue feared that globalization could erode values such as democracy and social justice. Power was shifting from elected local institutions to unaccountable transnational bodies. Western perceptions, which dominated global media, were not aligned with local perspectives; they encouraged consumerism in the midst of extreme poverty and posed a threat to cultural and linguistic diversity.

94. Elsewhere, as the Philippines dialogue emphasized, the experience of globalization was often of *"much talk of markets, but in reality very little access, much talk of jobs, but they were somewhere else, and much talk of a better life, but for others"*. One major reason was the lack of a level playing field, as industrialized country protectionism denied to others the very route that they themselves had used to grow. China's perceived success in attracting foreign direct investment (FDI) was also perceived as a threat, although participants in the Chinese dialogue rejected the notion that China was leading a "race to the bottom". In the Philippines dialogue, indigenous peoples highlighted the increasing conflict between their communities and mining corporations because of the liberalization of mining investments.

95. The economic volatility of globalizing countries was a key issue at the regional dialogue. A Thai participant described the violent reversal of capital flows during the Asian crisis as a *"punishment out of proportion to the sins committed"*. Capital market reforms were needed but there had to be prudent sequencing of liberalization and adequate social protection. Japanese participants emphasized that regional cooperation in trade and finance could increase stability.

Economic volatility

96. A more liberal regime was also necessary to cope with the growing movement of people across national borders. Trafficking of women and children constituted one of the grossest abuses of human rights and required concerted action.

Latin America and the Caribbean

97. The Latin American dialogues occurred at a time of crisis in the region as the economic problems of Argentina spilled over to its neighbours. Consequently, many were quite sceptical of the benefits of increased global trade and interaction.

98. On the whole, however, the dialogues showed a more nuanced attitude. While globalization needed reform to take account of people's needs, the region also needed reform to take advantage of globalization. The people and societies of the region should be at the centre of efforts to create a more *"humane"* globalization. The dialogue in Brazil highlighted the elimination of hunger, universal education and decent work as the key items in the new agenda, to counterbalance the aspects of trade, finance and technology which had been in the ascendant so far.

99. The challenge of globalization had to be seized. On a positive note, it was associated with the spread of democracy in the region and with growing public awareness of issues such as gender inequality, human rights and sustainable development. The "smaller" global world of today was making the cross-fertilization and circulation of ideas much easier. As noted by the participants in the dialogue in Chile, it was helping to shape a new global ethic based on universal values and principles shared by people all over the world. The challenge now was how to put the emerging rights agenda into practice.

100. For many, globalization was not delivering on its promises, and particularly not delivering decent work.[5] *"Workers can hardly trust the current model of globalization when they see every day a growth of the informal economy, a decline in social protection and the imposition of an authoritarian workplace culture"*, said a trade union leader. But even in a country as successful as Costa Rica the participants in the dialogue felt that the majority of citizens, regardless of their income level or social status, perceived more threats than opportunities in globalization. Unstable global financial markets, in particular, had had disastrous social consequences in many countries, due both to inadequate government policies and to poor understanding of local conditions by the IMF and foreign banks. The middle classes in Argentina and Uruguay had been hit particularly hard.

101. From many quarters came a call for a renewed role for the State. As the Prime Minister of Barbados said at the dialogue of Caribbean States, *"we cannot leave people-focused development to the serendipity of market forces. Rather than retreat, the State must forge new smart partnerships with the private sector and the institutions of civil society"*. This was echoed at the regional dialogue in Lima. It included more efficient public services but also a harmonious relationship between the private sector as generator of wealth and employment and the public sector as promoter of a competitive environment. Competitiveness needed to be enhanced by investment and human capital development, not by lowering wages or raising protective tariffs. Throughout this region, there was a particular need for policies to favour small and medium-sized enterprises and to oppose the informalization of the economy.

102. Migration had become an important issue throughout the whole region, from Mexico – where one worker in five was living abroad – to Argentina, where many young people with skills were moving to countries from which their grandparents had migrated in search of prosperity.

103. Much hope was placed on regional integration as a route to social and political goals. Integration within Mercosur in particular could be deepened. Wide-ranging regional institutions were already in place in the Caribbean, which needed to be strengthened. Regional solidarity could also be a means for the region as a whole to actively engage in the construction of globalization.

---

[5] According to a survey by Latinobarómetro (Santiago, Chile) in 2002, over 40 per cent of people in Latin America rated unemployment, labour market instability or low wages as their most important problem. The same survey indicated that a majority of respondents considered that government economic policies are responsible for the problems, while 22 per cent blamed globalization and 23 per cent the IMF (special tabulations from the regular Latinobarómetro survey. See www.latinobarometro.org).

Transition countries of Europe and Central Asia

104. The painful social upheavals of the transition from communism in the former Soviet Union and Eastern Europe were generally not blamed on globalization *per se*. Participants at the dialogues were wary of the pitfalls of globalization, but reluctant to return to the old, closed systems. They were acutely aware of the costs of change, particularly when there were no new social safety nets to replace the ones which had been discarded.

105. Few countries have taken better advantage of the new possibilities of engaging with the globalized world than Poland. Its experience in moving gradually towards the EU was a good illustration of how regional cooperation was a path towards beneficial integration in the global economy. But *"no matter how strongly involved in the mainstream of globalization we are"*, said the Polish Finance Minister, *"there is always an opportunity and an obligation to pursue a national policy of socio-economic development"*. Poland's communist past left it with a strong sense of State obligations to society. And despite the many benefits of change, people were frustrated by continuing high levels of unemployment and the problems involved in restructuring old industries and the large farm sector. In Lodz, the country's largest textile manufacturing centre, nearly 100,000 workers – mainly women – had lost their jobs because of competition from Asia.

106. The dialogue in Russia underscored the opportunities and challenges of globalization: increased investment flows, expanded export markets, and new possibilities to achieve higher growth and better standards of living. However, many adjustments were still needed, and a just distribution of both the costs and benefits of reform was important. The social costs of Russia's accession to the WTO had to be minimized, and there was need for improvement and enforcement of labour legislation, greater employment generation and reform of the educational system.

107. National culture and diversity had to be protected from globalization. Of particular concern was the failure of multinational enterprises to respect the law and labour standards. Migration was another serious problem – both the exodus of skilled workers due to poor local conditions, and illegal movements. Despite these concerns, the participants saw engagement with globalization as an inevitable process, while emphasizing the need to direct it in a more socially responsible manner.

Western Europe and North America

108. The greater international competition induced by trade and capital liberalization was blamed for increased income disparities within industrialized countries, placing particular strain on low-skilled work in older industries, the first to be transferred to lower-cost countries. However, the export of jobs due to globalization was only one of several causes of unemployment. Of greater concern to the participants in the dialogue in Germany was the effect of capital mobility on fiscal policy. International tax competition, it was claimed, was imposing severe limits on the financing of the welfare state. [6]

109. Throughout Europe, migration was a critical issue. People reacted strongly, often with unpredictable political consequences. However, this issue had to be

---

[6] Similar concerns were echoed in the report of the Flemish Commission on the Social Dimension of Globalization; see www.ilo.org/wcsdg/consulta/flemish/index.htm

addressed in the context of Europe's ageing population and of the social cohesion which is at the heart of the European social system.

110. Europe was constructing a social model which some believed could to a certain extent be replicated elsewhere. The dialogue in Finland gave one example of how integrated economic and social policies and a partnership approach had been instrumental in building a modern and competitive information society. The construction of the EU itself was an expression of that same model and, at the same time, a response to the pressures of globalization. Though a unique historical process, it contained elements that could inspire better, more inclusive management of the global economy.

111. The dialogues suggested that Europeans were in principle sympathetic to many developing country complaints about the pattern of globalization. It was acknowledged that the rules of globalization were set by the industrialized world and that if globalization was to become more inclusive the developing world should have a much bigger say. The importance of granting more development assistance to the poorest countries was generally recognized. The negative impact of the Common Agricultural Policy on the developing world was also recognized by some, but it was clear that there were political obstacles to reform.

112. There is an enormous amount of information on the perceived impact of globalization in the United States, with sometimes contradictory findings. Some recent major surveys report generally strongly positive attitudes to globalization accompanied by concern about jobs. Recent academic research found objections among a significant group of American voters to further exposure to globalization.[7] This study showed that perceptions of globalization were more positive the higher the level of education and skills.

113. Some limited focus group consultations were also held in the United States in the course of the Commission's work. Those consulted had little doubt that the world economy had changed radically over the past 20 years. Globalization was putting new pressures on companies to be more competitive, squeezing wages and leading to corporate mergers. Some domestic jobs had moved to other countries, but in general the process was leading to greater wealth and well-being. The United States itself was seen as the main driver of globalization, and this was regarded positively. However, it was recognized that there were also adverse effects. These included impact on the environment and the marginalization of those countries in Africa and the Middle East that were unable or unwilling to participate.

114. Views were divided on whether globalization would continue or be impeded by rising nationalism. There was a need for international organizations, official and otherwise, to help guide the process. These included the IMF, the United Nations, the World Bank, the WTO, the ILO and other specialized agencies as well as business, trade unions, churches and NGOs. There was also a need for better governance at all levels.

---

[7] Kenneth F. Scheve, and Matthew J. Slaughter: *Globalization and the Perceptions of American Workers* (Washington DC, Institute for International Economics, March 2001).

Business, labour and civil society

115. In the Commission's dialogues with business, chief executive officers did not see themselves as the main drivers of globalization. Business did not create globalization, but reacted to it, they said. For some enterprises the task was especially difficult. Businesses from poor countries and small enterprises everywhere found it hard to manage global competition without public support. For bigger firms, in the global environment *"the key to effectiveness is in the management of diversity"* – of markets, suppliers and workforce.

116. Business leaders also rejected the notion that they were imposing single models across their operations worldwide: *"The more we become global, the more we operate locally"*, said one participant. Business might even act as a two-way channel, transferring new technology to the South while at the same time bringing home awareness of the problems and concerns of developing countries.

117. A key issue for the social dimension of globalization was to achieve a better spread of FDI. This meant creating stable and corruption-free environments that would encourage long-term business commitment.

118. Predictable rules and an agreed framework of values were essential for markets to operate well. Governments had the overall responsibility to ensure that agreed rules were respected. But excessive regulatory zeal was undesirable when markets could correct many disturbances automatically. *"We need more dialogue and change in behaviour; not more rules and regulations."* The importance of respect for values was underlined. Progressive business is strongly committed to voluntary social responsibility. Good corporate citizenship was increasingly important for business development.

> Predictable rules and agreed framework of values

119. Yet the dialogue the Commission had with the World Economic Forum at Davos revealed that business confidence had been undermined by corporate scandals. There was concern about a possible backlash to globalization and its harmful effects. It was also felt that a dialogue with the World Social Forum could bring benefits to both sides.

120. Participants in the Commission's dialogue with trade unions considered that the economic base of developing countries was being progressively eroded by the policies of industrialized countries, the International Financial Institutions (IFIs) and the WTO. They were concerned by a continued emphasis on privatization of utilities such as water, electricity and health services that was exacerbating poverty. They were also concerned that the exploitation of women workers in Export Processing Zones (EPZs) had expanded dramatically. This included low wages, intimidation of workers trying to organize themselves, violence and sexual harassment.

121. It was especially important to ensure respect for workers' rights and labour standards in the global economy. Trade union leaders thought the ILO could play a leading role, working in greater cooperation with other international organizations, including the IFIs and the WTO, national governments and employers' and workers' organizations.

> Workers' rights and labour standards must be protected

122. Union leaders in industrialized countries maintained that dissatisfaction with corporate governance had reached a crisis point. It was *"time to save corporations from themselves"*. Deregulation and the emphasis on shareholder value had gone too far. Increased global competition encouraged employers to play *"fast and loose with labour practices"*, including the replacement of decent employment with insecure informal, casual and contract work. For many corporations,

voluntary corporate social responsibility was simply *"an attempt at a public relations repair job"*, without any real effect on mainstream business operations.

123. What was required was a global system of industrial relations including global works councils, social audits of companies, and mechanisms to monitor and verify the implementation of codes of conduct adopted by multinational companies.

124. Civil society groups were likewise concerned that corporate and financial interests dominated the pattern of globalization, and that there was insufficient accountability. The negative effect of extractive industries on indigenous peoples, local communities and environments was a common theme. Another was the adverse impact of international rules for intellectual property rights, which open the door to the privatization of indigenous knowledge. Many denounced a rise in the political influence of corporations, including through a marked concentration of private ownership of the media.

Critique of the economic model

125. This was part of a broader critique of an economic model which was imposed on countries, notably through the conditionality of the IFIs. It was evident in the WTO, which promoted a paradigm of competition in which the weak have to compete with the strong. *"A conversation between a cat and a mouse is not a conversation."* It led to the neglect of social and environmental goals, and so to an unsustainable pattern of growth which imposed high costs on people and communities. *"It is"*, said one participant, *"a deeply undemocratic and disempowering system."*

126. Civil Society Organizations (CSOs) are diverse in their interests, their action and in the level and focus of their anger, but few reject the idea of a more interconnected world. For many the goal is rather to change the principles on which the global economy works. The slogan of the World Social Forum is "another world is possible".

Emphasis on human rights and respect for values

127. Many CSOs put great emphasis on human rights and respect for values such as fairness, solidarity and gender equality. They see pervasive double standards in the gap between the rhetoric and the behaviour of many global actors. Policy proposals include making all actions of international organizations subject to a prior review of their consistency with universal human rights. Another widespread demand is a comprehensive solution to the debt crisis, preferably through simple debt cancellation.

128. There was frustration at the failure to deliver on the commitments made by the Member States at UN fora over recent decades. Some believed there had been a systematic effort to sideline the United Nations on issues of economic justice, peace and development, and called for it to be given greater authority over international economic and other policies. They stressed their concern at the apparent weakening of multilateral solutions and multilateral approaches to the problems of globalization, a concern that was echoed in many other dialogues.

129. A critical part of the solution, it was widely argued, lies in giving voice to the voiceless. A wider, more participative and democratic framework was needed at all levels: local, national and global. Women are still under-represented in most policy-making bodies. Many CSOs argued that public policies and economic systems must reflect local needs and local decisions. At the same time, there must be greater democracy in the functioning of the multilateral system, and particularly the Bretton Woods organizations and the WTO.

* * *

130. Overall, we found much encouragement for our work from the programme of dialogues and consultations in different regions. While there are many differences of view, there is also a shared belief that globalization can and must serve the needs and aspirations of people and communities everywhere. To achieve that, correctives are urgently needed at the local, national and international levels. As one participant said, *"We stand at a dramatic equilibrium between the best and the worst that could happen in the next decades"*. The dialogues underlined how we, as a global community, share a common fate, and reminded us that this fate lies in our hands.

II.2 Globalization: Its nature and impact

Introduction

Key characteristics of globalization

The institutional context

The impact of globalization

Introduction

131. Globalization is a complex phenomenon that has had far-reaching effects. Not surprisingly, therefore, the term "globalization" has acquired many emotive connotations and become a hotly contested issue in current political discourse. At one extreme, globalization is seen as an irresistible and benign force for delivering economic prosperity to people throughout the world. At the other, it is blamed as a source of all contemporary ills.[8]

Key characteristics and enabling conditions

132. Nevertheless, it is widely accepted that the key characteristics of globalization have been the liberalization of international trade, the expansion of FDI, and the emergence of massive cross-border financial flows. This resulted in increased competition in global markets. It is also widely acknowledged that this has come about through the combined effect of two underlying factors: policy decisions to reduce national barriers to international economic transactions and the impact of new technology, especially in the sphere of information and communications. These developments created the enabling conditions for the onset of globalization.

133. The effects of the new technology have also given a distinctive character to the current process of globalization, as compared to similar episodes in the past. The natural barriers of time and space have been vastly reduced. The cost of moving information, people, goods and capital across the globe has fallen dramatically, while global communication is cheap and instantaneous and becoming ever more so. This has vastly expanded the feasibility of economic transactions across the world. Markets can now be global in scope and encompass an expanding range of goods and services.

---

[8] The term "globalization" did not become popular until the 1990s. The final report of the Study Commission of the German Bundestag, *Globalization of the World Economy: Challenges and Answers* (14th legislative period, June 2002) notes that the number of times the word globalization was used in a major German newspaper, the *Frankfurter Allgemeine Zeitung*, increased from 34 in 1993 to 1,136 in 2001.

134. Another distinctive feature of the current process of globalization relates to what is conspicuously absent. Unlike earlier episodes of globalization that were characterized by massive cross-border movements of people, the current process largely excludes this. While goods, firms and money are largely free to criss-cross borders, people are not.

Goods, firms and money are largely free to criss-cross borders – but people are not

135. In this section, we highlight the salient features of the evolution of globalization, outline the emerging institutional framework governing it, and finally assess the impact this process has had on countries and people.

Key characteristics of globalization

136. The basic trends with respect to world trade, FDI, financial flows and technology are shown in figures 1 to 9.

Trade

137. World trade has expanded rapidly over the past two decades. Since 1986, it has consistently grown significantly faster than world gross domestic product (GDP) (figure 1). Throughout the 1970s, trade liberalization within the framework of the General Agreement on Tariffs and Trade (GATT) was modest and gradual, and involved the industrialized countries much more than it did the developing ones. However, from the early 1980s onwards, the extent of trade liberalization, especially in the developing countries, began to accelerate (figure 2).

138. This trade expansion did not occur uniformly across all countries, with the industrialized countries and a group of 12 developing countries accounting for the lion's share. In contrast, the majority of developing countries did not experience significant trade expansion (figure 3). Indeed, most of the Least-Developed Countries (LDCs), a group that includes most of the countries in sub-Saharan Africa, experienced a proportional decline in their share of world markets – despite the fact that many of these countries had implemented trade liberalization measures.

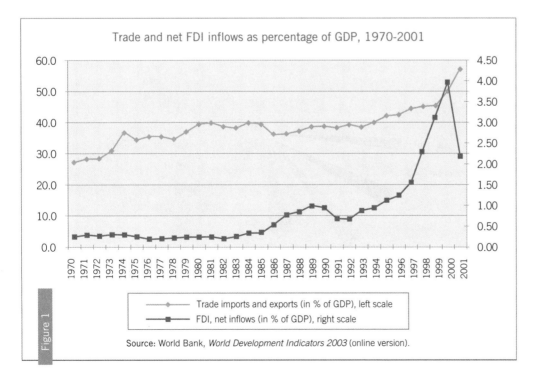

Trade and net FDI inflows as percentage of GDP, 1970-2001

Figure 1

Trade imports and exports (in % of GDP), left scale
FDI, net inflows (in % of GDP), right scale

Source: World Bank, *World Development Indicators 2003* (online version).

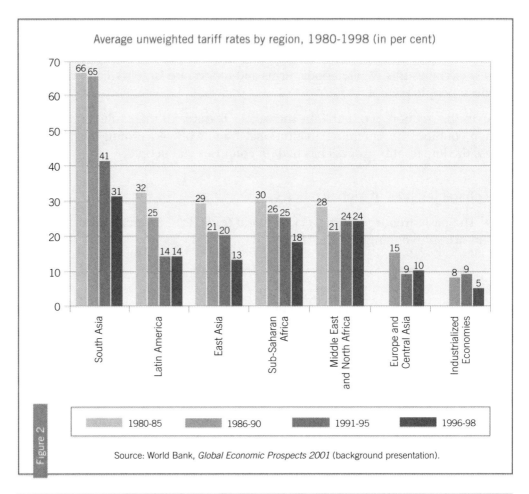

Average unweighted tariff rates by region, 1980-1998 (in per cent)

Legend: 1980-85 | 1986-90 | 1991-95 | 1996-98

Source: World Bank, *Global Economic Prospects 2001* (background presentation).

Figure 2

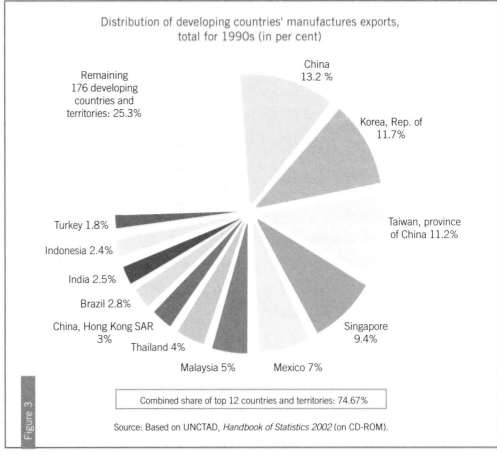

Distribution of developing countries' manufactures exports, total for 1990s (in per cent)

China 13.2 %
Korea, Rep. of 11.7%
Taiwan, province of China 11.2%
Singapore 9.4%
Mexico 7%
Malaysia 5%
Thailand 4%
China, Hong Kong SAR 3%
Brazil 2.8%
India 2.5%
Indonesia 2.4%
Turkey 1.8%
Remaining 176 developing countries and territories: 25.3%

Combined share of top 12 countries and territories: 74.67%

Source: Based on UNCTAD, *Handbook of Statistics 2002* (on CD-ROM).

Figure 3

Foreign Direct Investment

139. During the early 1980s, FDI accelerated, both absolutely and as a percentage of GDP (figures 1 and 4). Since 1980, the policy environment worldwide has been far more conducive to the growth of FDI. Over the 1990s, the number of countries adopting significant liberalization measures towards FDI increased steadily (figure 5). Indeed, there are only a few countries that do not actively seek to attract FDI. However, many of these hopes have not been fulfilled. Despite the rapid growth of FDI flows to developing countries, investment remains highly concentrated in about ten of these countries (figure 6).

140. Apart from their increased volume, the nature of these investments has also changed. The information and communications technology (ICT) revolution, coupled with declining transport costs, made the growth of far-flung, multi-country based production of goods and services both technically and economically feasible. Production processes could be unbundled and located across the globe to exploit economic advantages arising from differences in costs, factor availabilities and the congeniality of the investment climate. Components and parts can easily be trans-shipped across the world and assembled at will. The communications revolution has made feasible the coordination and control of these dispersed production systems.

Financial flows

141. The most dramatic element of globalization over the past two decades has been the rapid integration of financial markets. The Bretton Woods system, created after the Second World War, rested on the foundation of closed capital accounts and fixed exchange rates. Thus, in contrast to trade and FDI where gradual liberalization had been initiated, financial globalization was not even on the policy agenda at the time. The world lived with a system of separate national financial markets.

Rapid integration of financial markets

142. This began to change in 1973 with the breakdown of the Bretton Woods system. But there was no immediate rush to capital account liberalization. This began in the industrialized countries only in the early 1980s, with a subsequent increase in capital flows among them.

143. As has been pointed out, "the world monetary system underwent three revolutions all at once: deregulation, internationalization, and innovation." [9] Financial liberalization created the policy environment for expanded capital mobility. But the increase in capital flows was greatly boosted by the revolution in ICT. This made possible the improved and speedier knowledge of foreign markets, the development of "round the world and round the clock" financial transactions, and the emergence of new financial instruments, especially derivatives.

144. Since the late 1980s there has been a global trend towards financial liberalization. This ranged from relatively simple steps such as the unification of exchange rates and the removal of controls over the allocation of credit in the domestic market to full-blown liberalization of the financial sector that included the opening up of capital accounts. Within the developing world, the latter type of reform was initially confined to a group of middle-income countries with a

Emerging markets gained most from growth in North-South investments

---

[9] Philip Turner: "Capital Flows in the 1980s: A Survey of Major Trends", *BIS Economic Papers No.30* (Basle, Bank for International Settlements, April 1991).

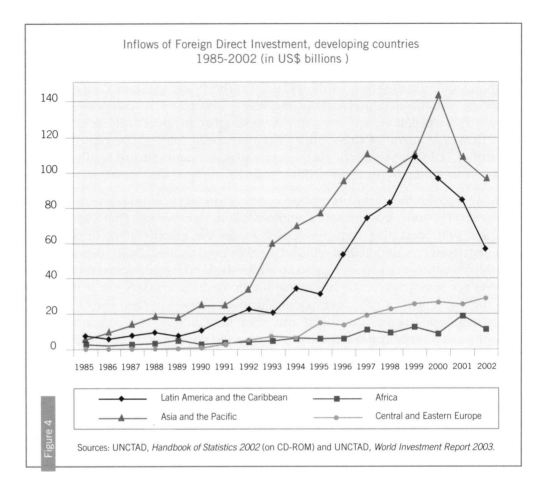

Inflows of Foreign Direct Investment, developing countries
1985-2002 (in US$ billions)

Latin America and the Caribbean   Africa
Asia and the Pacific   Central and Eastern Europe

Sources: UNCTAD, *Handbook of Statistics 2002* (on CD-ROM) and UNCTAD, *World Investment Report 2003.*

Figure 4

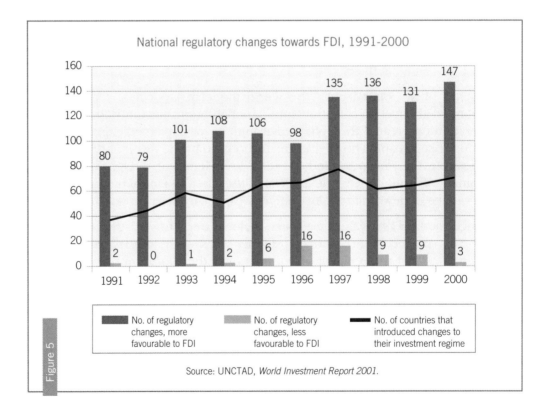

National regulatory changes towards FDI, 1991-2000

No. of regulatory changes, more favourable to FDI
No. of regulatory changes, less favourable to FDI
No. of countries that introduced changes to their investment regime

Source: UNCTAD, *World Investment Report 2001.*

Figure 5

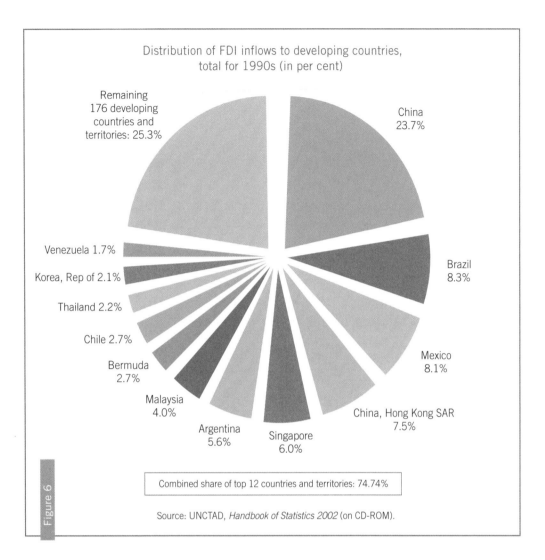

Figure 6

Distribution of FDI inflows to developing countries, total for 1990s (in per cent)

Remaining 176 developing countries and territories: 25.3%

China 23.7%

Venezuela 1.7%

Korea, Rep of 2.1%

Thailand 2.2%

Chile 2.7%

Bermuda 2.7%

Malaysia 4.0%

Argentina 5.6%

Singapore 6.0%

China, Hong Kong SAR 7.5%

Mexico 8.1%

Brazil 8.3%

Combined share of top 12 countries and territories: 74.74%

Source: UNCTAD, *Handbook of Statistics 2002* (on CD-ROM).

relatively greater range of institutions of financial intermediation that included bond and equity markets. The action in terms of the explosive growth in private financial flows from North to South was concentrated in these "emerging markets".

145. These flows consisted of elements such as investments in the equity markets of these countries by investment funds (a major part of which was on behalf of pension funds), bank lending to the corporate sector, and short-term speculative flows, especially into currency markets. Lending through the international bond market also increased in the 1990s in the wake of financial globalization (figure 7).

Technology

146. The industrialized countries were the source of the technological revolution that facilitated globalization but that revolution has also had ripple effects on the rest of the global economy. At one level, the new technology changed international comparative advantage by making knowledge an important factor of production. The knowledge-intensive and high-tech industries are the fastest-growing sectors in the global economy and successful economic development will eventually require that countries become able to enter and compete in these sectors. This implies that they will have to emphasize investments in education, training and the diffusion of knowledge.

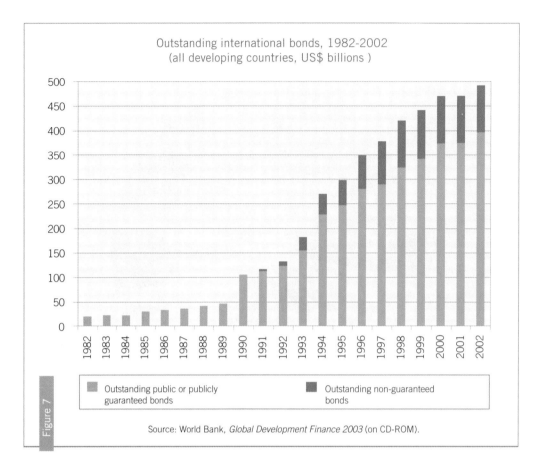

Outstanding international bonds, 1982-2002
(all developing countries, US$ billions)

Figure 7

■ Outstanding public or publicly guaranteed bonds   ■ Outstanding non-guaranteed bonds

Source: World Bank, *Global Development Finance 2003* (on CD-ROM).

Serious North-South imbalances in access to knowledge and technology

147. There have also been more direct impacts through the diffusion of these new technologies to developing countries. This has occurred principally, though not exclusively, through the activities of multinational enterprises (MNEs). However, as in the case of trade and FDI, there are serious North-South imbalances in access to knowledge and technology. Almost all the new technology originates in the North, where most research and development occurs. This is an important source of the dominance of MNEs in the global markets, and of their bargaining strength vis-à-vis developing country governments.

148. The effects of this new technology have also spread well beyond the realm of the economic, expanded though this now is. The same technology that enabled rapid economic globalization has also been exploited for general use by governments, civil society and individuals. With the spread of the Internet, e-mail, low-cost international phone services, mobile phones and electronic conferencing, the world has become more interconnected (figures 8 and 9). A vast and rapidly growing stock of information, ranging from science to trivia, can now be accessed from any location in the world connected to the Internet. This can be transmitted and discussed just as easily. At the same time, satellite television and the electronic press have created a veritable global fourth estate.

Inter-relationships

149. These changes in trade, FDI, financial flows and technological diffusion are increasingly part of a new systemic whole. An underlying common factor is that all these elements necessarily evolved in the context of increasing economic openness and the growing influence of global market forces. This is a profound change, affecting the role of the State and the behaviour of economic agents.

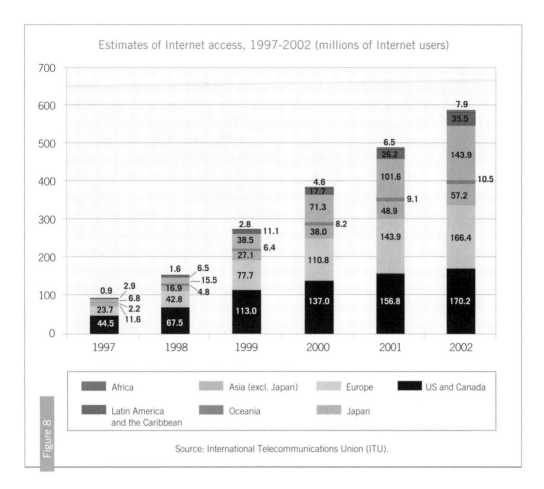

Estimates of Internet access, 1997-2002 (millions of Internet users)

Legend:
- Africa
- Asia (excl. Japan)
- Europe
- US and Canada
- Latin America and the Caribbean
- Oceania
- Japan

Source: International Telecommunications Union (ITU).

Figure 8

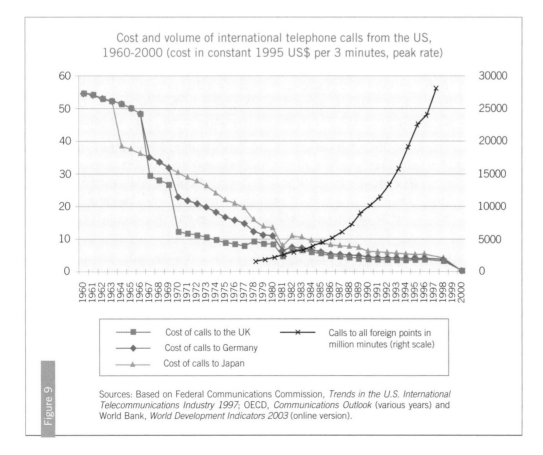

Cost and volume of international telephone calls from the US, 1960-2000 (cost in constant 1995 US$ per 3 minutes, peak rate)

Legend:
- Cost of calls to the UK
- Cost of calls to Germany
- Cost of calls to Japan
- Calls to all foreign points in million minutes (right scale)

Sources: Based on Federal Communications Commission, *Trends in the U.S. International Telecommunications Industry 1997*; OECD, *Communications Outlook* (various years) and World Bank, *World Development Indicators 2003* (online version).

Figure 9

150. Trade and FDI have become more closely intertwined as the global production system increasingly shapes patterns of trade, especially through the rapid growth of intra-firm trade in components. The MNEs are now estimated to account for two-thirds of world trade while intra-firm trade between MNEs and affiliates accounts for about one-third of world exports. At the same time, trade in components and intermediate goods has increased. The qualitative changes in the structure of world trade – specifically an increase in the trade in components and intermediate inputs – are perhaps as significant as the quantitative increase in trade. At the same time, portfolio investments and other financial flows have become an increasingly important determinant of the macroeconomic environment that shapes patterns of trade and investment in the real economy. Similarly, the diffusion of new technology has also had a profound effect on comparative advantage, the competitiveness of enterprises, the demand for labour, work organization and the nature of the employment contract.

The policy environment

151. One of the underlying factors behind increasing globalization was a shift in economic thinking that became pronounced in the 1980s. While the industrialized countries were experiencing stagflation, a significant number of developing countries had fallen into a debt crisis and experienced economic retrogression. This prompted a rethink on prevailing economic models in both industrialized and developing countries. One element of this revised thinking in developing countries related to import-substitution policies which had by then begun to run out of steam. This contrasted with the evident success of the export-oriented industrialization policies of the East Asian newly industrializing economies (NIEs).

Impact of
structural
adjustment
loans

152. The widespread recourse of indebted developing countries to structural adjustment loans from the Bretton Woods institutions in the aftermath of the debt crisis of the early 1980s played a pivotal role in the redefinition of trade and industrialization strategies. Prominent among the conditions attached to these loans was the liberalization of policies towards trade and FDI. This was in line with the rising influence of pro-market economic doctrines during this period. Under these structural adjustment programmes, there was a significant increase in the number of cases of trade and investment liberalization in many developing countries.

153. As discussed in the previous section on views about globalization, many trade unions and CSOs, as well as some policy analysts and developing country governments, maintain that the IFIs have imposed excessive conditionality on developing countries. In their view, this policy has been harmful both in confining them within an inappropriate neo-liberal policy straitjacket and in inflicting heavy social costs.

154. The rise of pro-market economic doctrines over the last 20 years played a key role in laying the foundations for the emergence of globalization. The collapse of communism in Europe in 1989-90 was a turning point. At a stroke it added to the global free market economy an additional 30 former communist countries with a combined population of 400 million people.

Free-market
globalization
boosted by
explosive growth
of Internet

155. To some analysts, the end of the bipolar world also meant the disappearance of any systemic alternative to the market economy. As a result, according to this view, free-market globalization took off in 1990. Coincidentally, this was also the period when the explosive growth of the Internet occurred, giving a fortuitous technological boost to this process.

The institutional context

The multilateral trading system

156. In the meantime, the institutional context for international economic relations also began to change. A new round of multilateral trade negotiations launched in 1986 set the stage for the transformation of GATT into the WTO in 1995. A key change was the broadening of the agenda of trade negotiations well beyond the GATT remit of reducing tariffs and other direct barriers to trade. Subjects that were hitherto not considered to be trade issues such as services, intellectual property rights (IPRs), investment measures and competition policy (the "behind-the-border" issues) were now argued to be within the scope of trade negotiations.

157. The rationale for this was that these measures were also impediments to the free flow of goods and services across borders. The harmonization of national policies in these areas was deemed to be essential for the deeper liberalization of world trade. This same logic could also be applied to a number of other aspects of national policy and regulation, especially when the objective of free trade is extended to encompass concerns over fair and sustainable trade. Hence there have been lingering tensions over the desirability of extending this list of "behind-the-border" issues.

158. With hindsight, many developing country governments perceived the outcome of the Uruguay Round to have been unbalanced. For most developing countries (some did gain), the crux of the unfavourable deal was the limited market-access concessions they obtained from developed countries in exchange for the high costs they now realize they incurred in binding themselves to the new multilateral trade rules.

Global production systems

159. The emergence of global production systems that drove the increasing flows of FDI has created new opportunities for growth and industrialization in developing countries. Some 65,000 MNEs, with around 850,000 foreign affiliates, are the key actors behind these global production systems. They coordinate global supply chains which link firms across countries, including even local sub-contractors who work outside the formal factory system and outsource to home workers. [10]

160. The growth of these global production systems has been most pronounced in the high-tech industries (electronics, semi-conductors, etc.) and in labour-intensive consumer goods (textiles, garments and footwear). It is also becoming significant in the service sector where technological advances have made it possible for services such as software development, financial services and call centres to be supplied from different countries around the globe. The high-tech industries have experienced the fastest growth and now constitute the largest single component of the manufactured exports of developing countries. [11] In these industries, the production of parts and components is carried out by subsidiaries of MNEs located in developing countries. Most of the research and development (R&D) and

Global production systems emerged, with MNEs the key actors

---

[10] See Marilyn Carr and Martha Chen: "Globalization, social exclusion and work: with special reference to informal employment and gender", background paper prepared for the World Commission, Geneva, 2003.

[11] S. Lall: *The employment impact of globalization in developing countries,* ILO mimeo (Geneva, October 2002).

other technologically sophisticated functions are carried out in the industrialized countries.

Global "just-in-time" production system

161. In the labour-intensive consumer industries the picture is quite different. The MNEs design the product, specify the product quality, and so on, and then out-source its production to local firms in developing countries. They also exercise control over the quality and timing of production, which is often subjected to changes in design and volume. The driving force is the flexible and timely adjust-ment to changes in consumer demand with minimal inventory costs. It is a global "just-in-time" production system. The MNEs also control the marketing of the product; branding and logos are an important source of market power and, incidentally, of large fortunes.

162. A notable feature of the growth of these global production systems is that it has occurred without the parallel development of multilateral rules to govern its key element, FDI. This has given rise to a number of concerns, which will be addressed in Part III.

The global financial system

Role and influence of private financial agencies greatly increased

163. The governance structure of the global financial system has also been trans-formed. As private financial flows have come to dwarf official flows, the role and influence of private actors such as banks, hedge funds, equity funds and rating agencies has increased substantially. As a result, these private financial agencies now exert tremendous power over the economic policies of developing countries, especially the emerging market economies. Rating agencies determine whether countries can have access to sovereign borrowing and, if so, the cost of this. The assessments of stock analysts have a profound influence on the flow of funds into stock markets, while the decisions of hedge fund managers often impact on national currencies.

164. Within the logic of perfect markets, there would be nothing wrong with these developments. The increased influence of private actors in the global finan-cial system should lead to greater efficiency in worldwide allocation of financial resources, as well as to the associated benefit of exerting greater, and much needed, market discipline on developing country governments. However, finan-cial markets, even at the national level, are typically one of the most imperfect of markets. There are severe problems of information failure, especially information asymmetries.

165. These problems are magnified at the level of global financial markets, where international lenders may have limited and poor information about local borrowers. For example, concerns have been raised over the operations of hedge funds and rat-ing agencies, and the probity of some large international investors in the light of recent corporate scandals. This leads to an over-extension of credit, including to unsound local banks and firms. Perceptions that there are implicit guarantees about the fixedness of exchange rates and bailouts compound this process.

166. A further important source of failure in this global financial market is the absence, at that level, of effective institutions for supervising it, such as exist at the national level.

Global financial system plagued by financial crises

167. Invariably, therefore, the global financial system has been plagued by a series of financial crises of increasing frequency and severity. The negative impact of these crises has been devastating, wiping out the gains of years of prior economic progress and inflicting heavy social costs through increased unemployment and poverty.

168. However, only a small minority of developing countries have become part of this new global financial system. As in the case of FDI, these private financial flows have remained highly concentrated in emerging markets. Thus the vast majority of developing countries, including almost all the LDCs, receive hardly any private financial flows.

169. For aid-dependent low-income countries, mostly in sub-Saharan Africa, their marginalization from financial markets means that they are deprived of any means to mitigate the effects of the significant decline in ODA. As a result, many of these countries are still, some two decades later, caught in the debt trap they fell into in the early 1980s.

Many LDCs remain caught in the debt trap

The impact of globalization

170. The combined and interactive effect of these developments in trade, FDI, finance and technology, has had a profound and varying impact on different economic sectors, types of enterprises, categories of workers and social groups. This section highlights some of the far-reaching changes that have occurred.

Primary concerns

171. We begin by setting out the perspective from which we will be evaluating the impact of globalization. Our primary concerns are that globalization should benefit all countries and should raise the welfare of all people throughout the world. This implies that it should raise the rate of economic growth in poor countries and reduce world poverty, and that it should not increase inequalities or undermine socio-economic security within countries.

172. It is thus widely accepted that the litmus test for the current process of globalization is whether it will significantly enhance the speeding up of development and the reduction of absolute poverty in the world, and whether it will ensure economic, social and environmental sustainability.

173. The social impact of globalization is not only confined to countries that have been marginalized from the process or less successful in their attempts to integrate into the global economy. Even in the relatively successful countries significant social costs are involved in the form of transitional adjustment costs, in some cases quite large. China, for example, despite sustained high growth, has faced problems of transitional unemployment that are likely to intensify with the stepping up of the reform of State-owned enterprises. Similarly, as evidenced by the Asian financial crisis, even countries with exemplary past records of economic performance can suffer heavy social costs.

Globalization can involve heavy social costs

The impact on economic growth

174. A basic step in evaluating the impact of globalization is to look at what has happened to rates of economic growth both globally and across countries. Here it is striking that since 1990 global GDP growth has been slower than in previous decades (figure 10), the period in which globalization has been most pronounced. At the very least this outcome is at variance with the more optimistic predictions on the growth-enhancing impact of globalization.

175. Growth has also been unevenly distributed across countries, among both industrialized and developing countries. In terms of per capita income growth, only 16 developing countries grew at more than 3 per cent per annum between

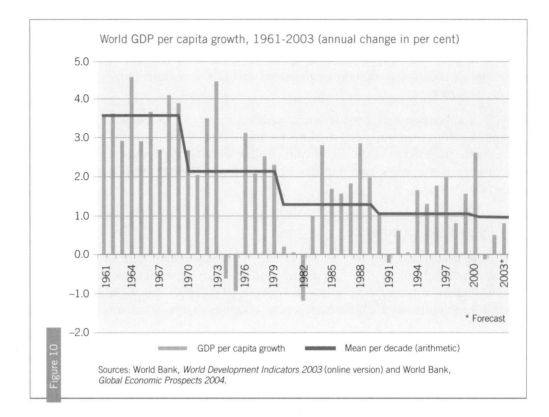

World GDP per capita growth, 1961-2003 (annual change in per cent)

* Forecast

GDP per capita growth ▬▬ Mean per decade (arithmetic)

Sources: World Bank, *World Development Indicators 2003* (online version) and World Bank, *Global Economic Prospects 2004*.

Figure 10

1985 and 2000 (table 1). In contrast, 55 developing countries grew at less than 2 per cent per annum, and of these 23 suffered negative growth.

176. At the same time, the income gap between the richest and poorest countries increased significantly (figure 11).

177. This uneven pattern of growth is shaping a new global economic geography. The most striking change is the rapid economic growth in China over the last two decades, together with a more gradual but significant improvement in the economic growth performance of India, two countries which together account for more than one-third of the world's population.

Table 1. The economic performance of developing countries (grouped by growth performance) compared to industrial and transition countries

		Industrial countries	Developing countries with growth rate per capita GDP of							Transition[1] countries
			← >3%[2] →		2%-3%	1%-2%	0%-1%	<0%		
Number of countries		22	16	(14)	12	20	14	23		17
% share of world population (2001)[3]		13.8	44.7	(7.1)	5.6	10.3	7.5	4.8		5.3
GDP growth (in %), 1985-2001		2.5	7.3	(6.2)	4.2	3.4	2.3	1.8		−1.1
Population growth (in %), 1985-2001		0.65	1.5	(1.6)	2.0	2.2	2.1	2.6		−0.3
% share in global trade (including transition countries)	1991	53.9	18.5	(10.3)	3.2	6.6	3.1	4.7		10.0
	2001	48.4	26.6	(11.3)	2.9	6.7	3.0	3.6		8.9
% share in global FDI (including transition countries)	1991	54.4	24.6	(13.7)	2.2	10.2	3.0	2.9		2.7
	2001	52.9	22.2	(2.7)	2.0	5.8	6.9	4.3		5.8

[1] Growth rates for transition countries are calculated for the period 1991-2002. [2] The second column excludes China and India. [3] The 124 countries included in the sample accounted for 92 per cent of the estimated world population of 6,129 million in 2001.

Source: The basic data are taken from the World Bank, World Development Indicators (CD-ROM, 2003).

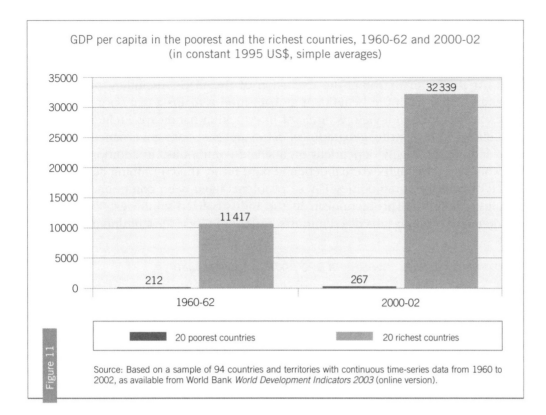

GDP per capita in the poorest and the richest countries, 1960-62 and 2000-02 (in constant 1995 US$, simple averages)

Source: Based on a sample of 94 countries and territories with continuous time-series data from 1960 to 2002, as available from World Bank *World Development Indicators 2003* (online version).

Figure 11

Uneven impact across countries

178. Significant though it is, the rise of China and India is only part of a larger picture which reveals highly uneven distribution of the benefits of globalization among countries. The industrial countries, with their strong initial economic base, abundance of capital and skill, and technological leadership, were well placed to gain substantial benefits from increasing globalization of the world economy.

179. Expanding global markets for goods and services provided new outlets for their exports while the emergence of global production systems and liberalized investment rules generated new opportunities for their MNEs, increasing their global reach and market power. Similarly, the growth of global financial markets provided expanded opportunities for investments with higher returns in emerging markets. In addition, their technological leadership, together with the strengthening of international rules on IPRs through the WTO, increased their earnings from royalties and licensing fees. However, these benefits were partly offset by internal problems of adjustment that generated losses for some workers.

180. The other clear group that reaped significant benefits was the minority of developing countries that have been highly successful in increasing their exports and in attracting large inflows of FDI. Foremost among this group have been the original NIEs of East Asia that have now converged on industrialized country income levels and economic structures. Some other middle-income countries in Asia, the EU accession countries, and Latin American countries such as Mexico and Chile also appear to be on track to achieve this.

A minority of developing countries reaped significant benefits

181. For the most part, these countries had relatively favourable initial conditions in terms of prior industrialization, the level of human resource development, transport and communications infrastructure, and the quality of economic and social institutions. But they have not all pursued the same development strategies. Notably, China, India and Vietnam, countries with large domestic markets, have

not followed orthodox liberalization strategies, while the Republic of Korea, for example, relied on strong government intervention to kick-start its industrial development.

The LDCs remain
excluded from
the benefits of
globalization

182. At the other extreme, the exclusion of the LDCs, including most of sub-Saharan Africa, from the benefits of globalization remains a stubborn reality. The LDCs are trapped in a vicious circle of interlocking handicaps including poverty and illiteracy, civil strife, geographical disadvantages, poor governance and inflexible economies largely dependent on a single commodity. In addition, many are also burdened by high external debt and hard hit by the continuing decline in the price of primary commodities. These problems have been compounded by continuing agricultural protectionism in the industrialized countries. This restricts market access while subsidized imports undermine local agricultural producers.

The impact of trade, investment and financial liberalization

183. More insight into how the key elements of globalization have affected countries can be gleaned from the growing body of country studies on these issues. A broad generalization that appears to emerge from these is that the impact has been mixed.

184. For example, a set of recent ILO studies on the impact of trade on employment and wages in the manufacturing sector showed sharply contrasting impacts among countries.[12] In the three Asian emerging economies studied, trade growth had a generally favourable effect on employment and wages in manufacturing. In contrast, in Latin American countries such as Brazil and Mexico, employment in manufacturing has either not risen appreciably or has fallen. Real wages of unskilled workers have tended to decline and the wage differential between skilled and unskilled workers has increased relatively sharply.

No universal
prescription for
the best approach
to trade
liberalization

185. These and similar studies suggest that the relationship between trade liberalization and growth and employment is likely to be "a contingent one, dependent on a host of countries and external characteristics".[13] Differences in country circumstances (such as the level of income or whether a country has comparative advantage in primary commodities or manufacturing) are likely to warrant different strategies of trade liberalization. There is thus no simple universally valid prescription on the best approach to trade liberalization.

186. With respect to FDI, the evidence suggests that, on the whole, foreign investment does increase growth. Although this should also have a positive effect on employment this may be negated by strong crowding-out effects on local firms unable to compete and by the introduction of capital-intensive technology by foreign firms. However, empirical evidence on the employment impact of FDI is sparse and does not permit simple generalization.

187. Cross-border investments can potentially also raise the rate of growth if there are spillover benefits from the transfer of technology and skills to the local economy. In this case, the investment raises labour productivity and incomes and hence exerts a positive effect on growth and employment. Once again, the empirical evidence reveals mixed outcomes. While countries such as Singapore and Ireland

---

[12] Ajit Ghose: *Jobs and Incomes in a Globalizing World* (Geneva, ILO, 2003).

[13] Francisco Rodriguez, and Dani Rodrik: "Trade Policy and Economic Growth: A Sceptic's Guide to the Cross-National Evidence", in B. Bernanke and K. Rogoff: *NBER Macroeconomics Annual 2000* (Cambridge, MA, MIT Press, 2000).

have experienced strong spillover effects, this has not been true of all countries. The main lesson learnt from the success stories is that a critical precondition is the presence of local firms able to absorb the new technologies and respond to new demands. Also vital are policies to develop local education, training and technology systems and to build supplier networks and support institutions.

188. However, the empirical evidence cited above on the impact of FDI on growth and employment provides only partial answers to the complex issue of what the net benefits from FDI have been to a host country. A full evaluation will have to give due weight to factors such as: the impact of FDI on small and medium-sized enterprises and on poor producers; the potential conflicts of interest between foreign firms and host countries; and the impact of FDI on the pattern of trade and the balance of payments. How the balance of costs and benefits works out largely depends on country characteristics and policies but international trends also matter. These include the increasing locational flexibility of FDI and the growing influence of MNEs in areas such as intellectual property and trade and financial flows in the global economy.

189. On capital account liberalization, there is emerging agreement that the growth benefits to be derived from it are small. Even setting aside the economic and social havoc caused by crises, the gains to developing countries from participating in the current global financial system have been increasingly questioned. The potential benefits in terms of increased access to international financial markets have often been reduced or negated by instability. This problem is particularly acute for countries with poorly regulated financial systems.

Growth benefits from capital account liberalization are small

190. A basic structural flaw has been the prominence of short-term speculative flows within the system. This has led to surges of capital inflows when the capital accounts are opened, which have then been swiftly reversed. This has been largely driven by a quest for short-term speculative gains that has not only failed to contribute to an increase in productive investment but has also created new constraints to development policy.

Short-term speculative flows have been damaging

191. Financial openness has also, in some cases, led to a misallocation of resources and an increase in the real cost of capital. The misallocation arises when information failures lead foreign lenders to finance unsound investments. The real cost of capital is also increased when governments raise interest rates in order to maintain exchange rate stability. Other side effects of financial openness have been the need to maintain a significantly higher level of foreign exchange reserves and greater vulnerability to the flight of domestic capital.

192. More fundamentally, financial openness has limited the scope for deploying countercyclical macroeconomic policy. The reason for this lies in the fact that with financial openness countries have to surrender autonomy over either exchange rate or monetary policy. Given open capital accounts, maintaining a fixed exchange rate implies forgoing the freedom to fix domestic interest rates, while control over the latter can only be regained by allowing the exchange rate to float. In addition, the scope for expansionary fiscal policies is often severely restricted by the demands of foreign financiers.

193. Globalization also affects public finances. In particular, tax rates have declined on relatively more mobile factors of production. In the world's 30 richest countries the average level of corporate tax fell from 37.6 per cent in 1996 to 30.8 per cent in 2003 (figure 12). Tax incentives to attract FDI contributed to their lowering of average tax rates. A similar phenomenon can be seen in the taxation of high-income earners, who are also relatively more mobile. Between 1986 and

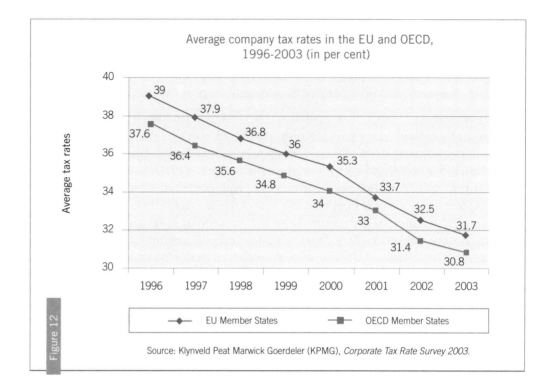

Average company tax rates in the EU and OECD,
1996-2003 (in per cent)

Source: Klynveld Peat Marwick Goerdeler (KPMG), *Corporate Tax Rate Survey 2003*.

Figure 12

1998, the top marginal tax rate on personal income declined in the vast majority of countries, both high- and low-income, often substantially.[14] These changes in tax rates do not necessarily reduce tax revenues overall, since lower tax rates can also reduce tax evasion and increase production incentives. Nevertheless, there is concern about the distributional impact of these reductions in tax rates for mobile factors of production. A greater reliance on indirect taxes and on taxes on relatively immobile factors such as labour makes tax systems less progressive at a time when income inequality has been increasing in several high- and middle-income countries.

Employment, inequality and poverty

194. In order to assess the social impact of globalization it is essential to go beyond economic performance and examine what happened to employment, income inequality and poverty over the past two decades of globalization.

Open
unemployment
rates have
increased

195. For the world as a whole latest ILO estimates show that open unemployment has increased over the last decade to about 188 million in 2003. However, employment performance over the past two decades has varied across regions (figure 13). It is also noticeable that within the developing world unemployment rates have increased since 1990 in Latin America and the Caribbean and South-East Asia, and since 1995 in East Asia. One factor behind the rise in unemployment in these regions was the financial crisis at the end of the 1990s. For example, in some major countries affected by crises, unemployment rates did decline after the crisis, but in many cases not to the pre-crisis level (figure 14).

196. The share of self-employment, which for most developing regions is a proxy indicator for the size of the informal economy, increased in all developing regions, except for East and South-East Asia (figure 15). Direct data on employment in the

[14] See Raymond Torres: *Towards a socially sustainable world economy* (Geneva, ILO, 2001).

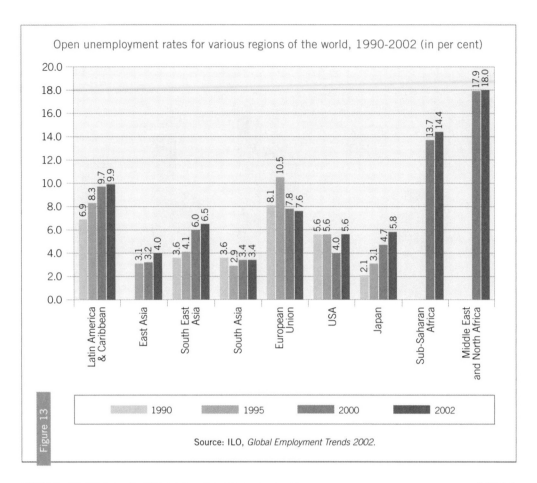

Open unemployment rates for various regions of the world, 1990-2002 (in per cent)

	1990	1995	2000	2002
Latin America & Caribbean	6.9	8.3	9.7	9.9
East Asia	3.1	3.2		4.0
South East Asia	3.6	4.1	6.0	6.5
South Asia	3.6	2.9	3.4	3.4
European Union	8.1	10.5	7.8	7.6
USA	5.6	5.6	4.0	5.6
Japan	2.1	3.1	4.7	5.8
Sub-Saharan Africa			13.7	14.4
Middle East and North Africa			17.9	18.0

Source: ILO, *Global Employment Trends 2002*.

Figure 13

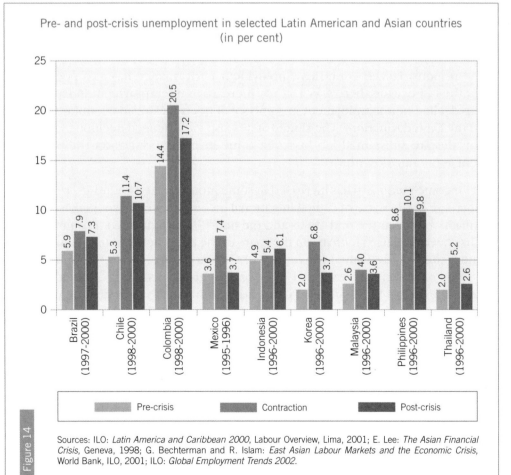

Pre- and post-crisis unemployment in selected Latin American and Asian countries (in per cent)

	Pre-crisis	Contraction	Post-crisis
Brazil (1997-2000)	5.9	7.9	7.3
Chile (1998-2000)	5.3	11.4	10.7
Colombia (1998-2000)	14.4	20.5	17.2
Mexico (1995-1996)	3.6	7.4	3.7
Indonesia (1996-2000)	4.9	5.4	6.1
Korea (1996-2000)	2.0	6.8	3.7
Malaysia (1996-2000)	2.6	4.0	3.6
Philippines (1996-2000)	8.6	10.1	9.8
Thailand (1996-2000)	2.0	5.2	2.6

Sources: ILO: *Latin America and Caribbean 2000*, Labour Overview, Lima, 2001; E. Lee: *The Asian Financial Crisis*, Geneva, 1998; G. Bechterman and R. Islam: *East Asian Labour Markets and the Economic Crisis*, World Bank, ILO, 2001; ILO: *Global Employment Trends 2002*.

Figure 14

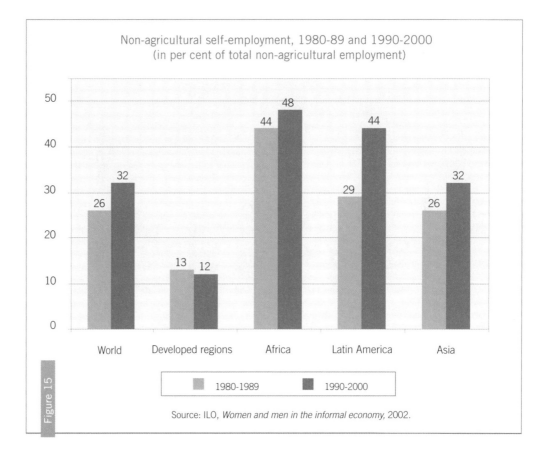

Non-agricultural self-employment, 1980-89 and 1990-2000
(in per cent of total non-agricultural employment)

Figure 15

1980-1989   1990-2000

Source: ILO, *Women and men in the informal economy*, 2002.

informal economy are not readily available. Such an increase is typically linked to stagnation or slow growth in modern sector employment and the consequent increase in labour absorption in the informal economy.

197. In industrialized countries employment performance has also been mixed. Over the last decade there was a steady increase in unemployment in Japan, but a sharp decline in unemployment in some small open European economies, as well as in the United Kingdom. The United States also experienced declining unemployment, despite substantial job losses in some manufacturing industries, until the recent economic downturn.

198. Income inequality has increased in some industrialized countries, reflected in an increase in the share of capital in national income as well as an increase in wage inequality between the mid-1980s and the mid-1990s (figure 16). Even more striking has been the sharp increase in the share of the top 1 per cent of income earners in the United States, United Kingdom and Canada (figure 17). In the United States the share of this group reached 17 per cent of gross income in 2000, a level last seen in the 1920s. This increased concentration in wealth has been the prime factor in the rise in income inequality in the United States; the declining share of the bottom decile of wage earners has been in reverse since 1995.

199. This emergence of wealth is important for the analysis of globalization since exceptionally high earnings have typically been linked to compensation paid by MNEs, the development of new businesses with a global reach and global "superstardom". The increased concentration in wealth is likely to imply increased market and political power, both nationally and globally, for those who have benefited from this. It is also an important influence on people's perceptions of globalization.

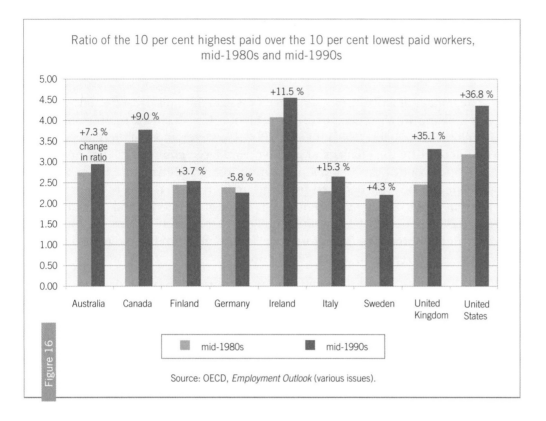

Ratio of the 10 per cent highest paid over the 10 per cent lowest paid workers, mid-1980s and mid-1990s

+7.3 %
change
in ratio

+9.0 %

+3.7 %

-5.8 %

+11.5 %

+15.3 %

+4.3 %

+35.1 %

+36.8 %

Australia   Canada   Finland   Germany   Ireland   Italy   Sweden   United   United
                                                                          Kingdom   States

mid-1980s   mid-1990s

Source: OECD, *Employment Outlook* (various issues).

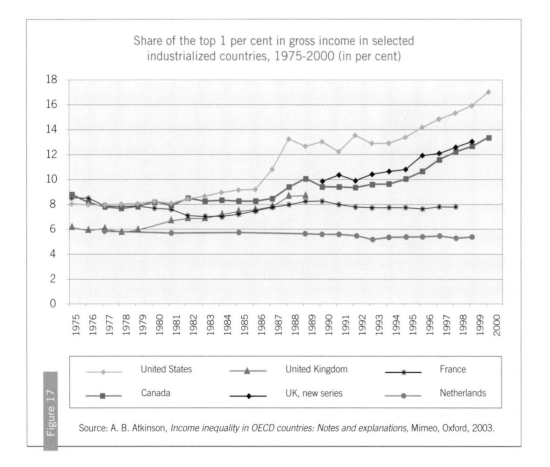

Share of the top 1 per cent in gross income in selected industrialized countries, 1975-2000 (in per cent)

United States   United Kingdom   France

Canada   UK, new series   Netherlands

Source: A. B. Atkinson, *Income inequality in OECD countries: Notes and explanations,* Mimeo, Oxford, 2003.

200. Outside the industrialized countries, there has been a similarly mixed picture on changes in income inequality (figure 18). While the large majority of countries have experienced a rise in income inequality, it remains an open question as to what extent globalization is to blame.

201. The impact of globalization on poverty is also difficult to assess. The number of people living in absolute poverty worldwide has declined significantly from 1,237 million in 1990 to 1,100 million in 2000. However, most of this improvement is accounted for by the changes in just two very large countries, China and India, where 38 per cent of the world's population live. In China alone the number of people living in poverty declined from 361 million to 204 million. Elsewhere, in sub-Saharan Africa, Europe and Central Asia, and Latin America and the Caribbean, poverty has increased by 82, 14, and 8 million, respectively (figure 19). However, regional and country-specific factors unrelated to globalization were also key factors in these differences in poverty reduction.

202. All this leaves a basic ambiguity in the interpretation of the data on trends in global poverty. While it is clearly a cause for celebration that world poverty in the aggregate has been reduced, this is little consolation to those outside the few countries where these gains have been concentrated.

203. An additional ambiguity is that there can be real social costs involved even if aggregate indicators such as the unemployment rate or the level of poverty do not show any deterioration. The reason for this is that the stability of these rates could mask considerable "churning" in labour markets and movements in and out of poverty. There is some evidence that these phenomena have become more marked with increasing globalization. Again, it is cold comfort to those who have lost jobs or fallen into poverty that others experiencing opposite fortunes have prevented a fall in the unemployment or poverty rate.

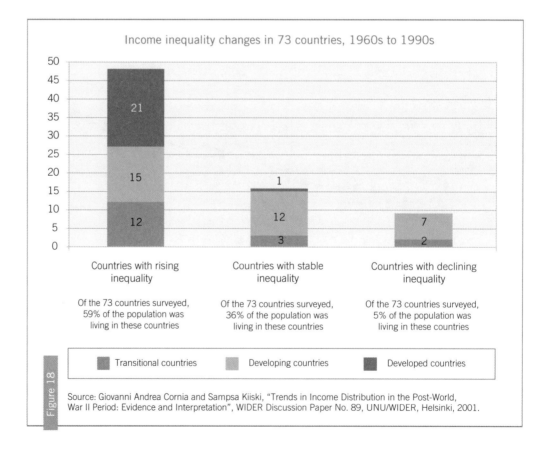

Figure 18

Source: Giovanni Andrea Cornia and Sampsa Kiiski, "Trends in Income Distribution in the Post-World War II Period: Evidence and Interpretation", WIDER Discussion Paper No. 89, UNU/WIDER, Helsinki, 2001.

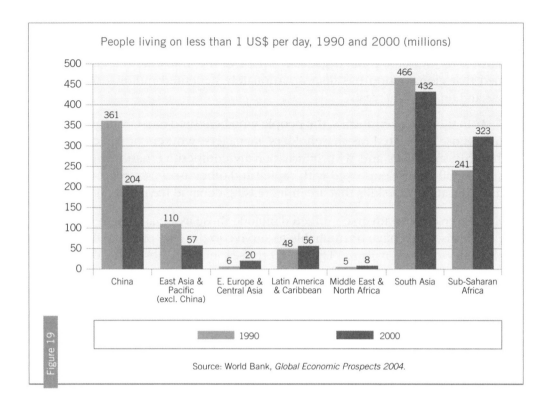

People living on less than 1 US$ per day, 1990 and 2000 (millions)

China: 361 (1990), 204 (2000)
East Asia & Pacific (excl. China): 110 (1990), 57 (2000)
E. Europe & Central Asia: 6 (1990), 20 (2000)
Latin America & Caribbean: 48 (1990), 56 (2000)
Middle East & North Africa: 5 (1990), 8 (2000)
South Asia: 466 (1990), 432 (2000)
Sub-Saharan Africa: 241 (1990), 323 (2000)

■ 1990   ■ 2000

Source: World Bank, *Global Economic Prospects 2004*.

Figure 19

204. This type of mobility is one of the main reasons why people have different perceptions of the social impact of globalization. Personal experience (or direct observations) of job or income loss by particular social groups or localities largely colours perceptions, regardless of what the overall picture may be. As a result, at least part of the heated debate over the social impact rests on such differences in perceptions and in the way aggregate social indicators are interpreted.

205. The mixed picture that emerges on economic performance and on changes in employment, inequality and poverty makes it extremely difficult to generalize on what the impact of globalization has been. In part this is because globalization is a complex phenomenon. Observed outcomes such as changes in the level of unemployment and of poverty reflect the combined results of a complex of factors of which globalization, however broadly defined, is but one. Domestic structural factors such as the degree of inequality in the distribution of income and wealth and the quality of governance are often important fundamental influences on these outcomes. It is important to avoid the common error of attributing all observed outcomes, positive or negative, entirely to globalization.

The impact on people

206. This section looks beyond economic variables to focus on how globalization has affected peoples' lives. Globalization involves changes in economic structure, relative prices, and consumption possibilities and patterns, which in turn affects peoples' jobs, livelihoods and incomes. Invariably some have been adversely affected while others have gained from this often intense process of change.

207. The economic benefits and social costs of globalization are not evenly distributed among social groups. In many countries some groups of workers have been adversely affected by trade liberalization and the relocation of production to lower-wage economies. While this has so far primarily affected unskilled workers, some skilled and professional workers have also been affected by developments

In many countries some workers have been adversely affected

such as the outsourcing of software development, the increasing trade in professional services and increased immigration of skilled professionals from developing countries. At the same time, organized labour in the industrialized countries has argued that globalization has disproportionately benefited multinational corporations and financial interests.

208. As in the case of countries, the people who benefited most from globalization include those associated (as shareholders, managers, workers or sub-contractors) with successful MNEs and with internationally competitive national enterprises. More generally, those endowed with capital and other assets, entrepreneurial ability and education and skills that are in increasing demand have all benefited.

209. Conversely, the adversely affected include those associated with uncompetitive enterprises that have been unable to survive in the face of trade liberalization or the entry of foreign firms. These enterprises include those previously highly protected by trade barriers, subsidized State enterprises, and small and medium-sized enterprises that had a limited capacity to adjust to a rapid liberalization of the economy. Impoverished producers of importables, whether in the urban informal economy or in agriculture, have been particularly vulnerable to the influx of cheap imports and sharp changes in the relative prices and availability of inputs. Such producers are also unable to seize the new economic opportunities that have been generated because they lack capital and access to credit, information and extension services.

210. Others who have lost out, except in countries that have experienced rapid growth, have been the poor, the assetless, illiterate and unskilled workers and indigenous peoples. This has occurred not only as a result of the primary economic impact of globalization but also because of its indirect effects. For example, the increased mobility of capital combined with high levels of unemployment has weakened the bargaining position of workers vis-à-vis employers. At the same time, increasing international competition for markets and for FDI have generated pressures to increase labour market flexibility and erode labour protection. Hence, in spite of the positive effects of FDI described earlier and the fact that workers in foreign firms often earn more than in local firms, there have been growing concerns over the inadequate quality of the employment that has been generated in some parts of the global production system. This is particularly true of employment in firms acting as sub-contractors to MNEs in labour-intensive industries such as garments and footwear. This has highlighted the importance of international action to protect fundamental worker rights in all countries.

211. A particularly vulnerable group is indigenous peoples. Where their integration into the global economy has occurred without their free and prior informed consent and without adequate protection of their rights, livelihoods, and culture, they have suffered severely. In such cases investments in extractive industries, mega-hydroelectric dams, and plantations have led to massive dislocations, disruption of livelihoods, ecological degradation, and violation of their basic human rights.

212. Increasing tax competition, together with the new doctrine in favour of a reduced role for the State, is widely believed to have reduced the fiscal capacity of governments. In many cases, this has led to a reduction in government expenditures vital to the poor such as those on health, education, social safety nets, agricultural extension services and poverty reduction. For example, figure 20 shows declines in expenditure on education in several regions of the world in the latter part of the 1990s.

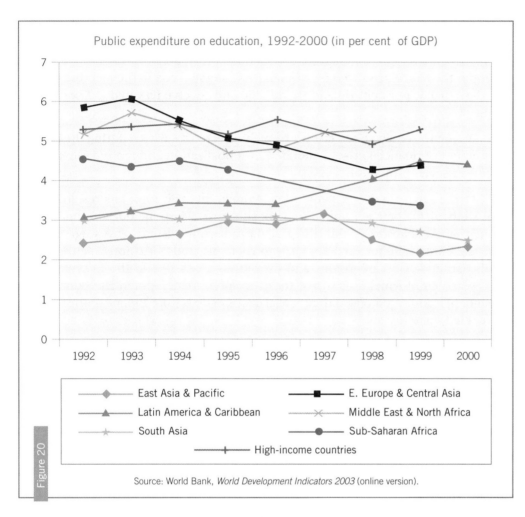

Public expenditure on education, 1992-2000 (in per cent of GDP)

Legend:
- East Asia & Pacific
- E. Europe & Central Asia
- Latin America & Caribbean
- Middle East & North Africa
- South Asia
- Sub-Saharan Africa
- High-income countries

Source: World Bank, *World Development Indicators 2003* (online version).

Figure 20

213. Such expenditures, used efficiently, are vital for poverty reduction and for enhancing the capabilities of people to benefit from globalization. Education, for example, is a key element in a global economy where education, skills and knowledge are increasingly important for economic survival, let alone success. Yet the level of investment in education is grossly inadequate. Of the 680 million children of primary school age in developing countries, 115 million are not in school, 65 million of them girls. And of the children who start primary school only one in two complete it.

Investment in education is grossly inadequate

214. In some countries, globalization has resulted in serious gender imbalances. The extent of this imbalance depends largely on the level of gender equality prevailing in the norms, institutions and policies of a country at the time when integration into the global economy takes place. In addition, women from different social groups in a particular country are affected differently. Nevertheless, in many developing countries deep-rooted and long-standing gender inequalities have meant that the social cost of globalization has fallen disproportionately on women.

215. There is a growing body of evidence illustrating the ways in which substantial numbers of women have been adversely affected by globalization, both absolutely as well as in relation to men. For instance, trade liberalization has often allowed the import of subsidized agricultural products and consumer goods that have wiped out the livelihoods of women producers. The increased entry of foreign firms has often had a similar effect through, for example, displacing farming women from their land or out-competing them for raw materials essential to their productive activities. At the same time, women producers face formidable barriers to entry

Many women adversely affected

into new economic activities generated by globalization. This is often because of biases, either against women directly or against the micro- and small enterprise sector in which they predominate, in the policy and regulatory environment. The extent of the handicaps faced by women producers is seen in the fact that women own less than 2 per cent of land worldwide and receive less than 10 per cent of credit. [15]

216. Women have also been more adversely affected than men during the increasing number of financial crises generated by globalization and more disadvantaged by cuts in social protection.

217. At the same time, for many other women, globalization has resulted in an improvement in their economic and social status. They include the millions of women workers absorbed into the global production system. This wage employment gave them higher incomes than in their previous situations – either intra-family servitude or a penurious and precarious existence in the informal economy. Wage employment also gave these women greater potential economic independence and often raised their social status even within the most oppressively patriarchal societies.

Wider effects

218. There are other far-reaching ways in which globalization has touched the lives of people. We focus on two key aspects of these: increased global interconnectivity and the growth of illicit cross-border activities.

Global interconnectivity has increased awareness of global disparities

219. The massive increase in global interconnectivity is affecting people's lives in different ways, some of them predictable and others unforeseen. One important change is an increase in global awareness. People anywhere are now much more aware of events and issues everywhere. This has vastly expanded awareness of global disparities in living standards and life chances, and political and social rights and liberties.

... improved the quality of democracy

220. For people living in the relatively deprived parts of the world, this both raises their expectations and lowers their tolerance of the situation they are in. This has probably been a significant factor in the spread of democracy and growing demands for political freedoms where these are still denied. The increased availability of information has also created better-informed and more critical pressure groups and electorates, a boon for the quality of democracy.

... and forged a greater sense of global community

221. For people in the richer countries, the information revolution is helping forge a greater sense of global community and transnational solidarity, as seen in the explosive growth of global coalitions of non-State actors around issues of universal concern such as globalization itself, the environment, human rights, humanitarian aid and labour exploitation.

222. This global information revolution has also clearly affected cultures and social values. However, these kinds of changes are difficult to pin down and document. One contentious issue is the impact of the information revolution on local cultures and values across the world. There is widespread concern at the overwhelming dominance of the culture and values of the United States, and other Western countries, in the global media and entertainment industry. The fear is that

---

[15] FAO: *Women and sustainable food security* (SD Dimensions, SDWW, 2003) (http://www.fao.org/sd/fsdirect/fbdirect/FSP001.htm).

constant exposure to the images of Western lifestyles and role models could lead to tensions which would be both culturally and socially divisive.

223. Another side-effect of globalization has been a sharp increase in the level of illicit cross-border activities. This has included increased tax evasion and the rise of multinational crime syndicates engaged in money laundering, trafficking in people, and the sex and drug trades. The same factors that facilitated the growth of legitimate cross-border economic transactions have also provided the means for illicit cross-border transactions. The ICT revolution has made the cross-border coordination of illicit activities easier, while global financial liberalization has facilitated tax evasion and money laundering. Similarly, the sharp fall in transportation costs and the growth of mass tourism has made the smuggling of people and drugs less costly and more difficult to detect.

Illicit cross-border activities

224. This inadvertent facilitation of cross-border crime has also been reinforced by two other factors. The first is the increase in the economic returns to cross-border crime through the expansion of lucrative opportunities for arbitraging across markets (e.g. the emergence of off-shore financial centres and tax havens, and the growing income disparity between poor and rich countries alongside tight immigration controls). The second factor is the slow development of multilateral arrangements for the detection and suppression of these illicit cross-border activities, which reduces the risks involved. Under such favourable conditions, these activities have flourished.

III. THE GOVERNANCE OF GLOBALIZATION

Introduction

225. The goals set out in our vision require concerted action on a wide front. The major thrust of our proposals for action relate to improving the governance of the global economy. We believe that globalization has vast potential for increasing economic efficiency and growth and thereby for delivering economic prosperity to all nations and people. But, as our preceding analysis has shown, we are still far short of fully realizing these potential benefits.

226. A basic reason for this is that the current process of globalization lacks effective and democratic governance. Some essential market-supporting and regulatory institutions are missing, making the system prone to various market failures. Moreover, the rules and institutions that do exist are unfair towards poor countries, both in the ways they were drawn up and in their impact. This is compounded by the weakness of mechanisms for redressing the vast inequalities between and within countries, and for delivering on important social priorities such as the provision of global public goods [16] and social protection.

227. In a world of nation States, the governance of globalization is bound up with governance at the national level. To take advantage of the opportunities of globalization, and ensure that they are widely and fairly distributed among different groups within nations, there is a need for effective political and legal institutions, strong economic and technological capabilities, and policies which integrate economic and social goals. More generally, well governed countries, whose domestic policies take into account the needs of other countries, will be more effective partners in bringing about a fair and more inclusive process of globalization. This is why the response to globalization can be said to begin at home.

228. We therefore start, in section III.1, by examining the instruments and options that governments and key national actors have available to strengthen national institutions and policies, with a view to improving their social and economic performance in the context of globalization. This calls in the first instance for action at the national level. But we believe that a fairer globalization also needs action and empowerment at different levels – in local communities and economies, and in the rapidly developing new forms of regional cooperation and integration. We examine some of the key issues at each level.

229. We then turn, in section III.2, to the large and complex agenda for the reform of global governance. We first lay out the analytical framework for the governance of globalization that is the basis for our subsequent recommendations. It highlights the deficiencies in the current system of governance and the unbalanced outcomes resulting from these. In doing so, it also identifies the key reforms that are required.

230. In section III.2.2 we address the first of these areas for reform, the current rules governing the global economy. We argue that there is a need for greater fairness and balance, both between and within countries and especially between rich and poor countries. This includes both the unfairness of some of the rules that do exist for the multilateral trading and financial systems, as well as the negative impact of the absence of adequate rules in areas such as international migration.

231. Next, in section III.2.3, we set out our proposals for a more equitable and coherent set of international policies covering development assistance and the

---

[16] For example the control of communicable diseases, protection of the environment and global security.

achievement of global social and economic aims. These policies exert a major influence on the distribution of the benefits of globalization and its impact on poverty. We highlight, in particular, the urgent need to substantially increase resources to meet global goals, to ensure that there is consistency and coherence between economic and social objectives, and to give higher priority to the goal of decent work for all.

232. Finally, in section III.2.4, we examine key institutions of the current system of global governance, and the role of the main actors concerned. We suggest steps which can be taken to strengthen the capacity of the multilateral system to address the social dimension of globalization by making it more democratic, coherent and accountable, and to mobilize all actors – both State and non-State – to support this process.

III.1 Beginning at home

National capabilities and policies

Empowering the local level

Regional integration as a stepping stone

233. All nations are increasingly interdependent, and we urgently need better and fairer global rules, policies and institutions. But before coming to those essential questions, we must start at home. People experience the problems and opportunities of an increasingly interconnected world, often different for women and men, within their own communities and countries. Policies within nations continue to be a key factor in determining whether or not countries and people benefit from globalization. We need to examine the means and instruments available to governments, and to social actors within countries, to enable citizens to participate effectively in the gains of globalization and to protect and provide assistance when adjustments are required.

Governments must manage change

234. Globalization leads to economic adjustment in all countries, industrialized and developing. New economic opportunities emerge, but they may demand new skills and appear in new locations. Relocation of production between countries can destroy jobs in one place and create employment in others. Whole regions where production is concentrated in declining sectors suffer, while others benefit from new opportunities. Governments need to manage these changes, in coordination with key social actors – supporting adjustment and new opportunities, empowering people through participation and skills and protecting citizens from insecurity. The challenges are especially daunting for many developing countries where institutions, capabilities and infrastructure need to be built while simultaneously facing an increasingly competitive economic environment.

235. While each national situation is different and there is no universal policy agenda, some issues recur. The following sections explore the contribution of democratic governance, the need for strong State capabilities to manage the process of integration into the global economy and the challenges of the informal economy. We look at investment in education, work and employment, and the need for coherence among economic, social and environmental goals.

236. This is not only a national agenda. How people set and meet their goals and aspirations depends to a large extent on their immediate economic and social environment. Successful policies to respond to globalization need to start with local

communities. Their empowerment is a central element in any strategy for making globalization work for people.

237. Finally, coordination among countries at the regional level offers an additional route to expand capabilities and strengthen institutions. We look at the role that regional integration can play in achieving a fairer pattern of globalization.

National capabilities and policies

Governance

238. We strongly believe in the fundamental importance of good governance in all countries at all levels of development for effective and equitable participation in the global economy. The basic principles which we believe must guide globalization are democracy, social equity, respect for human rights and the rule of law.[17] These need to be reflected in institutions, rules and political systems within countries, and respected by all sectors of society.

Good governance is the foundation

239. Poor governance is manifested in a host of interlocking problems that have appeared in varying combinations and degrees in different countries. Examples include dysfunctional States torn apart by civil strife, authoritarian governments of various hues, and States with democratic government but severe inadequacies in terms of the policies and institutions required to support a well-functioning market economy. In the most extreme cases there is little hope for improvement without international action and assistance. In others, where the basic preconditions for democratic governance are in place, there is considerable scope for bringing about improvement through national effort.

240. The basis for good governance is a well-functioning democratic political system that ensures representative and honest governments responsive to the needs of people. This involves more than simply the holding of regular, free and fair elections. It also implies respect for human rights in general, and notably for basic civil liberties such as freedom of expression and of association, including a free and pluralistic media. Every effort should be made to remove obstacles to the growth of representative organizations of workers and employers, and to fruitful social dialogue between them. In addition, proactive measures are needed to promote the growth of representative organizations of the poor and other socially disadvantaged groups. These are fundamental conditions for the development of a vibrant civil society that reflects the full diversity of views and interests. They are all means to ensure participatory processes of policy design and implementation, and provide continual checks and balances on the exercise of governmental authority and private power.

Good governance is built on democracy, the rule of law, and equitable social and economic institutions

241. The rule of law and the effective administration of justice is the foundation. An equitable legal framework, applied consistently to everyone, defends people from abuse of power by the State or by non-State actors. It empowers people to assert their rights – to property, education, decent work, freedom of speech and other "springboards" for human growth and advancement. Meanwhile, efforts are needed at both national and local level to ensure that the law is respected and

---

[17] "We will spare no effort to promote democracy and strengthen the rule of law, as well as respect for all internationally recognized human rights and fundamental freedoms, including the right to development", United Nations Millennium Declaration, 2000.

applied, and that all citizens, rich and poor, have the access, knowledge and resources to use it. This requires transparent and accountable government institutions at executive, administrative and parliamentary levels, as well as independent judiciaries. Public monitoring of budgets, contracts and procurement is also crucial – a role which is mainly the responsibility of parliaments, but in which employers' and workers' organizations, and representative CSOs also have an important part to play.

242. The need for good governance also extends to the formal institutions required for the efficient and equitable functioning of a market economy. The basic requirements include a sound financial system that mobilizes savings and promotes investment, the regulation of markets to prevent abuse and anti-competitive behaviour, mechanisms for ensuring transparent and socially responsible corporate governance, and an effective system for delineating property rights and for the enforcement of contracts. Without such institutions, countries are highly disadvantaged in access to global financial markets. Labour market institutions, including appropriate legal frameworks, freedom of association, and institutions for dialogue and bargaining are also essential in order to protect the fundamental rights of workers, provide social protection and promote sound industrial relations. Social dialogue is an important component of good governance, and an instrument for participation and accountability. Means are also required to ensure that the inequality of income and wealth remains within acceptable limits so that social cohesion can be strengthened.

243. One important aspect of national governance is the need for countries to adequately take into account the impact of their domestic policies on others. In an interconnected world, the economic policies of the major players in the global economy have a substantial impact on all other countries. Those countries with greater decision-making power in international bodies also have a special responsibility to consider all interests in the global market place. There is also a widespread failure to live up to commitments and agreements reached in the global United Nations conferences of the 1990s, especially where these involved financial resources. [18]

Poor governance is widespread

244. All countries are afflicted by some forms of poor governance. In the public sector, the accountability of public servants and public administrations is often inadequate in both high- and low-income countries. [19] Meanwhile in the private sector, poor corporate governance has become an issue of major concern. The enormous abuses in 2001 and 2002 by the management of Enron, Worldcom and Global Crossing were possible because of poorly functioning boards and deficient auditing and accounting practices. Corruption is widespread in many developing countries, where it is especially detrimental to the poorest who are excluded from services and are subject to arbitrary treatment. And industrialized countries are by no means corruption-free. [20] Moreover, corrupt practices in developing countries too often involve counterparts from developed countries willing to offer substantial bribes.

---

[18] For example, see the annual Social Watch publications which report on what governments have done to implement the commitments they have made in international fora (www.socwatch.org).

[19] See, for example, *Transparency Deutschland, Positionen, Aktionen, Perspektiven, 2003*, www.transparency.de

[20] Transparency International: *Global Corruption Report 2003* (Berlin, 2003).

245. Overcoming such deficiencies is a major challenge in the quest for improved economic performance. The process of economic transformation in Central and Eastern Europe illustrates this well. The former planned economies of this region were burdened with institutions unsuitable for the functioning of a market economy. There was a lack of clear laws and judicial institutions to enforce contracts, and of institutions to manage market entry and exit. The implementation of price liberalization and privatization policies was carried out before the institutions required for a market economy were in place, diverting effort into rent-seeking and asset-stripping activities. In the absence of open democratic processes, many institutions, including parts of the State, were captured by private interests in the transition process. The result was an extended period of declines in GNP and alarming growth in unemployment, inequality and poverty. The more recent shift of emphasis to institutional reform has led to improved economic response, although progress is uneven.

Economic liberalization and the State

246. The economic policies adopted by countries in their quest for success in the global economy have often involved far-reaching liberalization of trade, investment and financial policies. This has been associated with collateral liberalization of the domestic economy involving privatization, a reduction in the role of the State in economic management and regulation, and a general expansion in the role of the market. Starting in some industrialized countries in the early 1980s, the model has now been adopted in very diverse economic and social contexts.

Policies to manage economic liberalization must be tailored to differing circumstances

247. Policies for market liberalization must recognize the importance of the point of departure – the differing situations of industrialized and developing countries, the pre-existing policy and institutional environment, and the state of the economy and of the external economic environment at the time the policies are applied. Otherwise, there is no guarantee that liberalization policies will yield the universally positive outcome its advocates foresee. On the contrary, the results are likely to be mixed, with positive outcomes in some cases and strongly negative ones in others.

248. An important issue is the pace and sequencing of the liberalization process. In the past, a "big bang" approach to liberalization was often advocated and sometimes applied. This involved liberalization across the board, carried out simultaneously. Today, it is generally recognized that this was a mistake. The supporting institutions and regulatory frameworks required for a market economy need to be developed gradually, and require strong public administrative capacity. The comparison between Eastern European and East Asian experiences of reform is instructive.

249. This highlights the important role of the State in managing the process of integration into the global economy, and in ensuring that it meets both economic and social objectives. This role includes the provision of classical public goods which have positive externalities such as health, education, and law and order; the supervision of markets and the correction of market deficiencies and failures; the correction of negative externalities such as environmental degradation; the provision of social protection and safeguarding the vulnerable; and investment in areas of public interest where private investment is not forthcoming. These essential functions of the State need to be maintained in the context of globalization. In many parts of the world, the problem is the weakness of State action in these areas,

Role of the State in managing economic fluctuations and in macroeconomic policy

and the absence of any realistic expectation that private provision can fill the gap. Another important role of the State lies in limiting the impact of globalization on income inequality, through progressive taxation, wage policies, social programmes and other mechanisms.

250. The reduction in the role of the State that has occurred across the world may often have been desirable, but in many cases the pace has been too fast and the balance has tipped too far. While State economic intervention in the past may frequently have been ineffective or misdirected, globalization has created many new needs which the State now has to respond to. This role is especially important today in the absence of strong institutions for global governance.

251. The new challenge faced by the State in the context of integration into the global economy can be seen at several levels. Financial liberalization exposes countries to greater risks of economic fluctuations, including the devastation that can be inflicted by financial crises. This requires a strengthening of the role of the State in providing social protection, not its weakening. Similarly, the increased mobility of capital that is associated with globalization strengthens the hand of employers vis-à-vis workers. At the same time, labour markets are experiencing a higher rate of job creation, dislocation and destruction as economies adjust to greater openness. These have adverse effects on workers in both North and South. These labour-related developments underscore the need for a stronger role for the State in building effective and equitable social safety nets and labour market institutions.

252. Another important domain of State action is macroeconomic policy. The main objectives of this include: achieving the highest possible rate of economic growth; promoting full employment; and maintaining macroeconomic stability. The latter is essential for ensuring that the rates of growth of output and employment are sustainable and protected from the risk of economic crises. Macroeconomic policy must maintain business and consumer confidence, which requires keeping fiscal deficits and inflation within acceptable proportions. However, the objective of macroeconomic stability should not override the other two. The preferred policy stance is to seek to achieve the highest feasible rate of output and employment growth that is compatible with macroeconomic stability over the medium term.

253. One of the effects of globalization has been to reduce the space for national macroeconomic policy, notably because international capital markets sanction deviations from orthodoxy. However there remain policy instruments to achieve the objectives outlined above. The key instrument is the rate of growth of both public and private productive investment in the economy. That, together with the need to strengthen the State, underlines the importance of domestic resource mobilization and an effective, non-regressive taxation system. It also highlights the need to bring the informal economy into the economic mainstream. Taxes which only extend to the formal economy not only lead to revenue shortfalls, they also provide strong incentives for informal work.

254. The prospects of realizing the above strategy will be greatly enhanced by creating institutions that ensure wider participation in the formulation of economic policies. Such policies are often considered to be the exclusive preserve of technocrats, bankers and financiers. But consistency between economic and social policies requires close coordination between all the ministries concerned. Moreover, since workers, enterprises of all sizes and many other groups have a strong stake in the outcomes, existing institutions need to be strengthened and new mechanisms created to allow their voices to be heard and their interests taken into account.

255. Public investment and policy also have a strategic role to play in strengthening national capacity to benefit from integration into the global economy, and in sharing the gains more equitably. Partnerships between governments and private actors – business, trade unions, community organizations, cooperatives and others – are an effective means to develop the skills, infrastructure, technological and managerial capabilities, and frameworks that provide an enabling environment for private investment (both domestic and foreign) in the most dynamic productive activities. This is not about "picking winners", but establishing the preconditions for the growth of globally competitive enterprises.

256. The approach taken to strengthen national economic capability will vary greatly according to the initial conditions. In many low-income countries, agriculture accounts for a large proportion of economic activity and an even higher proportion of employment. The majority of the poor (75 per cent) live in rural areas and the incidence of poverty is highest in countries that are dependent on primary commodity exports. This calls for a series of policies to support agricultural growth including: the elimination of price distortions and practices which discriminate against some sectors of agriculture; support for niche markets; substantial public investment in education and health; and recognition of the key role of women in agricultural production, and therefore in poverty reduction. In many areas the priority is investment in transport networks, electricity and water management, which increases productivity and security and opens markets. Meanwhile, investment in agricultural research, extension services and financial support is also important. Many poor countries need better seeds, less harmful agronomic practices, and access to new knowledge and techniques. It is also vital that traditional knowledge be protected, used and extended. [21]

Rural development vital in low-income countries

257. At the same time, diversification of the rural production structure is usually essential. Growth of the rural non-farm economy is often hindered because it is largely within the informal economy. While policies required to support this growth will vary widely, they should generally aim to increase productivity and accelerate learning and technological progress. The upgrading of primary production exports and diversification of the export structure is often a priority.

258. Many middle-income developing countries are now competing among themselves to export similar labour-intensive manufacturing products to the same markets. As a result they are trading more, but earning relatively less. The challenge for these countries is to move into higher-value exports. A strategic response is needed to promote innovation, adaptation and the learning processes associated with it. [22] Key to the creation of national systems of innovation is the upgrading of skills and technological capabilities. This will both enhance the gains from trade and participation in global production systems, and expand the domestic market through increases in productivity and wages. Global production systems should

Upgrading skills and technological capabilities

---

[21] The UN Economic and Social Council recently called for a wide-ranging integrated approach to rural development which develops many of these points. See ECOSOC: Draft Ministerial Declaration, E/2003/L.9. National action can draw on programmes of policy advice, capacity building and technical assistance undertaken by FAO to support the development of sustainable rural livelihoods and food security, and by IFAD to enable the rural poor increase their organization, knowledge and influence on public policy. See www.ifad.org and www.fao.org

[22] A. Amsden: *The Rise of the Rest* (Oxford University Press, 2001).

provide opportunities for domestic firms to be engaged in a process of learning and adaptation in both industry and services, closely linked to "world-class" production experience. Policies are also needed to strengthen production linkages between leading economic sectors and the rest of the economy and to take account of the needs and constraints of small enterprises. Access to financing and financial institutions is particularly critical, as are specialized technical extension services for micro-enterprises and poor women entrepreneurs.

259. These issues are no less important for industrialized countries. Here too training, financial and technology policies and partnerships can support the phasing out of inefficient old industries and the growth of new high value-added activities. [23] Flanking policies for economic adjustment include not only social protection and income security, but also the supportive policies which help create new opportunities, notably in the knowledge economy and new service sectors.

260. Agriculture is a particular concern. Each nation is of course entitled to develop its own agricultural policies, but the excessive support and subsidies to this sector in many OECD countries illustrate how domestic policies can fail to adequately take into account the implications for other countries. Policies for this sector should be designed with the livelihoods of poor farmers in both industrialized and developing countries in mind, and reward rural producers for delivering public goods such as environmental services. Presently, in OECD countries only 4 per cent of support is targeted to environmental objectives.

The informal economy

The informal economy is large and growing

261. In most developing countries there is a large informal economy, where economic activity lacks recognition and protection under formal legal or regulatory frameworks. It typically consists of small-scale manufacturing, services or vending in urban areas, domestic work or agricultural work on small plots of land. In many of the lowest-income countries it accounts for the large majority of workers. There is often a high proportion of women workers. This work is very diverse, ranging from small enterprises to survival activities, including not only the self-employed and family workers but also wage labour in many forms. Typically such activities are of low productivity, and poverty levels among informal workers are high. But there is also a large reservoir of entrepreneurship and innovation. Informal work is less prominent in industrialized countries, but by no means absent, and includes the informalization of previously secure wage employment.

262. Like poverty, the informal economy long predates globalization. But it is growing. In many parts of the world today the bulk of new employment, both self-employment and wage work, is informal. As seen above, how far this is due to globalization is hard to establish, but the increased competitive pressures in global markets have not made informality any easier to control. At the same time, while some informal workers provide low-cost inputs to global production systems, the majority are excluded from the opportunities of globalization and confined to restricted markets.

---

[23] At the Lisbon European Council in March 2000, the European Union set itself a new strategic goal for the next decade: *to become the most competitive and dynamic knowledge-based economy in the world, capable of sustainable economic growth with more and better jobs and greater social cohesion.*

263. This is a major governance issue, with a considerable impact on the distribution of the benefits from globalization. First, the lack of rights and protections leads to vulnerability and inequality, undermining many of the principles of governance outlined above. Second, there is lack of access to markets and services, so that potential for growth and development is unrealized. Third, there is a failure to build a fair and participative economy, for the rules of the game are in effect not the same for all. Since private initiative and entrepreneurship will only thrive if people feel that the law is on their side, there is a need to set clear rules which are applied equally to all members of society.

264. The goal must be to make these informal activities part of a growing formal sector that provides decent jobs, incomes and protection, and can trade in the international system. This will be an essential part of national strategy to reduce poverty. That means increasing assets and productivity, appropriate regulatory frameworks, raising skills and ensuring that policy biases are removed. Policies to deal with the lack of recognition of qualifications and skills, and the exclusion of informal workers from social security and other protections are particularly important. So too are policies to improve the distribution of assets, and especially to increase access for self-employed women and men and small businesses to financial resources, technology and markets, and to increase opportunities for investment. But most workers and economic units in the informal economy have difficulty accessing the legal and judicial system to enforce contracts, and their access to public infrastructure and benefits is limited. A variety of bureaucratic and other restrictions create barriers and difficulties which hinder formalization, growth and sustainability. [24]

Policies to help raise productivity and shift informal activities to the formal sector

265. A fundamental problem is the lack of an adequate legal and institutional framework for property rights. Up to 4 billion people are effectively excluded from participation in the global economy because their property rights are not recognized. They are thus deprived of the legal identification, and the forms of business that are necessary to enter the global market place. In reality their assets – notably land and housing – are worth enormous sums. But this is "dead capital", because it generally cannot be used as loan collateral, discouraging credit and investment. Failure to deal with this issue frustrates the potential for growth and development of millions of small enterprises. And it encourages low quality economic activities, which fall outside the tax net. [25]

266. The legalization of *de facto* property rights is therefore a vital step in the transformation of the informal economy. To achieve this, governments need to:

- identify the people and the assets concerned;
- identify the practices and customs which govern the ownership, use and transfer of these assets, so as to root property law in the prevailing social context;
- identify administrative, bureaucratic and legal bottlenecks and obstacles to market access;

Governments should take steps to establish property rights and ensure gender equality and core labour rights

---

[24] See ILO, *Decent Work in the Informal Economy*, Report VI, International Labour Conference, 90th Session (Geneva, ILO, June 2002) for a review of a wide variety of policy issues concerning the informal economy, including legal frameworks, standards, financing and governance questions.

[25] Hernando de Soto: *The Mystery of Capital: Why Capitalism Triumphs in the West and Fails Everywhere Else* (New York, Basic Books, 2000).

- re-structure the legal framework so that the actors concerned have an incentive to operate under the rule of law and have their assets and transactions officially recorded; and
- design low-cost legal and administrative mechanisms that will allow formerly informal property holders and businesses to interface productively with creditors, investors, public services and international markets.

267. Establishing property rights should not be confused with privatization. There are a wide variety of ways in which land and other assets are held in traditional systems, many of them communal, collective or cooperative. National legal frameworks should acknowledge and recognize these patterns, and care is needed to ensure that all the implications, including the gender implications, are fully understood when legal rights are recorded. In some parts of the world, for example, in the traditional informal system land is controlled by women, but when formalized it is registered in the man's name. Formalization must enhance opportunity, not constrain it.

268. A balanced approach to upgrading the informal economy would require the systematic extension of property rights to be accompanied by similar action on core labour rights for all persons engaged in informal activities. There is a particular need to ensure that workers and employers in the informal economy have the right to freedom of association and collective bargaining. Women and youth, who make up the bulk of the informal economy, especially lack representation and voice. There is likewise a need to build adequate social protection systems. Action on all these fronts would be mutually supporting.

Enabling and empowering people – through education

People must have the capabilities to benefit from globalization

269. People can only contribute and benefit from globalization if they are in adequate health and endowed with knowledge, skills and values and with the capabilities and rights needed to pursue their basic livelihoods. They need employment and incomes, and a healthy environment. These are the essential conditions which empower them to lead a self-determined, decent life, and to participate fully as citizens in their local, national and global communities. These goals, which are at the heart of the Millennium Declaration, can only be reached if national governments allocate adequate resources to health, education, basic infrastructure and the environment, and create the institutional framework which ensures broad access and opportunity.

270. Effective education systems are the foundation of opportunities to lead a decent life. Ensuring that all children have adequate access to education is an essential public sector function for countries at all income levels. Education not only benefits the individual, but society as a whole. When children remain sufficiently long in school, and in particular when girls receive adequate schooling, this increases economic growth rates, lowers fertility rates, leads to a reduction in child mortality and improves the educational attainments of the next generation. Adequate primary and secondary education is more than the empowerment of the individual, it is the empowerment of the society.

271. While education deficits are obviously greater in developing countries, this is a major issue in industrialized countries too. In many industrialized countries there is a persistent problem of illiteracy and low skills, which is an important source of social exclusion, often stigmatized and unacknowledged. Unequal access to education also fuels growing wage inequality in the labour market, which we noted in

section II.1, and the uneducated and unskilled in industrialized countries face severe disadvantage in an increasingly competitive global market.

272. The provision of both primary and secondary schooling increased throughout the 1990s, but progress is inadequate and masks wide differences between countries and regions. The OECD countries, for example, spend 100 times more per pupil in primary and secondary education than low-income countries. Yet some low- and medium-income countries have achieved remarkable progress in educational achievement. Brazil, Eritrea, the Gambia and Uganda have registered a 20 per cent increase in the primary school completion rate in less than a decade. These experiences demonstrate that more rapid progress is possible if the political will and the resources exist, in high- and low-income countries alike. [26]

Progress in education masks wide differences between countries and regions

273. Nevertheless, in many countries today, especially in sub-Saharan Africa, educational achievements are threatened by the HIV/AIDS pandemic, which has claimed the lives of many trained teachers – mainly female teachers in both primary and secondary schools. HIV/AIDS prevention and treatment programmes need to focus on education services to avoid the collapse of already fragile education systems and the reversal of past gains.

Education threatened by HIV/AIDS and by child labour

274. Another widespread concern is child labour, which is both a serious problem in its own right and a major factor limiting school enrolment, retention and educational achievement. The poverty of parents today condemns working children to poverty tomorrow. Action to increase schooling and skills needs to go hand in hand with action to reduce child labour. The growing national consciousness of this issue is leading many countries to adopt strategies for the elimination of the worst forms of child labour. We fully support such strategies.

275. All countries which have benefited from globalization have invested significantly in their education and training systems. Today women and men need broad-based skills which can be adapted to rapidly changing economic requirements as well as appropriate basic skills which enable them to benefit from information technology, increasing their ability to overcome barriers of distance and budgetary limitations. While Internet technology is not particularly capital-intensive, it is very human capital-intensive. Sound education policy also provides an important instrument to offset the negative impacts of globalization, such as increasing income inequalities, with effects which may ultimately be stronger than labour market policies. [27] The educational needs and disadvantages of ethnic and religious minorities need careful attention. These issues apply across the board, in both high- and low-income countries.

276. While there is no universal model for investing in training, various mechanisms and incentives can be applied, including levy systems, public grants, training funds, tax rebates and the provision of sabbatical leave. Good practice in learning at work shows up in increased productivity, so business has an interest in funding such training.

---

[26] Christopher Colcough et al: "Achieving Schooling for All: Budgetary Expenditure on Education in Sub-Saharan Africa and South Asia", *World Development* 28 (11), pp. 1927–1944. Common features of successful primary education reform programmes in low-income countries include: a high share of national resources devoted to public primary school education; control of unit costs; higher than average spending on complementary, non-salary inputs; competitive pay for teachers; a manageable pupil-teacher ratio of around 40; average repetition rates below 10 per cent.

[27] See Martin Rama: *Globalization, Inequality and Labor Market Policies* (World Bank, Development Research Group Paper, 2001).

277. The development of a national qualifications framework is also an important foundation for participation in the global economy, since it facilitates lifelong learning, helps match skill demand and supply, and guides individuals in their choice of career. Access to training and skills development for women is often hindered by family commitments, indicating a need for childcare facilities and possibilities for distance learning. Other priorities include recognition and upgrading of skills for workers in the informal economy and the adaptation of training to accommodate workers with no formal education.

Work and employment

278. People see the world through the optic of their workplace. Success or failure in the labour market determine whether family needs and aspirations can be met, whether girls and boys get a decent education, whether youths are able to build a career or end up on the street. Youth employment is a critical area for action. Loss of work affects dignity and self-esteem, generates stress and other health problems, and undermines social integration.

279. People are most directly affected by globalization through their work and employment. That is how people experience the opportunities and advantages, as well as the risks and exclusions. For the gains from globalization to be widely shared, countries, enterprises and people have to be able to convert global opportunities into jobs and incomes.

Globalization affects people through work and employment

280. A major goal is to reduce unemployment, which has huge costs for people and society in industrialized and developing countries alike. But this alone is not enough. There are many people who are fully employed in unacceptable jobs – often in appalling working conditions, at low productivity or subject to coercion. Employment must be freely chosen and provide an income sufficient to satisfy basic economic and family needs. Rights and representation must be respected, basic security attained through one form or another of social protection, and adequate conditions of work assured. Taken together, these different elements make up what has come to be known as "decent work". This includes not only employment, but a wider set of goals which reflects the broader aspirations of women and men.

The goal is decent work

281. The most obvious route to the creation of decent employment lies in higher growth, and that is the aim of many of the economic policies discussed above. The key macroeconomic issue is whether a focus on employment calls for a different balance of fiscal or monetary policy. For this to be adequately assessed in each case, it would make sense for countries to adopt employment targets as part of the budgetary process, and to make an employment impact analysis an explicit criterion of macroeconomic policy decision-making. Gender sensitivity can be achieved through approaches such as "gender budgeting", which examines the differential impact of macroeconomic policy on women and men, notably through its effect on employment and the provision of public services.

282. It is particularly important to correct market failures that create biases against employment-intensive growth, and to ensure that tax patterns do not create unnecessary obstacles to investment, enterprise growth and employment creation. As discussed above, it is also essential to ensure that obstacles to the creation of enterprises, especially small and medium-sized enterprises (SMEs), are removed. In addition, structural policies are needed to foster the growth of the new economy, based on the rapid diffusion of ICT and other new technologies.

283. In many parts of the world, especially in industrialized and middle-income countries, problems of high or rising unemployment have been compounded by additional pressures on the quality of employment. Real wages and conditions of work have been under pressure, partly as a result of increasing competition for export markets and foreign investment. There has also been growing insecurity among those at work, due to interrelated factors such as the erosion of the welfare state, labour market deregulation and the declining power of trade unions. Changes in technology and work organization have placed a premium on greater labour flexibility, resulting in an increase in contingent work and less secure employment contracts. [28] The interests of both workers and employers need to be recognized, and balanced policies are essential. They need to be based on a new social contract that includes the following elements:

- commitment to social dialogue in the formulation of economic and social policies, especially those relating to the reform of labour markets and social protection;

- recognition that the drive for greater efficiency and higher productivity must be balanced against the right of workers to security and equal opportunities;

- commitment to take the "high road" of business-labour collaboration to achieve efficiency gains, and to eschew the "low road" of cost-cutting and downsizing. This is increasingly important in a knowledge economy that is dependent for success on the skills and motivations of a diverse workforce.

284. Policies to promote decent work are equally important in low-income countries, where reducing unemployment and underemployment is also the key to reducing poverty.

285. A two-pronged strategy is required. The first consists of maximizing the rate of growth of new jobs that yield incomes above the poverty line. The second consists of policies and programmes to raise the productivity and incomes of those that remain in sub-poverty employment in the rural and urban informal economy.

286. Programmes that expand employment opportunities and raise productivity for the poor – such as the development of rural infrastructure and extension services to small farmers, small and micro-enterprise development and micro-credit schemes – need to be strengthened. Particular efforts are needed to ensure equal access to assets for women, indigenous groups and ethnic minorities. Modernization policies in agriculture which do not pay attention to women's employment often end up marginalizing them.

287. Beyond the creation of jobs, it is important to strengthen policies that help countries to cope better with the social strains of globalization. In most developing countries, social protection systems and institutions are weak and under-resourced. The insecurities associated with globalization reinforce the need to give priority to extending unemployment insurance, income support, pensions and health systems. That is also true in industrialized countries, where the coverage of social protection is generally greater but often far from universal, and those who lose out from shifts in production often receive little in the way of compensation. Good social protection systems are important if the benefits from globalization are

---

[28] See, for example, ILO: *World Employment Report* (Geneva, 1996-97). Also OECD: *Employment Outlook: 2003 Edition: Towards More and Better Jobs* (Paris, 2003).

to be distributed fairly within countries. [29] It is vital that they reach those in the informal and rural economies, women, and other groups who are largely excluded, because this is an essential part of any strategy to reduce poverty. Innovative approaches need to be promoted, such as those based on local organizations and initiatives. Low pay commissions to examine the reasons for low pay and propose solutions may also help to protect the working poor from competitive pressures. All of these policies can contribute to the development of the components of a socio-economic floor for all citizens.

288. At the same time, the role of workers' basic rights and civil and political liberties in promoting decent work and equitable development must be emphasized. These rights provide the preconditions for developing, through a free and independent labour movement and organizations of the poor, the countervailing power necessary to promote improved wages for workers, combat and reverse any deterioration of labour standards and support a virtuous cycle of rising living standards and equitable growth. They are also essential for generating the constant democratic pressure that is required to ensure greater accountability and transparency in economic policies, as well as more equitable social policies.

289. In many countries, labour legislation has not kept pace with changes in the pattern of employment. As a result large numbers of workers fall outside the protection of labour laws. A substantial improvement in coverage and compliance is required, calling for better monitoring and stronger administrations, with particular emphasis on the informal economy. There is also a need to reverse the trend towards the erosion of collective organizations of both workers and employers, and of collective bargaining. Such economic reform must emphasize dialogue and greater efforts by the organizations concerned to adequately reflect the concerns of all sections of the society. Stronger social dialogue is an essential means for building a common perspective among different interests within countries on how to achieve both social and economic goals.

Sustainable development and resource productivity

Achieving more sustainable patterns of consumption and production

290. The interaction between economic, social and environmental goals is at the heart of a coherent policy approach. And while many environmental issues require global action, a great deal of the groundwork for sustainable development has to be done at national and sub-national levels.

291. One of the strategic ways of achieving sustainable development is opting for the right technologies. Developing country governments can ask international enterprises to apply identical pollution control technologies at home and abroad while granting a period of grace to domestic companies. More forward-looking would be the adoption of policies to systematically increase resource productivity, i.e. the amount of economic wealth and social welfare extracted from one unit of natural resources. More emphasis on resource productivity and less on labour productivity can lead to more employment and an improved environment at the same time. Incentive structures at national and supranational levels should be shaped to encourage this shift of emphasis.

---

[29] D. Rodrik: *Has Globalization Gone Too Far?* (Washington DC, Institute for International Economics, 1997); and ILO: *World Labour Report 2000: Income Security and Social Protection in a Changing World* (Geneva, ILO, 2000).

292. Local communities traditionally conserve and protect their local environment from deforestation and pollution. By helping them invest in sustainable natural resource management, two objectives can be pursued in parallel: securing and improving environmental quality, and generating local employment and income. There is a need to build on existing global mechanisms that reward the creation and maintenance at the local level of such global public goods. We support the efforts under way as follow-up to the World Summit on Sustainable Development in Johannesburg in 2002 to raise capabilities at all levels to achieve more sustainable patterns of consumption and production.

Empowering the local level

293. Our vision of globalization is anchored at the local level. The international policy agenda must respect diverse local needs and perspectives and respond to their demands. People live in their local environment. It is at this level that participatory democracy can be strongest, where much political mobilization occurs, where autonomy can be realized and solidarity is a part of daily life. At the same time, the local community is part of an integrating world. In the end, the local is part of the global and the pattern of globalization is influenced by what happens locally.

International policies must respect and empower local communities

294. At the same time, there are often major obstacles to local development. Greater decentralization is needed, but to be effective it must be accompanied by increased capacities and resources, and effective frameworks for democracy and participation. National governments have a critical role in ensuring redistribution from richer to poorer regions, and in raising the capacities of local governments and other actors. Decentralization must mean empowering local communities within the national economy and polity.

295. The notion of the "local" community varies enormously. For the majority of the world's population the local community means villages (many of which are isolated, remote and ecologically fragile) and urban shanty towns and slums. In such situations, there is typically a direct link between where people live and work. Rural communities subsist on local agricultural or non-farm activities, while poorer urban communities largely depend on various activities in the informal economy. Many of these communities face endemic poverty and, barring out-migration, the keys to poverty reduction lie in improving the local economic base and increasing the availability of basic social services.

296. The notion of the local community is equally important in high-income settings. Strong federal States, such as the United States or Germany, typically rest on clearly empowered subnational entities down to the local level. The celebration of the "local space" is also an explicit component of the architecture of the EU. While member States transfer some sovereignty over economic policy matters to the EU level, the diversity of cultures, values and languages is protected at the local level. Local systems of industrial or technological development are also the building blocks of national economic capability in many parts of the world.

297. Our concern for this issue of local space springs from the following considerations.

298. First, an increasing number of communities in the world have been directly affected by globalization. Some communities have been hit by job losses as a result of the decline of local industries in the face of trade liberalization or the relocation of firms to lower-wage countries. This often creates huge problems of local adjustment

Many local communities adversely affected

and places great stress on the social fabric. Even remote rural communities in the developing world are affected, as when cheap imports wipe out agricultural livelihoods or the entry of large mining or logging firms, or of some forms of tourism, disrupts traditional livelihoods and adversely affects the local environment.

299. Second, globalization may erode the resilience and vitality of local communities even where there has been no direct economic impact. The increasing reach of the global media, entertainment, and tourism industry is placing stress on traditional cultures and on the values, sense of identity and solidarity of local communities. Our vision is of a future global community which accommodates the multitude of local cultures and capabilities, not a tidal wave of homogenization.

300. Third, we believe that the global and the national must both be built on the local, and that this is one of the keys to a fairer, more generous globalization. Decentralized approaches to policy design and implementation are likely to be more effective, based on better knowledge of real situations and constraints, more participatory, closer to the needs and demands of people, and easier to monitor.

301. In order to strengthen this linkage between the local and the global, there is a need for a proactive and positive agenda focusing on local government, the local economic base, local values and cultural heritages.

Local government

Need for strong, democratic and accountable local institutions

302. Many social and economic policies are most efficiently implemented at the local level. In line with the general principle of subsidiarity, we believe that governance should take place at the lowest level at which it is effective. This calls for the creation of strong, democratic and accountable local institutions.

303. Protecting and nurturing the local space, and creating and supporting local authorities, are in the first instance the responsibility of States. Governments are notably slower to decentralize control over resources to subnational level than they are administrative structures and responsibilities. However, lack of local funds leads to inadequate public services and can be a cause of corruption. Local authorities thus need to be able to generate their own tax revenues or receive sufficient financial support from national budgets.

304. Their capabilities for implementation often need to be strengthened too. Non-State actors can play an important role provided they have sufficient resources. The territorial pacts which have been developed in Europe in recent years have shown that it is possible to empower local communities by bringing together many actors around a common project. [30] In turn, all local actors must be held accountable, nationally and locally, for their spending.

305. Local administration does not mean isolation. On the contrary, globalization offers many opportunities for national and cross-border networking, cooperation and exchange among local authorities; the local can be as open as the national,

---

[30] A territorial pact is a formal agreement among a wide range of actors – city councils, other local authorities, workers' and employers' organizations, trade unions, religious and cultural groups, NGOs, professional associations and schools – to jointly design and implement a coherent development strategy for a given territory. Since the late 1990s, hundreds of pacts have been launched throughout Europe to promote job creation and fight social exclusion through locally driven initiatives. See www.europa.eu.int/comm/regional_policy/innovation/innovating/pacts/en/

perhaps even more so. The networking processes established through the "mayors' networks" and those of community-based organizations deserve further support. [31]

The local economic base

306. Local production systems and markets play an important role in satisfying consumer needs and generating employment. Local economic space must be protected, while becoming more productive. National and international policies and support systems are required to reinforce local efforts through increasing access to micro-credit, support for management and protection from external interference. Rural industrialization which provides technologies and infrastructures to process raw materials locally should be supported. The value added gained from processing will further help in rural development. In addition to the policies required to support small enterprises, discussed earlier, local business development services should be encouraged. These can provide marketing assistance to local enterprises to ensure that they are not "locked in" to a single supply chain; support capabilities to meet global product standards; and encourage the clustering of enterprises to promote inter-firm cooperation and a more solid platform to become globally competitive. Clusters of small, local enterprises can be a major source of economic dynamism and employment creation, from furniture production in Central Java to software development in Silicon Valley. [32] Global networks of information exchange offer one means by which globalization can help promote local production of goods and services.

307. A variety of forms of economic organization can be both economically and socially efficient in the local environment. Cooperatives are an obvious example. They are a global force, with 800 million members worldwide, yet at the same time major local actors with a capacity which is built on trust and accountability. Their contribution needs to be recognized and strengthened.

308. Social entrepreneurs are also important at the local level. They have been successful in using individual initiatives to achieve social goals using the logic of markets. Probably the best-known example is the Grameen initiative in Bangladesh, which brings both information technology and education to the poor. One outcome of this enterprise is that today there are 40,000 "telephone ladies" selling mobile telephone services in half the villages of Bangladesh. The Grameen Bank not only provides financial services but also promotes an active social agenda. Other examples include the Self-employed Women's Association (SEWA) in India, its replication as the Self-employed Women's Union (SEWU) in South Africa, and micro-credit schemes for economic activities and local infrastructure provided through communities in Kosovo and Albania. Such schemes need to be supported and replicated. One way could be to link local initiatives, especially those which

Local production
systems need
support

---

[31] Among the main international networks of cities and local authorities are the newly founded United Cities and Local Government (www.iula.org); the World Associations of the Major Metropolises (www.metropolis.org); the World Associations of Cities and Local Authorities Coordination (www.waclac.org); the Cities Alliance (www.citiesalliance.org); and the International Council for Local Environmental Initiatives (www.iclei.org). For a comprehensive list see www.lgib.gov.uk/weblinks_3.htm The United Nations Human Settlement Programme (UN-Habitat) provides an important forum to expand those initiatives, see www.unhabitat.org

[32] For a comprehensive discussion covering both industrialized and developing countries, see *Clusters, Industrial Districts and Firms: The Challenge of Globalization*, conference in honour of Professor Sebastiano Brusco, University of Modena, Italy, 12–13 September 2003 (www.economia. unimo.it/convegni_seminari/CG_sept03/index.html). UNIDO is also an important source in relation to developing countries; see http://www.unido.org/en/doc/4297

offer opportunities for women entrepreneurs, within a global partnership, such as the Micro-credit Summit Campaign, which has mobilized thousands of micro-finance organizations and their actors. [33]

Local values and cultural heritages

Globalization is
seen as a threat
to local culture
but it can be a
source of strength

309. Globalization inevitably has an impact on local values and cultures. A particularly powerful force is the global media and entertainment industry. This projects the values and perceptions of the countries which dominate the industry and is often seen as a threat to impose those values. However, external cultural influences arrive in many other ways, such as through the movement of people and the spread of consumer goods and lifestyles.

310. Culture is never static, and most communities welcome exchange and dialogue with other communities. There are many ways in which they can be open to other realities and yet retain their own identity. What matters is whether they are empowered to live according to their own aspirations. The trust among people bound by common values and culture is the "glue" which binds local institutions to undertake joint actions. This social capital is essential for development. Globalization can both strengthen and weaken social capital. The media, trade and travel, and increasing competition can all erode interest in community concerns. Yet global interconnectedness, especially through ICT, can provide strong leverage for local action. The global role of civil society has resulted from the leveraging of local and national actions.

The rights and
cultures of
indigenous
peoples should
be recognized
and protected

311. An important issue at both the local and national level is the need to recognize and defend the rights of indigenous and tribal peoples to their territories and resources, their cultures and identity, their traditional knowledge and their right to self-determination. Their free and prior informed consent should be sought before any development project is brought into their communities. Their indigenous socio-political and economic systems, sustainable resource management practices and livelihoods should be allowed to co-exist with other systems and should be supported instead of destroyed because of the push for them to be integrated into the global market economy. The global economy operates under rules and legal frameworks which may be inconsistent with indigenous peoples' rights and destructive of their indigenous ways of life and cultures. There is a critical need for both national and local authorities to ensure that the rights of indigenous peoples are protected and discrimination against them is eliminated, including the effective implementation of legislation where it exists, and the development of appropriate legislation where it is absent. This includes support from governments for the adoption of the United Nations Draft Declaration on the Rights of Indigenous Peoples which is presently under negotiation. Similar concerns arise with respect to ethnic and religious minorities, who often need special attention if they are to have fair access to the opportunities of the global economy.

312. There should also be a recognition of prior rights of indigenous peoples over lands and resources they have occupied and nurtured since time immemorial. The refusal or inability of indigenous peoples to take advantage of modern land titling processes, which do not recognize their indigenous land tenure systems and re-

---

[33] See www.grameen.com, www.sewa.org, www.changemakers.net and www.microcreditsummit. org, among others.

source rights systems, should not be used as grounds for their dispossession in favour of other interests.

Regional integration as a stepping stone

313. Much can be done within countries to take advantage of global opportunities, and to ensure that the benefits are fairly distributed. But the national policy agenda is circumscribed, both by resources and level of development, and by global rules and policies. We turn to the latter in the next section. But there is also an intermediate stepping stone, that of regional integration.

314. Regional arrangements take many different forms. Of the over 250 economic integration agreements that have been notified to the WTO[34], the large majority are free trade areas. But there are also many efforts at deeper regional integration, very often as a political project as much as an economic one. The EU is a prime example, but similar goals can be seen in processes of integration in Latin America and Africa. Issues such as security, cultural links and the promotion of shared goals are at least as important as economic interests, and give rise to a wide range of regional institutions.

Regional integration can help countries manage global forces

315. Regional integration and cooperation can promote a more equitable pattern of globalization in at least three ways.

316. First, it can empower people and countries to better manage global economic forces. By effectively increasing the size of domestic markets, integration increases the capacity to withstand external economic fluctuations. Better regional coordination of economic policies can also help to dampen the spillover effects of external shocks between neighbouring countries. Common frameworks for financial regulation, rights at work, tax coordination and investment incentives are practical regional goals which can help prevent any risk of a "race to the bottom" in these areas. The development of common currencies such as the euro is also a potential source of stability.

317. Integration can also enhance the negotiating power of smaller countries, acting together, which would otherwise have little voice at the international level. When countries pool resources and develop common platforms, they gain political weight vis-à-vis international institutions and multinational enterprises.

318. Second, it can help build the capabilities needed to take advantage of global opportunities. Investment in skills, infrastructure, research, technology and support for innovation will often require a critical mass of effort more readily achieved at regional level. In larger markets it is easier to take advantage of economies of scale. More ambitious regional objectives are also possible, such as regional strategies for industrial transformation or a coordinated broader development strategy.

319. Third, it can improve the conditions under which people connect to the global economy. The promotion of human rights and democracy has been high on the agenda in Europe (where the Council of Europe has played an important role), Latin America (especially through the Inter-American Commission on Human Rights), Africa (initiatives of the new African Union (AU)) and elsewhere. Other major regional concerns include cross-border movements of people, the prevention and treatment of HIV/AIDS, and the prevention of trafficking. More generally,

---

[34] WTO: *World Trade Report, 2003* (Geneva, WTO, 2003); and World Bank: *Trade Blocs* (Washington DC, Oxford University Press, 2000).

when social goals are built into regional integration and regional institutions this provides a starting point for building them into the wider global economy.

The experience of regional integration

Experience of regional integration

320. The EU provides an interesting example of deeper forms of integration. It has been built on a strong legal framework and a number of policy principles:

- openness to the world economy and an effective internal market economy;
- supportive national social protection systems and common minimum work standards;
- respect for the rule of law, human rights, gender equality and political democracy.

... in Europe

321. There has been a growth in democratic supervision and involvement, and the European Parliament has played an increasingly important role in this. Other institutions contribute to legitimacy, including, for example, the European Court of Justice. The social partners are also engaged in and contribute to regional policies. The latest development is the proposed European Constitution, presently under review, which codifies and enshrines the key principles and goals. The process of integration is clearly seen as an economic success, as witnessed by the current enlargement process to many of the countries of Central and Eastern Europe.

... the Americas

322. Regional integration has been consistently high on the policy agenda in the Americas.[35] The commitment to integration in Latin America and the Caribbean has gone beyond trade liberalization to include finance, macroeconomics, and social and political integration. Rights at work, working conditions and employment are also widely on the agenda. This has also given rise to regional political institutions such as the Latin American Parliament, financial ones such as the Latin American Reserve Fund, as well as fora for the participation of non-State actors.

... Africa

323. In Africa, regional economic integration is seen as an important route to peace and stability, and to more effective participation in the global economy. The aim is to attract both foreign and local investors, and to develop a pool of regional expertise. Many regional and subregional institutions and organizations have been created with mandates to pursue economic integration.[36] African leaders clearly signalled their commitment to this process with the launch of the AU in 2001. The programmes of the AU include the New Partnership for African Development (NEPAD), an integrated development strategy that has among its goals "to halt the marginalization of Africa in the globalization process".

... Asia and Pacific

324. Regional integration in Asia tends to concentrate on trade and economic cooperation, peace and security, and less on deeper aspects of integration.[37] Subregional arrangements known as "growth triangles" have been established to enhance economic relations between the participating countries. Several major inter-regional initiatives involve economies in Asia – the foremost being the Asia and Pacific Economic Cooperation (APEC) arrangement, which involves many of

---

[35] Major processes of integration include Mercosur, the Andean Community of Nations (CAN), the Common Market of the Caribbean (CARICOM), the North American Free Trade Agreement (NAFTA) and the Central American Integration System (SICA). There are ongoing negotiations on a continent-wide Free Trade Area of the Americas.

[36] Including six major subregional organizations in eastern and southern Africa, and five covering western and Central Africa.

[37] However, recent developments in the Association of Southeast Asian Nations (ASEAN) point towards a deepening of integration over the coming decade.

the Pacific Rim States of Asia and the Americas. The Arab countries, too, are developing free trade agreements both within and beyond the region.

325. In sum, regional integration is on the agenda worldwide. However, the rhetoric and the reality do not always coincide. In the EU there are complaints of bureaucratization, distance from people, trade diversion and problems of unequal weight and influence between countries and social actors. In addition, coordination of economic policy is proving difficult. Yet there has been enormous progress overall. Elsewhere, progress has been uneven. In Latin America, the strengthening of regional institutions has been impeded by resource constraints and by a series of economic and political crises. In Africa, efforts to open up and interconnect African economies require considerable investment, which has been hard to mobilize. The danger of creating another layer of bureaucracy is real and the difficulty of the task should not be underestimated.

326. It is also important to distinguish between agreements among countries with broadly similar living standards (such as those within Latin America, Asia, Africa and Europe) and those which involve both industrialized and developing countries (such as those foreseen in current negotiations on the Free Trade Area of the Americas and the Euro-Mediterranean Free Trade Area). These are very different. Regional integration arrangements between low- and high-income countries can generate significant economic gains from increased market access, for much the same reasons as the wider process of globalization. But as in this wider process, agreements between countries of different weight may result in unbalanced outcomes, such as a more limited space for national development policies in lower income countries, or difficulties of economic adjustment that lead to job losses without resources to compensate those adversely affected. In the process of European integration significant resource transfers from richer to poorer regions have helped to reduce inequalities and facilitate adjustment, but such mechanisms face considerable political hurdles. These issues recur in bilateral, regional and global agreements and are considered further at the global level in the next section.

The social dimension of regional integration

327. Many of the deeper forms of integration incorporate policies and institutions focusing on employment, education, the environment, labour standards, human rights, gender equality and other social goals. However, these social goals tend to be a secondary issue, well behind economic and political aims. We consider that if regional integration is to be a stepping stone towards a fairer globalization, a strong social dimension is essential.

Social goals can be strengthened by ...

328. In order to incorporate these broader social goals in the process of regional integration, the following issues need to be taken into account.

329. First, the principles of participation and of democratic accountability are an essential foundation. Representative bodies, such as regional parliaments, have an important role to play. We believe that regional integration should be advanced through social dialogue between representative organizations of workers and employers, and wider dialogue with other important social actors, on the basis of strong institutions for democratic and judicial accountability. The creation of tripartite or wider councils and forums at the regional level (such as the Consultative Economic and Social Forum of Mercosur or the European Economic and Social Committee) provides an important institutional framework for such dialogue. Particular attention should be paid to the need to increase the participation of women, given persistent patterns of gender inequality.

more democratic accountability and social dialogue

330. Second, regional integration needs to incorporate social targets, backed by regular measurement and reporting of results. Such targets might cover respect for basic rights, the overall employment rate, poverty incidence, educational opportunities and the extent of social security coverage, all disaggregated by sex. Measurement is particularly useful at the regional level since progress, or lack of it, can create political pressures for coordinated action. A formal review process by regional organizations can help improve national policies.

331. Third, regional resource mobilization is required for both investment and adjustment. This is particularly important when integration involves countries at very different levels of development. The Structural and Cohesion Funds in the EU have helped promote upward convergence of poorer areas within the Union. Regional financial institutions are also vital in order to channel resources to regional investment. The building of these institutions and funds should be given priority in all processes of regional integration. Donors and international organizations should also support countries' efforts to develop common regional strategies for promoting social and economic development. The social dimension of regional integration requires an integrated policy approach, based on a political commitment at the highest level. Only Heads of State and Government have the necessary authority, which is why most significant steps towards regional integration are made at that level.

Globalizing regions

332. Our image of globalization comprises a set of linked, interacting regions, not an Orwellian world of competing blocks. It is a world in which each region is open to ideas, goods, capital and people. Such a process of "open regionalism" is not a constraint on the global economy; on the contrary, it can address some of the imbalances of globalization, while promoting development and equity within regions in a multilateral framework. Within each region, the process of integration is pursued through mechanisms which are most appropriate to that region – there is no uniform model. And regional action complements and supports the policies of the nations within them.

333. The logic of choosing a regional route is that difficulties of integration are greater at the global level, and so it makes sense to take the regional step first. But at the same time globalization can act as a linkage between open regions and deliver resources to support regional goals. It can help to support the common framework of values, grounded in democratic choice and universal human rights. And if there are strong policies and institutions at the regional level, it is easier to construct fair global policies. That provides a basis for better governance of the world economy.

334. We believe that institutions are required at the global level which can bring together different regions around global integration, and that this should be part of the future agenda for global governance. Regional integration can be a base for global governance; and good institutions for global governance can in turn be a powerful support for regional integration.

III.2 The reform of global governance

III.2.1 Analytical framework

Globalization and governance

335. Up till now the increasing international attention to issues of governance has been almost exclusively focused on the national level. The issue of global governance now warrants serious attention. Global governance is the system of rules and institutions established by the international community and private actors to manage political, economic and social affairs. Good governance, at both the national and global level, should further values such as freedom, security, diversity, fairness and solidarity. It should also ensure respect for human rights, international rule of law, democracy and participation, promote entrepreneurship and adhere to the principles of accountability, efficacy and subsidiarity.

336. Increasing globalization has generated a need for better global governance. [38] The growth of interdependence among nation States has meant that a broader range of issues now affects more countries more strongly than ever before. The growing nexus of links between countries through trade, FDI and capital flows means that changes in economic conditions or policies in major economies have strong spillover effects on the rest of the world. Similarly, new global rules also have a strong impact on the policy options and economic performance of countries.

337. More specifically, increasing globalization has given rise to a broadening range of issues that cannot be effectively dealt with except through collaborative global action. Examples of these include the problems of financial contagion, communicable diseases, cross-border crime, security concerns, tax havens and tax competition. More generally, there is a growing need to develop institutional arrangements to support and supervise global markets in the interests of all partici-

Growing need for collaborative global action

---

[38] See Deepak Nayyar "Existing System and Missing Institutions" in Deepak Nayyar (ed.): *Governing Globalization: Issues and Institutions* (Oxford University Press, 2002) and Joseph Stiglitz: *Globalization and its Discontents* (London, Allan Lane, 2002).

pants. This includes the need to ensure their smooth and equitable functioning, eliminate uncompetitive practices and abuses, and correct market failures.

Haphazard response to the new challenges of globalization

338. The response to these new challenges so far has been haphazard. What has emerged to date is a fragmented and incoherent system consisting of a patchwork of overlapping networks and agencies in the economic, social and environmental fields. There is a wide range of diverse arrangements including laws, norms, informal arrangements and private self-regulation. In some cases, private actors such as bond rating agencies have created important *de facto* standards that governments and markets cannot afford to ignore.

339. The coverage of these arrangements is also incomplete. There are many important areas such as international migration and foreign investment where there are no rules or only partial and inadequate ones. While in a few areas the rules function well, in many they are too confining and often unfair.

Major deficiencies in contemporary global governance

Vast inequality in the power and capacity of nation States

340. There are thus serious problems with the current structure and processes of global governance. Foremost among these is the vast inequality in the power and capacity of different nation States. At the root of this is the inequality in the economic power of different nations. The industrialized countries have far higher per capita incomes, which translates into economic clout in negotiations to shape global governance. They are the source of much-needed markets, foreign investments, financial capital and technology. The ownership and control of these vital assets gives them immense economic power. This creates a built-in tendency for the process of global governance to be in the interests of powerful players, especially in rich nations.

341. In an ideal world, there would be a balancing of the interests of the powerful and the weak, of the rich and the poor. Global governance would be based on democratic and participatory decision-making processes that lead to fair outcomes. However, the reality falls far short of this. The major victorious powers defined the governance structure of the post-war world, centred on the United Nations and the Bretton Woods institutions – a system which still constitutes the core of world governance today. Since then much has changed. Today there are over 190 independent States compared to about 50 then. Over this period a few developing countries have joined the ranks of high-income countries while middle-income and populous ones such as China, India and Brazil have emerged as significant players in the global economy. When the latter countries act collectively on particular issues they can also exert significant influence in global governance. In spite of these developments, however, the dominant influence of the industrialized countries in global governance has not been fundamentally altered.

342. There has also been a spread of democracy across the globe. Today, more people than ever before are aware of their rights and demand a say in national and, increasingly, global governance. Their ability to do so has been greatly facilitated by the ICT revolution and accelerating global connectivity. There is vastly expanded access to information as well as the means for CSOs and trade unions to form cross-border coalitions around a myriad of good causes. The struggle for the establishment of democracy in Poland and South Africa was greatly assisted by the pressures exerted by such coalitions.

343. The influence of global civil society is exerted in various ways. CSOs lobby governments both at home and in international conferences. They are actively engaged in advocacy and mobilizing public opinion. They promote transparency and democratic accountability through criticism and monitoring compliance with international commitments. But their influence is confined to these indirect channels. Apart from a few exceptions, they have no formal representation in international organizations and global conferences. Nevertheless, their emergence has enriched the process of global governance by bringing to bear a wider array of opinion and interests. They have also helped to advance fairness in global governance through their efforts to secure a better deal for the poor. But their role in global governance is questioned by some.

344. Other non-State actors, especially business and business organizations, have also come to play a larger role in global governance. In part, this is a natural reflection of the increasing importance of the private sector in an increasingly free market global economy. In the case of MNEs and international financial houses, their growing influence clearly springs from their global reach and economic power. They can influence global governance structures by exerting pressure on the policies and practices of governments in both industrial and developing countries. They are now often part of the national delegations of the developed countries in international negotiations on economic and financial issues. Their growing importance is also seen in the increasing number of public-private partnerships established to address specific global problems.

345. There has also been a growth of private self-regulation efforts at the global level. The harmonization of accountancy standards is an oft-quoted example. Another is the focus on the corporate social responsibility of MNEs, with an emphasis on issues such as the environment and labour standards. This has been partly in response to much-publicized NGO activism on these issues. Indeed, some of the new forms of private self-regulation involve cooperation with other parties.

346. In contrast, the influence of trade unions in the rich countries has come under pressure from increasing globalization. This has come from the increasing mobility of capital and growing competitive pressures in the global economy. The traditional counterweight to the power of business has thus weakened, both nationally and globally. However, there are indications that the trade union movement worldwide is adapting to these pressures, as evidenced by a growing number of agreements and accords with the multinational enterprises active in the globalization process.

347. The problems posed by the above structural inequalities are reflected in the democratic deficit in global governance. A key element of this is the unequal decision-making in some international bodies such as the United Nations Security Council and the Bretton Woods institutions. But the problem is more pervasive than this. Even in organizations with a formal equality in decision-making such as the WTO, this is no guarantee of fair outcomes. The underlying inequalities in economic power translate into bargaining strength in negotiations that poor countries are often unable to resist. There has also been growing differentiation in the ranks of developing countries, with the LDCs generally finding themselves in the weakest bargaining position.

348. These inequalities are compounded by the many important decisions on global governance which are taken outside the multilateral system. Limited membership groups of rich nations such as the Group of 7 (G7), the Organization for Economic Cooperation and Development (OECD), the Basle Committee, and the

Group of 10 (G10) within the IMF have taken important decisions on economic and financial issues with a global impact.

349. The developing countries face other handicaps in making their influence felt in global governance. Global governance now spans a wide range of issues and many of these are of increasing technical complexity. This makes it extremely difficult for most poor countries to be even present at all negotiations, let alone represented at an adequate technical level. In addition, the increasing differentiation among developing countries adds to the problem of collective action among them at the global level to compensate for their individual weaknesses.

350. These problems are compounded by the low democratic accountability in the process of global governance. The positions taken by governments in international fora are rarely subject to close and regular scrutiny by national parliaments. Neither are there stringent requirements for public disclosure of information on positions taken and the rationale for these. Similarly, in spite of recent improvements, the lack of transparency and accountability in international organizations remains a serious problem. These are rarely subject to independent evaluations of the impact of their policies and operations on countries and people. In most cases there are no procedures for people who are adversely affected by their operations to lodge complaints and seek redress.

351. Fuller disclosure of information and stronger pressures on governments and international organizations to account for their decisions and actions would make the impacts of their decisions and policies clearer and provide the basis for beneficial public debates on these issues. Indeed a global freedom of information act and an obligation for governments in the industrialized countries and international organizations to undertake *ex ante* assessments of the global impact of major policy decisions would be welcome developments.

352. Another aspect is the lack of coherence in global decision-making. Negotiations on global governance take place in compartmentalized sectors such as trade, finance, health, social affairs and development assistance. International organizations focus on their specific mandates and, as a result, the impact of their actions on other important objectives is often lost sight of. However, actions taken in one field now increasingly affect outcomes elsewhere. For example, decisions taken on trade can nullify the good done in developing countries through aid. Similarly, the actions taken by the IFIs can be at cross-purposes with those in agencies engaged in advancing social objectives. Mechanisms for ensuring coherence in global governance as a whole are either weak or non-existent. To a large extent this lack of coherence in global governance is a reflection of the fact that within national governance separate ministries rarely coordinate the actions each takes in their respective spheres of global governance, a failing that is perpetuated by the lack of accountability discussed earlier. The normal pressures in national politics to strike a compromise based on a trade-off between competing economic, social and environmental goals are typically absent in the global context.

Unbalanced outcomes

353. These weaknesses in global governance have contributed to the uneven social and economic impact of globalization. There are two main channels through which this has happened. The first is the creation of a system of rules governing the global economy that has been prejudicial to the interests of most developing countries, especially the poor within them. The second is the failure to put in place

a coherent set of international economic and social policies to achieve a pattern of globalization that benefits all people.

354. The evolving system of multilateral agreements and rules has revealed a bias in agenda setting towards measures to expand markets. In contrast, only limited attention has been paid to measures to achieve a more balanced strategy for global growth and full employment. This is the essential underpinning for policies to achieve a more inclusive pattern of globalization. Together with this, it will be important to pursue complementary initiatives such as the development of a multilateral framework on the cross-border movement of people; measures to regulate global markets, including curbing anti-competitive practices in global production systems; avoidance of tax havens; correcting serious failures in the global financial market; and the development of new sources of funding for aid and global public goods.

355. Most of the agreements that have been reached have been imbalanced. For example, in the multilateral trading system significant trade barriers remain in key sectors that are vital for expanding the exports of developing countries. In addition, the developing countries have, to their detriment, had to cede policy autonomy in important areas of development policy where they still need to develop their capacity.

356. Unfortunately, there is far less emphasis on policies to help developing countries to cope with the strains of adjustment and to strengthen their capacity to thrive in a competitive global economy. Relatively little attention is paid to the development of their technological capacities in an increasingly knowledge-based global economy. The goal of full employment and achieving decent work for all receives low priority in current international policies.

357. Another major weakness in global governance is the absence of global mechanisms and policies for ensuring socio-economic security. In rich countries, a significant proportion of national revenue is allocated to reduce poverty, provide social security and meet the needs of vulnerable people. However, in many countries these funds are being cut back drastically. At the global level, this role is meant to be performed by the multilateral agencies, voluntary organizations and bilateral development cooperation programmes. However, the resources available for this purpose are minuscule in relation to the needs for poverty eradication.

Absence of global mechanisms for ensuring socio-economic security

358. Any reform of global governance must be inspired by our vision of a fair and inclusive globalization. It must promote universal values and norms endorsed by the international community such as the rule of law, respect for human rights and fostering of democracy. It should contribute to the achievement of social and economic goals embodied in the Millennium Declaration and other key international agreements. The reform proposals should strengthen the global legal and institutional infrastructure for promoting growth, equity, human development and decent work. They should seek to enhance the representative, participatory, transparent and accountable character of global institutions. They should give voice to all men and women to articulate their concerns and interests. They should mobilize the energy and commitment and sense of solidarity and responsibility of key actors of the global community. A reform of global governance on this scale is clearly required, one that transforms the process and substance of globalization to meet the aspirations of people throughout the world.

III.2.2 Fair rules

Introduction

359. Our central concern is the unfairness of key rules on trade and finance, and their asymmetric effects on rich and poor countries. We are also concerned at the lack of adequate rules in areas such as global competition, investment and international migration. In this section we discuss: the need to preserve freedom for all countries (provided there is no conflict with collective interests) to pursue development policies that are in their best interests; the need to redress current inequities in terms of market access in international trade; the need to strengthen the emerging framework for global production systems; and the reform of the international financial system.

360. In most cases our primary concern is the need to redress current imbalances between rich and poor nations. But the issue of fairness extends beyond this; the global economy needs to benefit working men and women in rich and poor countries alike. The rules of the global economy should therefore be devised in the light of their impact on the rights, livelihoods, security and opportunities of people around the world. In particular, we address measures to strengthen respect for core labour standards and a coherent framework for the cross-border movement of people.

The space for national development

National policy responses constrained by global rules

361. As the previous section highlighted, globalization requires strong efforts to improve national governance as well as strategic policy responses from governments in order to maximize the benefits. Yet paradoxically, the present set of global rules encroaches on this essential policy space.

362. A key area is industrial development. Historically many of the now industrialized nations adopted a variety of policy instruments to foster the development of domestic industries at crucial stages in their industrialization. They also had extensive controls on FDI in terms of entry, ownership and performance requirements.[39] Similarly, the NIEs of East Asia based their industrial strategies on export promotion, conditional subsidies and protected domestic industries. Trade policies formed part of home-grown development strategies within which the State worked together with business to strengthen and monitor the performance of domestic industry. The State played a central role in mobilizing domestic investment and influencing its allocation, and in restricting or regulating FDI.[40] Measures such as minimum local content, export and technology transfer requirements, reverse engineering, and the indigenous adaptation of imported technology were also used effectively.

363. Of course the basis for international competitiveness has changed, and it may not be desirable or even feasible for all countries to imitate these strategies since much depends on initial conditions and capabilities. Nevertheless, these early experiences of industrial development highlight the important role that an appro-

---

[39] Including policy tools such as export subsidies, tariff rebates on inputs used for export, government sanctioned monopoly rights and cartel arrangements and directed credits. See Ha-Joon Chang: *Kicking Away the Ladder* (London, Anthem Press, 2002) and *Foreign Investment Regulation in Historical Perspective* (Third World Network, 2003).

[40] A. Amsden, op. cit.

priate set of home-grown policies can play in creating a competitive industrial base. At the same time, not all home-grown policies are necessarily effective; there have been serious errors in the past, such as the excessive reliance on import-substitution policies and on inefficient State enterprises.

364. The Uruguay Round agreements have significantly restricted the policy options now available to "latecomers". While the GATT Article XVIII continues to allow some infant industry and safeguard protection, the Agreement on Subsidies and Countervailing Measures (SCM) prohibits subsidies that are conditional on export performance and those that are contingent on the use of domestic rather than imported inputs. [41] In addition, it permits the use of countervailing measures to offset injury to domestic industries caused by a set of actionable foreign production subsidies. The Agreement on Trade-Related Investment Measures (TRIMs) requires the elimination of a number of measures such as local content and trade balancing requirements. [42] While recognizing the benefits to be derived from an international agreement to IPRs (discussed further in paragraph 383), some elements of the Agreement on Trade-Related Aspects of Intellectual Property Rights (TRIPS) made reverse engineering and imitation less feasible and raised the cost to developing countries of acquiring technology.

Fewer policy options available to "latecomers"

365. In totality, WTO rules now make the selective protection, or strategic promotion of domestic firms vis-à-vis foreign competition much more difficult than it was under the GATT. The limits these rules impose are aggravated by some aspects of policy conditionality of the Bretton Woods institutions. Taken together these rules and policy conditions can curb the use of industrial, technology, trade and financial policy as strategic forms of intervention to foster industrialization. [43]

366. Another area which can potentially circumscribe policy space is the emerging framework for financial regulation in the global economy. New standards and codes are being promoted through the Review of Standards and Codes (ROSC) and Financial Sector Assessment (FSA) processes. While the objective of strengthening financial systems is laudable, there is a risk that these instruments, as currently formulated and promoted, will impose standards that are inappropriate for many developing countries. Many of them are still too institutionally underdeveloped to be able to embrace all these codes. Requiring them to do so runs the risk of undermining viable growth and development strategies.

367. We strongly urge that all these global rules be reviewed to allow greater policy space for developing countries to adopt measures to accelerate their development in an open economic environment. In addition, the policies of international organizations and donor countries must shift more decisively from external conditionality to national ownership of policies. They should recognize more firmly the need to balance rights, equity and efficiency. At present this is mainly recognized in the WTO provisions for Special and Differential Treatment, and we propose a strengthening of that provision in the next section on multilateral trade rules.

Global rules should be reviewed to allow greater policy space

---

[41] Although LDCs and other countries listed in Annex VII of the SCM agreement (with GDP per capita under US$1000) are exempted from the prohibition of export subsidies.

[42] The Agreement does not define a 'trade-related investment measure'. Instead, it provides an illustrative list of measures inconsistent with the application of GATT Articles III.4 on national treatment and XI.1 on quantitative restrictions.

[43] Deepak Nayyar (ed.), op. cit.

Multilateral rules for trade

368. We fully support a multilateral approach to trade and encourage efforts to make multilateral trade liberalization mutually beneficial to all countries and socially equitable within them.

Multilateral rules for trade should be balanced and fair

369. In order to achieve this, multilateral rules for trade should be balanced and fair. A glaring inequity in the global trading system is the persistence of trade barriers in the North against labour-intensive goods produced in the South. These are items in which the South has comparative advantage, and which are vital for their growth and development prospects. On this, we share the broadly held view that unfair barriers to market access must be substantially reduced, and that this will provide important opportunities to developing countries. But we must also point out that this will not be a panacea. The interests of the LDCs will have to be safeguarded through the WTO provisions for Special and Differential Treatment to nurture their export potential. South-South trade barriers remain high and developing countries can do much to help themselves through reducing these. In addition, certain principles other than just fair market access must also be respected in order to make the global trading system fully fair to all.

370. One such principle is that trade liberalization should not be enthroned as an end in itself. It is but a means for achieving ultimate objectives such as high and sustainable growth, full employment and the reduction of poverty. As such, trade policies should be framed with these ends in mind and be evaluated accordingly.

Workers in industrialized countries may also face difficult adjustments

371. At the same time it is important to recognize that trade liberalization will often entail difficult adjustments. For example, greater market access for developing country exports will impose high social costs on some workers in the industrialized countries. In response, feasible national policy options to provide adjustment assistance to affected workers should be vigorously pursued. Doing so would ensure that greater fairness to developing countries is not achieved at the expense of vulnerable workers in rich countries. This is a good illustration of the need for greater coherence between national and international policies in achieving a fairer pattern of globalization.

Strategy for global growth and full employment

372. We should also, at the outset, recognize that the overall growth performance of the global economy is an important determinant of the extent and distribution of the benefits from multilateral trade liberalization. Improved market access for developing country exports will be far easier to achieve in the context of a more balanced strategy for sustainable global growth and full employment. Experience shows that unbalanced growth across countries is a basic source of economic tensions among trading partners. Countries experiencing persistent current account deficits and job losses through industrial relocation abroad often face mounting domestic pressure to increase protection.

373. We also recognize the need to protect and promote the rights of workers in both industrialized and developing countries. The best means to achieve this is adherence to the ILO Declaration of Fundamental Principles and Rights at Work. Assuring fundamental rights at work is not only desirable in its own right and an essential aspect of fair trade, but also provides the means to empower workers to gain a fair share of the increased productivity they are creating in all countries.

Agricultural protectionism

374. Agricultural protectionism is a major obstacle to the reduction of poverty, negating much of the good that is being done through ODA. Agricultural subsidies in the industrialized countries are now estimated to amount to over US$ 1 billion per day, while 70 per cent of the world's poor live in rural areas and subsist on less

than US$1 a day. This is a clear injustice. While acknowledging the legitimacy of national policies for agricultural development, we strongly recommend that new export credits and subsidies, and domestic support measures which distort trade should be prohibited and existing measures rapidly phased out. In addition, every effort should be made to achieve a substantial lowering of tariffs and address the present discriminatory tariff rate quota system, giving priority to products which originate in developing countries.

375. The problem of falling prices for non-oil commodities is related to this issue of agricultural protectionism. Many developing countries and LDCs still depend on agricultural commodities for more than half their export earnings. Yet from 1980 to 2000, world prices for 18 major export commodities fell by 25 per cent in real terms. This fall was particularly significant in the case of cotton (47 per cent), coffee (64 per cent), rice (60.8 per cent), tin (73 per cent) cocoa (71.1 per cent) and sugar (76.6 per cent). [44]

376. There is no simple answer to this problem. However, as a minimum, it is essential that the aggravating effect of agricultural protectionism be removed. The World Bank estimates that the removal of protection and support in the cotton sector would increase prices by 13 per cent over the next 10 years and world trade in cotton by 6 per cent. Africa's cotton exports would increase by 13 per cent. [45] Technical support should be stepped up to assist developing countries to diversify their exports and add value to commodities before exporting them. In this regard, the issue of tariff escalation for processed commodities needs to be addressed. [46] In addition, a global coordinated effort should be made on particular commodities such as sugar, cotton, wheat and groundnuts. [47]

377. There is no doubt that trade barriers in textiles and clothing need to be addressed. Developing countries have a strong comparative advantage in textiles, especially in clothing, accounting for around 50 per cent and 70 per cent respectively of world exports in these items. Many developing countries are heavily dependant on these exports. In addition, tariffs on textiles and clothing remain significantly higher than on any other sector except agriculture, ranging from three to five times the average for manufactures.

Trade barriers in textiles and clothing need to be addressed ...

378. However, we must also understand the difficulties that countries face. Substantial numbers of workers and enterprises are involved in industrialized and some developing countries. They will face significant hardship if they lose their jobs and income, especially where there is insufficient assistance and social protection. In all cases, the industrial disruption and restructuring which is likely to occur highlights the responsibilities for governments to put in place policies to protect the security of workers and their families, support the development of new opportunities, and improve access to new skills and capabilities. In the garment sector in many countries this particularly concerns women workers. In low-income countries, a national effort in this direction will often need international support.

but difficulties involved for countries

379. Another barrier to development is the escalation of tariffs in the industrialized countries. This undermines the efforts of developing countries to add value to

[44] IMF: *International Financial Statistics Yearbook*, various issues, cited in Oxfam: *Rigged Rules Double Standards* (Oxford, 2002).

[45] World Bank: *Global Economic Prospects, 2004* (Washington DC, 2003).

[46] See WTO: *World Trade Report, 2003* (Geneva, 2003).

[47] See World Bank, op. cit. for an analysis of possible global action in each of those commodity groups.

their exports of industrial products and raw materials. Despite the Uruguay Round agreements, industrialized countries have maintained tariff escalation, particularly on "sensitive products" not covered by the Generalized System of Preferences (GSP), such as food industry products, textiles, clothing and footwear.

Technical standards on products

380. In addition to these overt market barriers, developing countries are also increasingly concerned about the proliferation of technical standards on products ranging from packaging to food hygiene and pesticide residues. These are of course driven primarily by the legitimate need to protect consumers and citizens, and there is strong political pressure in the industrialized countries to set standards with an ample safety margin. These should be set in an objective way. However, compliance with standards implies large costs for exporters from developing countries, giving rise to accusations of protectionism. One recent example is the decision by the EU to apply restrictions on the level of aflatoxins in imports of nuts, cereals and dried fruits which go beyond international standards.[48] While WTO agreements attempt to prevent abuses by encouraging the use of international standards, the LDCs in particular often lack the resources and capability to implement them. They also often lack the institutional capacity to participate effectively in the international organizations and programmes overseeing these standards.

381. A number of offsetting measures should be undertaken in this area. Developed countries must commit themselves to assisting developing countries to facilitate the upgrading of product standards. At the same time, developing countries must be allowed a greater say in the formulation of product standards and efforts undertaken to minimize the impact of these standards on market access.

Abuse of anti-dumping measures

382. It is likewise important to prevent the abuse of anti-dumping measures as this can constitute a barrier to market access. The scope for abuse is increased by the fact that a lower standard of proof is required in anti-dumping than in domestic antitrust cases. This discrepancy between legal principles needs to be reviewed as part of efforts to revise disciplines and rules, which clearly need to be made more transparent and predictable. In this process, due attention also needs to be given to the vulnerability of developing countries. Technical support should be provided to assist them with procedural matters and thus eliminate the bias in the cost and ability to pursue or defend anti-dumping actions.

Intellectual property rights

383. Concerning TRIPS, we acknowledge that this is a complex issue. There is a need to protect intellectual property rights in both industrialized and developing countries so as to provide incentives for innovation and technology creation. At the same time, it is important to ensure broad access to knowledge and for it to be shared as widely as possible, which is of particular importance to developing countries. Fair rules are needed that balance the interests of technology producers and technology users, particularly those in low-income countries for whom access to knowledge and technology is limited. An important issue for the poorest developing countries is the problem of lack of institutional capacity, and the competition for resources with other development objectives when it has to be built. Efforts must be made to seek a balance. However, many argue that the TRIPS Agreement went too far. For one thing, it prevented access to life-saving medicines at afford-

---

[48] A study by the World Bank estimated that the implementation of this higher standard would have a significant negative impact on African exports of these products to Europe, which could be expected to fall by 64 per cent (US$670 million per year) compared to exports under current international aflatoxin standards. See T. Otskui, J.S. Wilson and M. Sewadeh: "A Race to the Top? A Case Study of Food Safety Standards and African Exports", *Working Paper No. 2563*, World Bank (Washington DC, 2001).

able prices. For another, it did not adequately protect open access to traditional knowledge that has long been in the public domain. The recent agreement in the area of TRIPS and public health shows that means can be found to address development concerns.[49] Efforts are under way in relation to other concerns.

384. With respect to investment and competition policy we note the deep division on these and other "Singapore Issues" within the WTO, which contributed to the impasse at the Cancun Ministerial Conference in September 2003. A significant number of developing countries are strongly opposed to their inclusion in the negotiating agenda and to their becoming part of a single undertaking. At the same time, some developed countries argue that both investment and competition policy are important complements to trade liberalization and should, for this reason, be negotiated within the WTO. It appears unlikely that progress on these issues will be made in the WTO.

Investment and competition policy

385. Instituting fair rules in the multilateral trading system would be a major step forward. However, unless stronger development provisions are built into the system, developing countries will find it difficult to take advantage of them. The current Special and Differential Treatment provisions for developing countries generally allow longer grace periods for implementing agreements and commitments and provide support to these countries to strengthen their capacity to comply with WTO agreements (e.g. the implementation of technical standards) and to handle disputes. There are also some special provisions for LDCs. However, these are insufficient and need to be strengthened.

386. More time to implement the rules is not enough. Uniform rules for unequal partners can only produce unequal outcomes.[50] Given the vast differences in levels of development, we believe that there is a need for affirmative action in favour of countries that are latecomers and do not have the same capabilities as those which developed earlier. It is possible to have a set of multilateral rules in which the obligations of countries are a function of their level or stage of development. A simple starting point would be to allow flexibility to these countries for joining in, or opting out of proposed disciplines or new issues in the WTO to permit greater policy space for them to pursue national development policies.

Need for affirmative action in favour of developing countries

Rules for global production systems

387. The globalization of production has provided important new opportunities for developing countries to accelerate their industrialization. However, as we have seen, except for a few countries, restrictions on market access have been a serious obstacle to realizing this. In particular, continuing tariff escalation makes it extremely difficult for most developing countries to graduate to high value-added activity within the global supply chain. In addition, there are two other important concerns that need to be addressed.

---

[49] A special Declaration on TRIPS and Public Health at the Doha Ministerial Conference in November 2001 stressed the importance of implementing and interpreting the TRIPS Agreement in a way that supported public health. It underscored countries' ability to use the flexibilities that are built into the TRIPS Agreement, including compulsory licensing and parallel importing. In August 2003, WTO member governments agreed to legal changes that would make it easier for countries that are unable to produce pharmaceuticals domestically, to import cheaper generics made under compulsory licensing.

[50] Deepak Nayyar, op. cit.

388. First, while MNEs have in many instances contributed to higher growth and an improved business environment, their dominance in global markets can present formidable barriers to entry for new firms, especially those from developing countries. In addition, the wave of cross-border merger activity in the 1990s has intensified concerns over industrial concentration in global markets and the barriers to competition that it gives rise to.[51]

389. Second, there has also been growing concern that incentive competition between developing countries to attract FDI is inducing these countries to go too far in lowering regulations, taxes, environmental protection and labour standards. In countries with inappropriate domestic regulatory and tax barriers, measures to reduce these are clearly required. They not only impede the entry of FDI but also impair the competitiveness of the domestic economy and impose higher prices on consumers. However, the problem of incentive competition that we are addressing goes well beyond such reforms. It centres on concerns that countries may be pushed by competitive bidding for FDI to offer concessions that are unnecessary and reduce the overall benefits received. EPZs are often presented as examples of this phenomenon. These are important concerns which need to be addressed.

390. With respect to competition, while there is strong antitrust legislation for most national markets, there is no equivalent for the global economy. And as pointed out earlier, there is little consistency between measures applied to anti-dumping investigations in global markets and legal principles governing anti-competitive behaviour in domestic markets. New initiatives are needed to make global markets more transparent and competitive.

391. A coordinated effort is needed to reduce private barriers or other restraints in global markets. These include the abuse of dominant positions in global markets, and international private cartels that fix prices, allocate markets and restrain competition.[52] In addition, vertical constraints in the supply chain such as exclusive distribution agreements, exclusive purchasing agreements and selective distribution systems may also restrict market entry.[53]

392. We recommend enhancing dialogue and cooperation on the issue of making global markets more transparent and competitive, and encourage the exchange of information and cooperation in respect of the extra-territorial enforcement of antitrust laws. Fora such as the International Competition Network, the OECD Global Forum on Competition and the WTO working group on Trade and Competition Policy provide important opportunities to discuss these issues.

393. Over the longer term, there may be a need to establish an International Agency on Competition Policy that monitors concentration in global markets, facilitates national competition policy reviews, and provides technical assistance to developing countries and international dispute resolution in the event of contradictory interpretations by national authorities on cross-border antitrust issues. We acknowledge that the environment is not yet ripe for a new institution of this type.

---

[51] P. Nolan et al: "The Challenge of the Global Business Revolution", *Contributions to Political Economy*, 21, 91.110, Cambridge Political Economy Society (Oxford University Press, 2002).

[52] The World Bank estimates that the total overcharge to developing countries for imported products sold by those cartels which were prosecuted during the 1990s for price fixing would have been US$2 billion for 2000. See World Bank: *Global Economic Prospects 2003* (Washington DC, 2002).

[53] For example, the United States against Japan in the WTO Kodak-Fuji case in which important distribution channels were alleged to have been foreclosed from the American company.

However, existing platforms for dialogue and cooperation could begin to delineate the role and functions of such an agency.

394. With respect to the problem of "beggar-thy-neighbour" investment policy competition, greater international effort is needed to construct a balanced development-friendly framework for FDI. Multilateral rule making in the area of investment, and specifically FDI, has a troubled history. It proved impossible to reach agreement on the United Nations Code of Conduct on Transnational Corporations in the late 1970s and 1980s. The draft code attempted to delineate both the rights and responsibilities of transnational corporations in their international operations. Efforts to negotiate a Multilateral Agreement on Investment (MAI) in the OECD met with particularly strong opposition from trade unions, NGOs and other groups and was finally abandoned in 1998. Many commentators have noted that the draft articles of the MAI established a series of rights for foreign investors with no attendant responsibilities in respect of investor conduct. Two important lessons emerged. First was the need to have the relevant actors at the table so as to balance the interests of home and host countries, investors (both domestic and foreign), workers and the public. Second was the need for a transparent and open process. Its absence fuelled public suspicion and opposition to the MAI.

Controversy over multilateral rules for investment

395. The site of controversy over multilateral rules for investment has shifted to the WTO, with strong objection from developing countries, trade unions and civil society. Opponents argue that the principles of non-discrimination and national treatment are not suitable for an investment agreement. There are legitimate instances (e.g. infant industries) where countries may wish to give advantage to domestic SMEs over foreign capital.

396. In the absence of coherent multilateral rules, the present framework for FDI regulates this domain in a piecemeal and fragmented way through Bilateral Investment Treaties (BITs), regional agreements such as NAFTA and other WTO agreements (the General Agreement on Trade and Services (GATS), SCM and TRIMs). [54] The recent surge in the number of BITs shows that the desire to protect and promote FDI is strong, regardless of whether or not consensus can be reached on a multilateral framework. We are concerned that developing countries may be accepting unfavourable terms in BITs as a result of unbalanced negotiations with stronger developed country partners.

397. There is clearly a need to put in place a more transparent, coherent and balanced development framework for FDI so that, in addition to the overall benefits to all countries, entry into global production systems by developing countries can be a win-win process.

FDI needs a more transparent, coherent and balanced development framework

398. We recommend that as a first step toward a balanced development framework for FDI, countries begin to act collectively to resolve the issue of investment policy competition by making incentives more transparent. While all may benefit from a more transparent system, no country or investor would want to act alone and place itself at a competitive disadvantage, requiring transparency, while others did not. Thus it is in the interests of countries to do this collectively and develop agreed disciplines. Countries could begin to do this on a regional basis. This would also be a valuable stepping stone for developing countries to define their collective

---

[54] For a review of the content of these agreements see UNCTAD: *World Investment Report, FDI Policies for Development: National and International Perspectives*, www.unctad.org/wir

interests on other issues, such as national treatment in the pre- and post-establishment phase, dispute settlement procedures, expropriation and compensation provisions, balance-of-payments safeguards, performance requirements, and other measures to balance private and public interests. It could also enhance their negotiating capabilities in bilateral negotiations.

399. We believe that efforts should then be stepped up to find a generally agreed forum, in which to work out a balanced development framework for FDI, perhaps starting with a "Policy Development Dialogue" of the type proposed in Part IV. Any such framework should be negotiated as a separate and coherent entity, and not be tied to concessions on the trade negotiating agenda at the WTO. It should provide a stable, predictable and transparent framework for investors; balance private, workers', and public interests, rights and responsibilities – both foreign and domestic; and ensure a fair, transparent and appropriate dispute resolution procedure. It would need to allow flexibility and policy space for countries to manage investment in a way that ensures that the benefits are realized, and the adverse effects, such as the crowding out of domestic investment, are minimized or controlled.

Reform of the financial architecture

400. Progress in terms of market access in international trade and entry into global production systems can, however, be negated by failure to adequately address the issue of reform of the global financial architecture. Gains in the spheres of trade and FDI run the risk of being set back by financial instability and crises. Even the basic ability to seize the new opportunities created by fairer rules governing trade and investment will be strongly influenced by the functioning of the global financial system.

Global financial system unstable – with middle-income countries worst affected

401. The current global financial system is highly imperfect. More than other markets, the global financial market is heavily dominated by financial interests in the industrialized countries. The governments of these countries, especially the economically strongest, determine the rules governing the market through their influence on the IFIs. These latter institutions in turn exercise great leverage over the macroeconomic and financial policies of developing countries. At the same time, the banks and financial houses from these same countries enjoy tremendous market power within the global financial system. The system is also characterized by severe market failures and is unstable. The upshot of all this is that most of the risks and the negative consequences of financial instability have been borne by the middle-income countries, currently the weakest players within the system.

402. Net private capital flows to developing countries, as conventionally defined, totalled over US$ 50 billion in 2002, a rebound compared to 2001 but still less than a quarter of the peak reached in 1996 before the Asian crisis. However, net private FDI was the only positive component of these net private capital inflows (US$ 110 billion in 2002). [55] Two other major components, net portfolio investment and net bank lending, saw an outflow of US$ 68.2 billion in 2002, continuing the negative trend for the sixth consecutive year. Thus the global financial system has worked in such a way that, in the aggregate, the net flow of private capital, excluding FDI, has been from poor, capital-scarce developing countries to rich and capital-abundant ones.

---

[55] See UNCTAD: *Trade and Development Report 2003* (Geneva, 2003).

403. Over the past decade, increased global capital mobility has also been accompanied by an increase in the frequency of financial crises in developing countries, often with high social costs. These financial crises reflect the interrelated problems of volatility and contagion. Volatility, as noted in section II.2, reflects the growing role of short-term financial flows. These are often characterized by surges in capital inflows and outflows in response to changes in financial market perceptions of the economic outlook in host countries. Information failures in these markets often magnify the warranted responses to a given real change in the economic outlook for particular countries. This problem is aggravated by contagion effects wherein "herd behaviour" by financial market operators leads to the extension of their judgments to countries where the economic fundamentals do not justify this. These contagion effects were particularly severe in the Asian financial crisis of 1997-98. These serious defects need to be corrected if we are to attain a fairer and more inclusive pattern of globalization.

404. Today there is a consensus on the need to reform the international financial architecture. This rests on the recognition that interdependence and openness, combined with volatility and contagion, have made the governance of financial markets far more difficult. Our goal should be to build a stable financial system that stimulates sustainable global growth, provides adequate financing for enterprises, and responds to the needs of working people for decent employment. A stable financial system will provide incentives for productive investment, while preventing the devastating employment effects of a financial crisis. It will also encourage a predictable role for foreign capital as a complement to domestic savings. The bottom line is that the international financial system should support the integration of developing countries into the global economy in a manner that promotes development.

International financial architecture in need of reform

405. Progress towards attaining this goal has been slow and limited. So far, reform has been mainly focused on crisis prevention measures such as greater disclosure of information, attempts to develop early warning systems, and the formulation of international standards and codes in financial sector supervision. While these initiatives are useful, their impact will be gradual and probably insufficient. It is true that international standards and codes have an important role to play in strengthening national financial systems across the world. They are a part of the strong need to improve the institutional framework within which international financial markets operate, whether through principles of sound corporate governance or through common minimum standards in prudential regulations, supervision and accounting. It is also clear that achieving this would contribute to greater stability in the global financial system and enhance the access of developing countries to international financial markets. There are, however, serious concerns over how the process of developing and implementing these standards and codes has been proceeding.

... but progress has been slow and limited

406. Of particular concern is the fact that developing countries are not being adequately involved in the design of these new standards and codes.[56] In addition, insisting on these standards would make it more difficult and more expensive for developing countries to access the global financial market. For example, "revisions

---

[56] There are some signs of a change in this. In the wake of the emerging market financial crises of the late 1990s the Group of 20, an international forum of finance ministers and central bank governors, was formed. It included ten systemically important emerging market economies in its membership.

of capital standards increasing the cost of risky loans by international banks may make it more difficult for such countries to fund development projects".[57]

407. We therefore urge that there should be a determined effort to ensure greater participation in the process of reforming the international financial system. There should also be a more open and flexible approach to the formulation of standards and policy guidelines, one that is more sensitive to the different circumstances and needs of developing countries. As has been pointed out, "neither G7 ministers nor multilateral officials have a monopoly of knowledge of which [development] model is best".[58]

408. In strict logic, policy guidelines are distinct from formal rules that govern the functioning of the international financial system. But this distinction is often unclear in practice. For example, the policy guidelines of the IFIs on issues such as capital account liberalization often operate as *de facto* rules for developing countries. This is because of the strong influence these institutions have over the policy choices of developing countries.

Pace of capital account liberalization should be tailored to country circumstances

409. The policy of capital account liberalization, for example, is one where a dogmatic approach should not be pursued. The experience of the 1990s has shown that countries with underdeveloped and poorly regulated financial systems should adopt a cautious and gradual approach.[59] Such an approach would be preferable since it would allow the required breathing space for strengthening financial systems in advance. More generally, countries with weak financial systems that have liberalized prematurely should not be discouraged from reintroducing selective instruments for managing capital accounts. In spite of the disadvantages associated with these measures, the use of such instruments as interim measures in the face of financial crises should, on balance, also be considered acceptable. Important lessons can be drawn from experience: from Chile and Malaysia on their use in crisis situations, and from India and China on prudent strategies towards capital account liberalization.

410. More generally, we believe that the reform process should confront the fundamental issues of the instability of the post-Bretton Woods exchange rate system and the destabilizing influences of macroeconomic and financial policies. There is a need for a mechanism to facilitate consultation, consistency and surveillance of national macroeconomic policies. The problem of global macroeconomic management cannot be left entirely to the market and it must extend beyond the G7 countries.[60] In the next section we discuss this issue of the coordination of macroeconomic policies, not simply to manage financial flows and exchange rates in the short term, but also to support economic growth, productivity increase and employment creation over the long term.

Urgent efforts needed to reduce financial volatility and contagion in emerging markets

411. It is also imperative to accelerate progress towards reducing the problem of financial volatility and contagion in emerging markets. There is a need to increase the supply of emergency financing in times of crisis so that it is made available before rather than after financial reserves are depleted. Such financing should also be made available to countries facing contagion. We appreciate the efforts that are under way on this issue but we urge speedier progress.

---

[57] Barry Eichengreen: *Financial Crises and What To Do About Them* (Oxford University Press, 2002).

[58] Ibid.

[59] See, for example: E. Prasad et al: *Effects of Financial Globalization on Developing Countries: Some Empirical Evidence*, IMF Mimeo (17 March 2003).

[60] Deepak Nayyar, op. cit.

412. In addition to the problems of debt relief, which will be dealt with in the next section, efforts to devise effective and equitable mechanisms for debt resolution should also be intensified. Among other things, such a mechanism should provide for a fair allocation of responsibilities and burdens between debtors and lenders. We note with regret that up till now there has been little headway in redressing the unfairness of the current system; this continues to place the interests of lenders above those of indebted countries and the poor within them.

413. A related issue is that of allowing sufficient policy flexibility for countries in crisis to adopt a more socially sensitive sequencing of adjustment measures. This requires giving higher priority to the objective of minimizing the social costs of adjustment packages. This will often imply the acceptance of a longer period of adjustment and less abrupt corrections in macroeconomic policies.

Labour in the global economy

414. These fairer economic rules of the game will not, by themselves, be sufficient to ensure that globalization delivers for people. As noted in Part I, there must also be respect for the international framework of agreed indispensable human rights and measures to promote social justice.

415. An important concern, highlighted by the international labour movement and others, has been the impact of intensified competition on labour standards. There is a consensus that core labour standards provide a minimum set of global rules for labour in the global economy. The question is what can be done to further strengthen respect for these core labour standards.

416. A second important concern is the lack of a coherent framework for the cross-border movement of people. Fair rules for trade and capital need to be complemented by fair rules for the movement of people, a difficult but crucial issue.

Core labour standards

417. There is general acceptance by the international community of the value of international labour standards as a means to improve the conditions of employment and labour worldwide.

418. In 1995, the Copenhagen World Summit for Social Development defined a set of "fundamental" workers' rights, based on seven International Labour Conventions. The ILO launched a campaign for their universal ratification, and at its 1998 Conference they were taken as the reference for the adoption of its Declaration on Fundamental Principles and Rights at Work and its follow-up. The Declaration restates the obligation of all member States to respect, promote and realize the principles concerning fundamental rights dealt with in the Conventions, namely:

•   Freedom of association and the effective recognition of the right to collective bargaining;

•   The elimination of all forms of forced or compulsory labour;

•   The effective abolition of child labour; and

•   The elimination of discrimination in respect of employment and occupation.

ILO's core labour
standards
establish
minimum rules
for labour in the
global economy

419. With the addition of a new Convention on the worst forms of child labour, eight ILO Conventions are now widely recognized as defining fundamental rights at work. [61] There is thus now international consensus that this particular set of core labour standards with universal reach constitutes the minimum rules for labour in the global economy.

420. The international community has frequently reaffirmed the role of the ILO in setting and dealing with the standards concerned. [62] This has avoided a situation in which different organizations work on the basis of different sets of labour standards, with conflicting interpretations of their meaning and application.

421. In both the WTO Singapore Ministerial Declaration of 1996 and the ILO Declaration on Fundamental Principles and Rights at Work of 1998, the member States of both organizations affirmed their commitment to the observance of the core labour standards. [63] They specifically underlined that these standards should not be used for protectionist trade purposes and that the comparative advantage of any country should not be called into question. Implicit in this pledge, of course, is that no country should achieve or maintain comparative advantage based on ignorance of, or deliberate violations of, core labour standards. These principles have been reaffirmed in very clear terms, in mutually reinforcing ways, in different fora.

422. The approach that has been agreed in the ILO is a promotional one, supplementing States' formal commitments where the Conventions have been ratified. The basic approach consists of regular reporting on respect for these fundamental principles and rights, combined with substantial technical cooperation programmes to assist countries to put them into effect. The ILO's regular supervisory mechanisms, which provide fair and appropriate procedures to ensure the implementation of labour standards and principles, are explained in the box in the paragraph below.

But blatant
violation of labour
and trade union
rights still occur

423. The practice on the ground often belies the commitments that have been taken at the highest political level – revealing a picture of widespread discrimination and blatant violations of labour and trade union rights. It shows discrimination based on sex, age, disability and HIV/AIDS status to be virulent in the world of work today. Growing economic insecurity and inequality have exacerbated

---

[61] These are: Forced Labour Convention, 1930 (No. 29); Abolition of Forced Labour Convention, 1957 (No. 105); Freedom of Association and Protection of the Right to Organise Convention, 1948 (No. 87); Right to Organise and Collective Bargaining Convention, 1949 (No. 98); Equal Remuneration Convention, 1951 (No. 100); Discrimination (Employment and Occupation) Convention, 1958 (No. 111); Minimum Age Convention, 1973 (No. 138); Worst Forms of Child Labour Convention, 1999 (No. 182). The Conventions themselves have each between 130 and 162 formal ratifications, which indicates near-universal acceptance of their obligations.

[62] "Governments should enhance the quality of work and employment by: [...] (b) Safeguarding and promoting respect for basic workers' rights, including the prohibition of forced labour and child labour, freedom of association and the right to organize and bargain collectively, equal remuneration for men and women for work of equal value, and non-discrimination in employment, fully implementing the Conventions of the International Labour Organization (ILO) in the case of States parties to those Conventions, and taking into account the principles embodied in those Conventions in the case of those countries that are not States parties to thus achieve truly sustained economic growth and sustainable development." (Programme of Action of the World Summit for Social Development, para. 54, 1995); "We renew our commitment to the observance of internationally recognized core labour standards. The International Labour Organization is the competent body to set and deal with these standards and we affirm our support for its work in promoting them." (WTO Singapore Ministerial Declaration, adopted 13 December 1996, para. 4.)

[63] At the Doha Ministerial in 2001, WTO members reaffirmed the Singapore Declaration provision on internationally recognized core labour standards. See WTO Doha Ministerial Declaration, 20 November 2001, para. 8.

ILO action to promote the implementation of international labour standards

The ILO combines different means of action to promote worldwide implementation of international labour standards and to settle controversies about compliance with standards. Its regular reporting and complaints procedures bring together member States and business and union representatives to assess compliance on a country or case basis.

International labour Conventions, including the eight fundamental ones, are adopted by the tripartite ILO Conference and submitted by governments to their national parliaments for ratification.

Regular reporting procedures
Under *article 22* of the ILO Constitution, the principal reporting mechanism, States report regularly to the ILO on how the Conventions they have ratified are given effect in law and in practice. Under *article 19*, governments report on the effect given to non-ratified Conventions and to Recommendations. The ILO Committee of Experts on the Application of Conventions and Recommendations reviews articles 22 and 19 reports, which are discussed within the tripartite Conference Committee on the Application of Standards.

Follow-up to the *1998 Declaration of Fundamental Principles and Rights at Work* provides for annual reports which permit a group of expert advisors to monitor the application of the Declaration and recommend action to the tripartite ILO Governing Body. A separate Global Report is prepared each year on one of the four fundamental principles and rights and is discussed in a plenary session of the International Labour Conference. Together, the Annual and Global Reports promote the ratification of the core Conventions and identify needs for technical assistance.

Workers' and employers' organizations are able to submit their observations on government reports in all these procedures. Dialogue in these reporting processes ensures that difficulties can be identified and measures proposed to overcome them.

Complaints procedures
ILO has constitutional procedures to address disputes relating to member States' compliance with standards under ratified Conventions or, in the case of freedom of association, as a result of constitutional membership. Under *article 24*, the ILO Governing Body examines *representations* made by workers' and employers' organizations that Members have failed to observe ratified Conventions. Under *article 26*, an independent Commission of Inquiry issues conclusions and recommendations for action, after investigation of a *complaint* by a government or Conference delegate (workers' and employers' organizations) alleging a Member's failure to observe a ratified Convention. *Article 33* remains available to authorize enforcement measures in extreme circumstances, when other measures have failed.

In a process derived from the Constitution itself, the tripartite Governing Body Committee on Freedom of Association (CFA) reviews complaints alleging violations of *freedom of association*, brought by any government or concerned workers' or employers' organization against any Member, whether or not it has ratified the Conventions on freedom of association.

---

problems of xenophobia and racial and religious discrimination. [64] An estimated 246 million children are involved in child labour – two-thirds of them engaged in hazardous forms of work. Over 8 million children below the age of 17 are forced to become child soldiers, trafficked into domestic service, working in debt bondage in agriculture and brick-making or forced to work in the illicit drugs and sex industry. [65] Bonded and forced labour is also prevalent among adults, ranging from human trafficking into domestic, drug-related or sex work to forced labour in the military, agriculture and prison services. [66] Violations of trade union rights continue to be a daily occurrence and many workers face both political and

---

[64] ILO: *Time for Equality at Work*, Global Report Under the Follow-up to the ILO Declaration on Fundamental Principles and Rights at Work (Geneva, 2003).

[65] ILO: *A Future without Child Labour*, Global Report Under the Follow-up to the ILO Declaration on Fundamental Principles and Rights at Work (Geneva, 2002).

[66] ILO: *Stopping Forced Labour*, Global Report Under the Follow-up to the ILO Declaration on Fundamental Principles and Rights at Work (Geneva, 2001).

administrative hurdles when trying to make their voices heard.[67] There are continued reports of the imprisonment, disappearance or murder of trade unionists who try to exercise these rights.[68]

424. Some observers call for stronger action. Attention has been focused on the WTO because of the possibility of applying trade sanctions to countries that do not respect these standards. Respect for core labour standards or enforcement of national labour legislation have also been included in the provisions of some bilateral trade agreements.

425. There are a number of difficulties here but the main problem is political. Core labour standards are regarded by many developing countries as part of a broader development agenda, both as a goal and also a principal means of development. They demand that the rules of the global economy be set to support their development goals as a whole, which also include rectifying inadequate access to markets, promoting stable flows of capital, and reducing commodity price fluctuations – issues addressed above. New proposals to strengthen respect for core labour standards should be part and parcel of stronger international policies to deal with these other imbalances and to support developing countries' efforts to meet objectives such as growth and employment. Any suggestion that the trade and human rights agendas be directly linked has been rejected by many developing countries, despite the fact that most of them subscribe fully to the human rights concerned.

Need to strengthen capacity of ILO to promote core labour standards

426. We believe that it is essential that respect for core labour standards form part of a broader international agenda for development, and that the capacity of the ILO to promote them be reinforced. This involves mobilizing the multilateral system as a whole, and strengthening this goal in the actions of governments, enterprises and the other actors concerned:

- First, all relevant international institutions should assume their part in promoting the core international labour standards and the Declaration on Fundamental Principles and Rights at Work. They should ensure that no aspect of their policies or programmes impedes implementation of these rights.

- Second, where the failure to realize these fundamental principles and rights at work is due to a lack of capacity rather than political will, existing technical assistance programmes for the implementation of standards should be stepped up, including the strengthening of labour administrations, training, and assistance to the organization of workers and enterprises. This should include reinforcement of existing action to eliminate child labour.[69]

- Third, the ILO itself should be strengthened by increasing the resources available for fair and appropriate supervision and monitoring, for promotional assistance, and for the Follow-up to the Declaration on Fundamental Principles and Rights at Work and other procedures established in the ILO's Constitution.

[67] ILO: *Your Voice at Work*, Global Report Under the Follow-up to the ILO Declaration on Fundamental Principles and Rights at Work (Geneva, 2000). Also see Reports of ILO Committee of Experts to the International Labour Conference at www.ilo.org, in particular the *General Survey: Freedom of Association and Collective Bargaining*, Report III, Part 4B, International Labour Conference, 81st Session, Geneva, 1994.

[68] See Reports of the ILO Committee on Freedom of Association submitted to the Governing Body at www.ilo.org

[69] This issue has moved sharply up the priority agenda in recent years. ILO's International Programme for the Elimination of Child Labour (IPEC) now works with national authorities, social partners and other actors in 85 countries.

- Fourth, where persistent violations of rights continue despite recommendations of the ILO's supervisory mechanisms, enforcement of these labour standards could be pursued through Article 33 of the ILO's Constitution, which in the event of non-compliance with a ratified Convention authorizes the ILO to take action to secure compliance.

427. In addition to the action of international institutions, market forces are increasingly encouraging enterprises to ensure that respect for these core labour standards is an integral part of doing business. Ethical consumer and fair trade initiatives provide incentives in a variety of product markets for private action. A growing number of investors are engaging in Socially Responsible Investment (SRI), evaluating companies not only on their financial, but also on their environmental and social performance, including respect for core labour standards. Enterprises large and small are making public their commitment to respect these core labour standards, whether in codes of conduct or other voluntary initiatives. The UN Secretary General's Global Compact brings together companies, UN agencies, labour and civil society to support the labour principles contained in the ILO Declaration on Fundamental Principles and Rights at Work. Efforts such as the Global Reporting Initiative are developing concrete reporting guidelines on these and other standards.

The cross-border movement of people

428. A major gap in the current institutional structure for the global economy is the absence of a multilateral framework for governing the cross-border movement of people. The GATS "Mode 4" provision is restricted to the temporary movement of service providers and covers only a tiny fraction of the cross-border movement of labour. There are also a number of international conventions which seek to protect migrant workers and combat trafficking in people.[70] However, no comprehensive multilateral framework exists for the cross-border movement of people. This is a serious omission for several reasons.[71]

Absence of multilateral framework for cross-border movement of people

429. The cross-border movement of people is a substantial and widespread phenomenon involving more than 10 million people a year over the past decade, as well as a growing number of countries. In some cases this movement has been temporary, while in other cases it has involved migration leading to permanent settlement. What was once a predominantly South to North flow, now has a significant intra-developing country dimension. These cross-border movements have

---

[70] The International Convention on the Protection of the Rights of All Migrant Workers and Members of Their Families, adopted in 1990, came into force in July 2003. This complements the ILO Migration for Employment Convention, 1949 (No. 97) and the ILO Migrant Workers (Supplementary Provisions) Convention, 1975 (No. 143). Together, these three International Conventions provide a framework for addressing the rights of migrant workers and questions of irregular migration. They operate within a broader policy context including recently-adopted UN treaties that address trafficking, smuggling and exploitation, such as the UN Convention against Transnational Organized Crime (2000), its Protocol to Prevent, Suppress and Punish Trafficking in Persons, Especially Women and Children (2000) and Protocol against the Smuggling of Migrants by Land, Sea and Air (2000), the Optional Protocol to the Convention on the Rights of the Child on the sale of children, child prostitution and child pornography (2000), as well as the earlier 1951 Convention and 1967 Protocol relating to the Status of Refugees. While relatively few countries and, where relevant, regional economic organizations have ratified these conventions to date (with the exception of the refugee treaties), these instruments provide important elements for a more comprehensive agenda.

[71] For a more extensive discussion on this issue see Deepak Nayyar: "Cross-Border Movements of People" in Deepak Nayyar (ed.), op. cit.

occurred despite a tightening of immigration controls in the industrialized countries and (in contrast to the cross-border movement of goods, services and capital) without any concerted effort to promote it.

Migration linked
to increasing
globalization

430. This pattern of migration is clearly linked to increasing globalization. Declining costs of transportation and the advent of cheap mass travel have greatly reduced one important barrier to movement. The ICT revolution and the universal reach of the media have meant a vast diffusion of awareness of differences in living standards between rich and poor countries that has added to the allure of migration. New market institutions have emerged which facilitate the process, in the shape of intermediaries and agents. Transnational enterprises move managers around the world, while the practice of "shopping" overseas for specialized skills has grown ("body-shopping"), and labour markets for some highly skilled professionals are effectively already global. The globalization of higher education systems has reinforced this trend. [72]

431. From the perspective of developing countries the absence of a multilateral framework for the cross-border movement of people reflects yet another gap in the rules governing the global economy. Many of them maintain that freer migration to the industrialized world would be a swift and powerful means of increasing the benefits they receive from globalization. From a labour perspective, the lack of a multilateral framework on migration is a clear illustration of the imbalance in the current rules of the game. While the rights of foreign investment have been increasingly strengthened in the rules set for the global economy, those of migrant workers have received far less attention.

Potential benefits
of migration

432. A multilateral regime for the cross-border movement of people that makes the process more orderly and eliminates the exploitation of migrants could offer considerable gains to all. Most industrialized countries have ageing populations that are tending to decline, while most developing countries have young and growing populations. Many of the problems of an ageing population, such as a declining labour force and the difficulties of financing social security in the face of rising dependency ratios, could be attenuated by increased immigration on terms which respect the rights of migrant workers. More generally, global labour productivity would increase through this process since the migration would be from low-productivity, surplus labour countries to higher-productivity ones. This would benefit not only the individual migrants involved but also their home countries through remittances, as well as the transfer of skills and the stimulus given to business activity by the diaspora. Remittances to developing countries currently amount to US$ 75 billion annually (1.5 times the value of ODA), while the "diaspora effect" has stimulated the growth of high-tech and other industries in several East Asian countries and India. In short, such movements of labour can be mutually beneficial to both North and South.

Current problems

433. The lack of an orderly multilateral regime on the cross-border movement of people has, by default, allowed a number of serious collateral problems to emerge. One is that of the brain drain from poor to rich countries. This has deprived poor countries of the very category of workers that they need most, while the loss from the investment in training them has been uncompensated. At the same time, there has been a sharp increase in illegal immigration and the international trafficking of people by criminal syndicates. It has been estimated that there are 15 to 30 million illegal or irregular immigrants worldwide, and the number is growing. A parti-

---

[72] Deepak Nayyar, ibid.

cularly disturbing aspect of the rise in human trafficking is that an increasing proportion of the victims are women, often trapped in degrading conditions in the sex and entertainment trades. This has occurred in the context of the increasing feminization of international migration, with women now comprising half of all international migrants. While women used to migrate primarily as dependants, they are increasingly doing so on their own as breadwinners. Given their greater vulnerability, this gives added urgency to the problem of the protection of the rights of migrant workers.

434. Before setting out our proposals for improving upon this situation we should note that there is a strong polarization of views on the desirability of expanding opportunities for international migration. However, the middle ground is that there are costs and benefits involved that should be seriously weighed. We have already referred to the significant potential benefits, both for the migrants themselves, and for the countries of origin and destination. But this needs to be tempered by the recognition of the potential costs such as the displacement of local workers, the disruption of labour market institutions and social protection systems, and the weakening of social cohesion.

435. Much can be done to improve significantly upon the current situation. The issue of developing a multilateral framework to govern international migration should now be placed firmly on the international agenda. The objectives of such a framework should be: to facilitate mutually beneficial ways of increasing migration opportunities, with due regard to States' legitimate interests to ensure that the process is fair to both sending and receiving countries; to make the process orderly, predictable and legal; to eliminate trafficking and other current abuses where women are especially vulnerable; to ensure full protection for the rights of migrant workers and facilitate their local integration; and to maximize the developmental benefits of international migration.

Need for multilateral framework for cross-border movement of people

436. We believe a multilateral framework for the cross-border movement of people to be a realistic project given the evident benefits to be gained. Some promising ideas have already been floated.

437. A number of these relate to the problem of the brain drain. The migration of skilled workers to industrialized countries yields both benefits and costs to the labour-exporting developing countries. The workers involved obviously gain, while the skills, technological know-how and business knowledge they acquire benefit their countries of origin through the contacts they maintain and upon their return when this occurs. However, these positive effects do not always occur spontaneously and to the full extent possible. The benefits to developing countries can be increased through the adoption of measures to facilitate the return of such workers to their home countries, including for temporary spells. The measures to stimulate such a process of "skills circulation" that could be considered include the acceptance of dual citizenship by both host and sending countries, the easing of re-entry conditions for non-permanent migrants, and tax and other incentives to stimulate the return of skilled migrants to their home countries. An increase in this type of "skills circulation" would benefit both industrialized and developing countries. The former could still continue to hire skilled labour from developing countries. At the same time it would reduce the current inequities arising from a permanent brain drain from poor to rich countries. [73]

---

[73] Deepak Nayyar (ed.), op. cit.

438. There are, however, also costs to developing countries, especially in cases where there is a scarcity of the skilled labour that is being lost to industrialized countries. In such cases, the outflow aggravates skill shortages. The problem is particularly acute in essential social services such as education and health. While domestic policies to increase the incentives and opportunities for skilled labour to remain at home are an important part of the solution, it has also been suggested that the industrialized countries should coordinate their hiring policies with developing countries facing such skill shortages in essential services.

439. Another interesting and practicable idea relates to measures that could be adopted to increase the developmental benefits of international migration. This involves the more effective tapping of the remittances of migrants through the lowering of transaction costs and risks, tax incentives for migrants to reinvest in their home countries, and the adoption of measures in host countries to allow return migrants to repatriate their social security contributions. Various other ideas have been proposed to return some of the gains from migration to the countries that have invested in the skills and education of the migrants concerned. A simple one would involve assigning a share of all income tax payments by migrants to a development fund.

440. There is therefore a large and productive agenda for multilateral action. The issues and problems associated with the movement of people across national borders cannot be addressed by single countries acting in isolation or on a unilateral basis. To move forward on this agenda, we recommend action at three levels.

441. The first concerns international conventions and binding obligations. Building on the foundation of existing instruments, we believe that in several areas international consensus can be reached on the need to revitalize and extend multilateral commitments, including issues such as the basic rights and protection of migrant workers and their families, trafficking, discrimination and exploitation. Action on such issues needs to be taken within the multilateral bodies concerned, notably the ILO and the UN bodies concerned with human rights and crime prevention.

Dialogue needed between countries of origin and destination

442. The second concerns dialogue between countries of origin and destination on key policy issues of common interest. Such dialogues could aim to develop and agree on procedures, recommendations and non-binding codes, complementing the formal obligations under ratified Conventions. This could begin on a bilateral or plurilateral basis, but it should extend to the regional level. Such dialogues should endeavour to:

- Exchange information on surpluses and shortages of labour
- Develop coordination of policies among labour-exporting countries
- Create some harmonization of policies among labour-importing countries
- Work towards a regime of discipline to be imposed on intermediaries
- Build a more effective system for the prevention of trafficking in people
- Address the problems of illegal immigrants.

443. These dialogues could also help build common approaches to major policy issues such as the rules for temporary migration, the brain drain and the contribution of migration to development, and the alignment of social security and labour market policies; and develop an information system on such matters.

444. The third level would be to initiate a preparatory process towards a more general institutional framework for the movement of people across national borders. This means a transparent and uniform system, based on rules rather than dis-

cretion, for those who wish to move across borders. The ultimate objective would be to create a multilateral framework for immigration laws and consular practices, to be negotiated by governments, that would govern cross-border movements of people. This would be similar to multilateral frameworks that already exist, or are currently under discussion, concerning the cross-border movement of goods, services, technology, investment and information.

445. A global forum is needed for regular exchange of information and views on this issue among all the countries and interests concerned. Such a forum could help identify both problems and opportunities, and point to ways to ensure that the movement of people occurs on an orderly basis. It should engage not only governments but also both sides of the world of work. In Part IV we recommend a dialogue to develop policy on this issue in order to examine how best to develop this agenda.

A global forum for regular exchange of information and views on migration

446. Moving this agenda forward would imply strengthening the existing multilateral organizations dealing with the movement of people – notably the ILO, the International Organization for Migration (IOM), the United Nations human rights mechanisms and the United Nations High Commissioner for Refugees (UNHCR) – and improving the coordination among them. We welcome the initiatives under way such as the Geneva Migration Group and the newly established Global Commission on International Migration, co-chaired by Dr. Mamphela Ramphele of South Africa and Mr. Jan O. Karlsson of Sweden which is due to start work in early 2004. We call on the ILO to take the lead on these matters and we look forward to the outcome of the General Discussion on labour migration at the International Labour Conference in Geneva in 2004.

III.2.3 Better international policies

Introduction

447. The proposals we have made for fairer rules, combined with effective action at the regional, national and local levels, will go a long way towards achieving our vision of globalization for all. But they are far from sufficient. Even on a level playing field many countries, especially the least developed, will not be able to succeed in the global economy. Substantially increased international action is required to ensure that opportunities and benefits are widely distributed, and that common goals are realized. In this section we examine how to promote a better coordinated, integrated approach to some of the key goals.

448. We begin by reviewing the resources available to meet global targets and commitments, notably the MDGs, and look at ways in which they might be increased and used more effectively.

449. We then turn to some of the main international policy domains where action is needed to address the social dimension of globalization. We believe that it is possible to achieve significant improvements and set out our proposals for doing so, in particular by raising capabilities, assuring security and promoting decent work.

Resources for global goals

More external resources needed for development and to meet the MDGs

450. Achieving growth and development goals depends in the first instance on the quality of national governance and the mobilization of domestic resources. In section III.1 we have highlighted the many actions which are necessary at the national level. But for many developing countries, moving ahead on all those issues constitutes a heavy burden. It simply cannot be met without substantial external resource support. That is why the urgent need for more resources for development is high on the international agenda. The Monterrey Consensus[74] states that "Mobilizing and increasing the effective use of financial resources and achieving the national and international economic conditions needed to fulfil internationally agreed development goals ... will be our first step to ensuring that the twenty-first century becomes the century of development for all". At the Third Conference on the Least Developed Countries in 2001, the 193 participating governments agreed to "take upon ourselves not to spare any efforts to reverse the declining trends of ODA".

451. Today the MDGs, which we discuss below, provide an important frame of reference. Available estimates suggest that for all countries to meet the MDGs by 2015, at least US$ 50 billion a year in additional ODA would be needed.[75] While donors made commitments at Monterrey to increase ODA by US$ 16 billion by 2006, that still leaves over two-thirds of the total to be met, even if all commitments are honoured. And the need for international resources is by no means limited to the MDGs, since these are minimum figures.

452. Where might these resources come from? We look at ODA, debt relief, possible new public sources and private investment.

---

[74] The *Monterrey Consensus* is the official document adopted by the International Conference on Financing for Development, held in March 2002 in Monterrey, Mexico.

[75] Recommendations of the High-Level Panel on Financing for Development, United Nations General Assembly, A/55/1000, June 2001.

Official Development Assistance (ODA)

453. In recent years, net ODA flows have been decreasing. Although there are signs that the bottom of the curve has been reached, with the beginnings of a recovery in 2002, most national ODA levels are far below the long-standing target of 0.7 per cent of GDP, with the average now only 0.23 per cent (figure 21). Meeting the 0.7 per cent target would increase assistance by over US$ 100 billion a year. We add our voices to those demanding that this commitment be respected. If all countries had met the target over the last 30 years, an additional US$ 2.5 trillion would have been available for development.

454. There are a number of reasons why countries are failing to meet this target. They include public concern about other priorities such as unemployment and insecurity at home and, among some, a belief that aid is not well spent. In the end, the resources come from taxpayers in industrialized countries, whose solidarity must be encouraged. However, there is also a political failure here: public support for ODA has remained high [76] but in too many countries the political response has been weak. The political process inclines governments towards giving priority to their immediate constituencies over more distant international commitments. We call on political leaders in all industrialized countries to make this commitment part of their core policy platform. We must deliver what has been promised.

455. However, exhortation is not enough. New initiatives are also required. Mobilizing opinion to meet the MDGs is an example of how it is possible to raise the political profile of key global issues. Increased global pressure around visible concerns such as HIV/AIDS and child labour has generated substantial new commitments of resources.

456. Public support needs to be converted into commitment. Many NGOs play an important advocacy role, and research efforts such as the Commitment to Development Index, which measures how far rich countries support development through aid, trade and other policies, help to reinforce the message. [77] Efforts are needed to ensure that people are aware that the poverty and injustice which ODA aims to reduce is a source of global instability and insecurity, and that they are informed about what their governments are doing about it.

457. Reaching the MDGs will require more effective delivery of ODA. Too much aid has been driven by strategic geopolitical objectives, instead of targeting poverty reduction. Much goes to middle-income countries rather than to the poorest countries, and aid is often provided in ways that benefit donor country exporters and visibility. Moreover, the impact of foreign aid is often weakened as it is delivered in a highly fragmented way, imposing a variety of donor requirements for preparing, delivering and monitoring development assistance. This generates unnecessarily high transaction costs, undermines national systems, and overwhelms the limited public administration capacity of recipient countries. A gradual shift from bilateral to multilateral channels, without losing the recognition of the identity of the donor, would help avoid overlap, inconsistency and reduced effectiveness of aid.

---

[76] See OECD: *Public opinion and the fight against poverty* (Paris, 2003). In one global survey, seven out of ten citizens said that they would support paying higher taxes if they were sure the proceeds would be spent on improving the lives of the world's poor. See *Global Issues Monitor 2002* (Toronto, Environics International, 2002) pp. 67–68.

[77] Foreign Policy Magazine and the Center for Global Development: "Ranking the Rich" in *Foreign Policy*, September–October 2003.

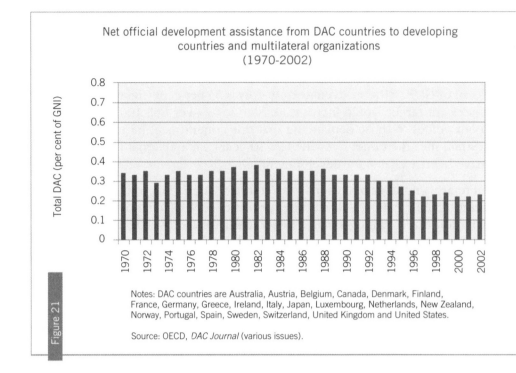

Net official development assistance from DAC countries to developing countries and multilateral organizations (1970-2002)

Notes: DAC countries are Australia, Austria, Belgium, Canada, Denmark, Finland, France, Germany, Greece, Ireland, Italy, Japan, Luxembourg, Netherlands, New Zealand, Norway, Portugal, Spain, Sweden, Switzerland, United Kingdom and United States.

Source: OECD, *DAC Journal* (various issues).

Figure 21

458. Donors should focus their aid on the poorest countries and on the achievement of the MDGs. Aid should be particularly directed towards sub-Saharan Africa and to countries which are sufficiently well governed. Aid has to back home-grown strategies and has to be demand-driven. Donors should not attempt to substitute for domestic governance. While a degree of conditionality is inevitable, if only to maintain political support for ODA in donor countries, this should not undermine national decision-making. The whole notion of national ownership of development policies can be undermined by conditionality. Aid should be committed in a credible, predictable way, binding donors as well as recipients. There is often scope for more parliamentary scrutiny in both donor and recipient countries. Effective aid needs to be untied, as tied aid is less efficient for the recipient and invites corruption. It is essential that aid should be provided to finance local as well as recurrent expenditures, especially in the health and education sectors. Moreover, donors need to harmonize procedures with those of partner country systems to improve the effectiveness of development assistance. All donors adopted the Rome Declaration on Harmonization in February 2003. It should now be implemented.

Debt relief

Resolving the debt issue

459. In many poor countries, mostly in Africa, external debt is still at unsustainable levels. Between 1990 and 2001, external debt as a percentage of gross national income rose from 88.1 per cent to 100.3 per cent in the severely indebted countries.[78] In 2001, the LDCs were still spending almost 3 per cent of GDP on servicing debt – an indication of how debt relief can rapidly free up resources for development.

460. It is vital that the debt problem is resolved as soon as possible to enable the countries concerned to face their difficult development challenges with a clean

---

[78] World Bank: *Global Development Finance*, 2002, 2003.

slate. The Debt Initiative for Heavily Indebted Poor Countries (HIPC), launched by the IMF and the World Bank in 1996, and enhanced in 1999, was recognition of the severity of this problem. However, this now needs to be accelerated and deepened. The majority of countries that reached the intermediate phase of this process have yet to reach the final stage. Even for countries meeting all the criteria, the initiative may not result in a sustainable debt burden.[79] The Jubilee 2000 campaign for debt cancellation demonstrated that this is a crucial issue which has large-scale public support worldwide.

461. Debt reduction processes must be designed and owned nationally – as is the intent in the Poverty Reduction Strategy Papers (PRSP) process – and ensure that there is accountability to people within countries. Conditions attached to debt relief and cancellation[80] are legitimate if they ensure that the savings are channelled into growth-enhancing, employment-creating and poverty-reducing programmes which respond to the needs of people. But they must not reproduce past structural adjustment policies that have not worked, such as dogmatic demands for privatization and reduced public services. The heads of the Bretton Woods Institutions have indicated that this is no longer the case, and recent evidence now shows increases in public spending on education and health associated with the HIPC. However, legitimate concerns remain, and the political consequences of conditionalities have to be monitored very carefully. Governments need to deliver on people's needs. If their hands are tied, the credibility of political systems and of democracy itself suffers.

Respecting national ownership

462. It is also important to ensure that debt relief is accompanied by an increase in ODA from developed countries. Much of the remaining debt problem for LDCs concerns multilateral sources. When such debt is not repaid this directly reduces the resources available for future loans. To compensate for this, there is a need for increased funding from donor countries. In addition, special attention must be given to countries whose debts have been rendered unsustainable by a collapse in commodity prices.

New public financial resources at the international level

463. We believe that achievement of the 0.7 per cent goal for ODA, together with debt relief, are the most promising immediate routes for raising new resources, notably for the priority goal of poverty reduction, and that efforts should be concentrated there. Countries have made firm commitments and it is everyone's responsibility to ensure that they are held to them. However, additional sources of funding are also needed. The goal of a fairer globalization cannot be achieved unless resources are available on a larger scale to support countries in their efforts to participate in the global economy, and to provide other important global public goods. It is essential to consider a wider range of options, provided they generate additional funding and do not replace current or future commitments.

New ways of increasing funding

464. An important first step would be increased international tax cooperation to support domestic resource mobilization. As we have seen in section II.2, globalization can put constraints on tax collection. Moreover, offshore capital markets have

---

[79] UNDP *The Human Development Report 2003* suggests that for HIPC countries, external financing and debt relief should be such that debt service does not exceed 2 per cent of GDP, including in the event of an external shock such as a natural disaster or a collapse in commodity prices.

[80] Debt cancellation was already foreseen in Commitment 7 of the Plan of Action at the 1995 Social Summit.

Better international policies 103

increased the options for tax avoidance and made it harder to combat tax evasion. The large-scale use of tax havens deprives countries of funds to build social and economic infrastructure. Oxfam has estimated that the loss of tax revenue to developing countries amounts to at least US$ 50 billion per year, an amount equivalent to total development assistance.[81]

International tax cooperation

465. An International Tax Dialogue has already been launched by the IMF, OECD and the World Bank to encourage and facilitate discussion of tax matters among national tax officials and international organizations.[82] There is a strong sense amongst many countries and experts that a comprehensive and accessible basis for international tax cooperation needs to be created and that the United Nations would be the appropriate forum for this. The Secretary-General has recommended that the Ad Hoc Group of Experts on International Cooperation on Tax Matters be upgraded into an intergovernmental body, either in the form of a committee of governmental experts or of a special new commission, as a subsidiary body of the Economic and Social Council (ECOSOC), and that it be supported by a small, expert secretariat. We support this initiative as a vital element in strengthening the integrity of national tax systems in all countries, increasing public resources for development and facilitating the fight against tax havens, money laundering and the financing of terrorism.

466. A proposal which has been on the table for some time is to restart regular issues of Special Drawing Rights (SDRs) to increase liquidity in the global economy. These resources could be voluntarily allocated to developing countries, and so provide them with additional resources for investment. The already approved Fourth Amendment to the Articles of Agreement of the IMF should immediately be ratified, thus allowing the cumulative SDR allocations to double.

467. Another recent proposal is to establish an International Development Trust Fund. Donors would make a series of long-term pledges for a flow of annual payments to an International Financing Facility (IFF). On the back of these pledges the IFF would issue bonds, turning the long-term income stream into immediately available development capital. The proposal, initially made by the United Kingdom Chancellor of the Exchequer, Gordon Brown, seeks to raise the amount of development aid from just over US$ 50 billion a year today to US$ 100 billion a year up to 2015. This idea should be pursued, provided it generates new resources in addition to existing commitments.

Proposals for new taxes at the global level

468. There is also a variety of proposals for new taxes at the global level, many of them controversial. Probably the best known is the Tobin tax, designed to tax speculative capital flows, but there are a number of others. One proposal which has been suggested is to tax the use of global resources, in particular the global commons. That is the rationale of a carbon tax, which would thereby contribute to environmental sustainability. At the World Summit on Sustainable Development in Johannesburg in 2002, Jacques Chirac said "Trouvons de nouvelles sources de financement. Par exemple par un nécessaire prélèvement de solidarité sur les richesses considérables engendrées par la mondialisation".[83] A global lottery has also been suggested as a source of revenue.

---

[81] Oxfam: *Tax Havens: Releasing the hidden billions for poverty eradication* (Oxford, Oxfam, 2000).

[82] www.itdweb.org

[83] "Let us find new sources of financing. For example, a necessary levy, in the interest of solidarity, on the considerable wealth that has been generated by globalization."

469. Historically, the growth of responsibility for action at community, national and, most recently, regional levels has led to a corresponding growth in the capability to raise revenues. In due course, growing global responsibilities are likely to lead to a similar response. However, quite apart from the debate over whether or not global taxes are desirable, there are at present insuperable political obstacles to putting them in place. The problem is not so much a question of what or how to tax, since a variety of technically feasible proposals exist. The point is that taxes are collected by governments within countries, and there is no global institutional framework with the necessary political authority to determine tax burdens and decide resource utilization. We believe that this is an important issue, on which discussion of possible practical actions should be encouraged.

470. It would of course be both possible and desirable to generate resources through reallocation of military expenditures to development in both industrialized and developing countries. Total world military spending for 2001 has been estimated at US$ 839 billion. If the 15 largest military spenders agreed to divert just 5 per cent to ODA, this would generate US$ 30 billion a year. This would surely make a greater contribution to global peace and security than it does through military expenditure.

471. However, if governments cannot agree to commit themselves to raising more funds at the global level, people can. They can decide to assume a global responsibility for solidarity, just as they did in neighbourhood schemes and friendly societies at the outset of the European welfare states in the 19th century. The development work of many NGOs is based on voluntary contributions, some of them on a large scale. Oxfam, for example, spends over US$ 300 million a year and has over a million "monthly pledge" donors. We also welcome new initiatives which permit voluntary contributions to be used for international solidarity, such as the idea of a "Global Social Trust".[84] A variety of methods can be developed to facilitate voluntary contributions to such schemes, such as permitting individuals to earmark resources in their national tax declarations. Again, such resources should be additional to existing ODA commitments, which also often support the work of NGOs.

<aside>International solidarity</aside>

472. Private philanthropic initiatives by foundations and wealthy individuals have also been making a major contribution to global social goals for many years. Estimated international grants by United States foundations alone reached a yearly average of more than US$ 3 billion over the 2000–2002 period, of which about two-thirds went to programmes for health, education, international development and the environment.[85] International giving grew faster than overall giving, spurred mainly by record commitments of a few large foundations such as the Ford Foundation, the Bill and Melinda Gates Foundation, the David and Lucile Packard Foundation, the United Nations Foundation, the John D. and Catherine T. MacArthur Foundation and the Rockefeller Foundation. However, less than 2 per cent of charitable giving in the United States goes abroad. Many organizations and networks are engaging in exploring the largely untapped potential of global philanthropy.[86]

---

[84] This is an ILO proposal aimed at increasing voluntary support from industrialized countries for social security schemes in developing countries. See ILO: *Exploring the feasibility of a Global Social Trust*, GB.285/ESP/4, November 2002.

[85] See Loren Renz and Josefina Atienza: *International Grantmaking Update*, The Foundation Center, October 2003 (www.fdncenter.org/research).

[86] For a detailed list, see the Global Philanthropy Forum website (www.philanthropyforum.org).

Private capital flows to low-income countries

Private capital flows need to be spread more widely

473. Cross-border investments have grown very rapidly. Today, 75 per cent of net capital flows to developing countries are private. However, as we saw in Part II, poorer developing countries do not appear to have benefited much from financial globalization. Private capital flows remain concentrated in a small number of mostly middle-income countries.

474. How private capital can be attracted and contribute to development was discussed in previous sections. Section III.1 argues the need for governments to invest in skills, infrastructure and institutions and to understand the motivations of private investors. Section III.2.2 suggests the need for a development-friendly multilateral framework of rules for investment. These two elements should be supported by more public-private initiatives and institutions such as country investment guides, common principles and investment routes. The latter can include global investment funds which channel resources to start-ups, micro-credit initiatives and socially responsible projects. The large number of successful socially responsible investment initiatives[87] suggests that this is a promising route, and more effort should be devoted to developing ways for them to channel resources to low-income countries. The complementarities between private and public capital flows also need to be on the agenda.

475. Good data on social and environmental sustainability are important too. Ratings agencies emphasize economic rather than socio-political indicators, and it is desirable to broaden assessment criteria to get a more accurate picture of long-term prospects and stability, as is attempted for example in the Calvert-Henderson index or the Wealth of Nations Triangle index of the Money Matters Institute. [88]

Achieving key goals

476. At the Millennium Summit, Heads of State and Government agreed to work together to build a safer, more prosperous and equitable world for all by 2015. They adopted eight global goals, all of them to be achieved by 2015. These goals commit the entire global community – rich and poor countries together. We regard them as a minimum for a decent world. We should move, on this foundation, towards a common understanding of a socio-economic floor for the global economy.

The Millennium Development Goals

In September 2000, 189 Heads of State and Government committed their countries – rich and poor – to meet a set of time-bound and measurable goals by 2015:

- Eradicate extreme poverty and hunger
- Achieve universal primary education
- Promote gender equality and empower women
- Reduce child mortality
- Improve maternal health
- Combat HIV/AIDS, malaria and other diseases
- Ensure environmental sustainability
- Develop a global partnership for development.

---

[87] In the United States, one out of every nine dollars under professional investment management is in "socially responsible" investing, amounting to over US$ 2 trillion. See Social Investment Forum, 2003 Report on Socially Responsible Investing Trends in the United States, Washington DC, www.socialinvest.org

[88] H. Henderson, J. Lickerman and P. Flyn (eds): *Calvert-Henderson Quality of Life Indicators* (Bethesda, Calvert Group, Dec. 2000). Money Matters Institute: *Wealth of Nations Triangle Index*, (Boston, March 2002).

477. Much of this depends on policies within countries, as we have discussed in section III.1. But the Millennium Declaration also represents a global commitment to international action. Achieving these goals will be important steps towards a fairer world. However, they will not be achieved with current levels of resources.

478. Many of these goals reiterate commitments that have been made many times, notably in the programmes of action of the major global conferences of the 1990s.[89] They also reflect internationally agreed instruments which protect the basic rights of peoples necessary to social, economic and cultural development.[90] Such universal human rights are the bedrock. They reflect internationally agreed norms and standards which are legal expressions of universally shared values and principles. They provide a framework for holding social actors accountable, including governments, citizens, corporations and international organizations.[91]

479. Among the key goals of social development, health has been given particular attention by the international community. The concept of "health for all" has been an important factor in recent debates on making medicines more affordable. The rapid spread of infectious diseases is one of the global ills of our interconnected world. Most recently the rapid action of the World Health Organization (WHO) on SARS has been effective in containing the spread of the disease. The 2001 WHO-supported Commission on Macroeconomics and Health argued for large-scale financial commitment by rich countries to scaling up the access of the world's poor to essential health services, contending that this will pay off in accelerated economic growth. The converse is also true. Poor health impedes development, as the catastrophic effects of HIV/AIDS in Africa testify. HIV/AIDS erodes development gains and risks crippling a whole generation. The ILO estimates that at least 26 million prime age workers (15–49) worldwide are infected. In Africa, 11 million children have lost at least one parent to AIDS – a number that is expected to rise to 20 million by 2010. Women are disproportionately affected by the disease. In Africa, 58 per cent of those with HIV/AIDS are female, and among the teenagers affected, 75 per cent are girls.[92] Initiatives launched to combat the disease require urgent attention and support. We have already referred to the debate on access to essential medicines in relation to the TRIPS agreement. Multilateral institutions and programmes, such as UNAIDS, the Global Fund to Fight AIDS, Tuberculosis and Malaria and the WHO '3 by 5' strategy to deliver antiretroviral therapy to 3 million people by 2005 remain under-funded and need to be adequately resourced.

Health and sustainable development are key goals

---

[89] See especially the Rio Declaration and Agenda 21 (UN Conference on Environment and Development), Vienna Declaration and Programme of Action (World Conference on Human Rights), Copenhagen Declaration and Programme of Action (World Summit on Social Development), Cairo Declaration and Programme of Action (World Conference on Population and Development), Beijing Declaration and Programme of Action (Fourth World Conference on Women).

[90] These include the International Covenant on Civil and Political Rights and International Covenant on Economic, Social and Cultural Rights, the Convention on the Elimination of All Forms of Discrimination Against Women, the Declaration on the Right to Development, the Convention on the Rights of the Child, ILO Convention No. 169 on Indigenous and Tribal Peoples and the Convention on the Elimination of All Forms of Racial Discrimination.

[91] See www.unhchr.ch; and on the relationship between globalization and human rights, Mary Robinson: "Making Globalization Work for all the World's People", speech delivered at the Aspen Institute Summer Speakers Series, Aspen, Colorado, July 2003.

[92] UNAIDS, *AIDS Epidemic Update 2003* provides a report on the overall progression of the epidemic.

480. We have also referred in this Report to national efforts in favour of sustainable development. Globalization has put additional stress on natural resources and the environment. Large-scale deforestation and greenhouse gas emissions are important factors in global climate change. Agenda 21 of the 1992 Earth Summit of Rio de Janeiro and the Declaration of the 2002 World Summit on Sustainable Development of Johannesburg laid out frameworks for action which show the complementarity between ecological, social and economic goals. Environmental goals must be pursued as part of the social dimension of globalization.

481. We do not go further into these issues, which are already the subject of a great deal of international attention. We focus instead on a number of goals closely related to globalization where greater international effort is particularly needed: first, education, skills and technological capability; second, issues of security and adjustment; and third, the goal of decent work.

Education, skills and technological capacity

482. In today's global economy and information society, knowledge and information are the keys to social inclusion and productivity, and connectivity is the key to global competitiveness. Yet in our unequal world the networked economy is able to incorporate all that it regards as valuable, but also to switch off people and parts of the world that do not fit the dominant model.

483. Technological capability is essential. Countries need the communications infrastructure and the production system which can process and use information for development; and people must have access to the knowledge and the ability to use it, in order to participate, take advantage of and be creative in the new technological environment. That puts education and skills at the centre of a fair and inclusive globalization.

484. Yet the foundation is not being laid in many parts of the world. Universal primary education is one of the MDGs that is furthest away from attainment. As for the skills and capabilities developed at secondary level and beyond, crucial for the information society, the gap is greater still.

International action on education must be reinforced

485. Education is a core element of society, and the foundation of democratic choice. The large differences in opportunities in education between countries are one of the basic causes of global inequality. Furthermore, international migration allows rich countries to benefit from the investments in human capital made in poor countries – giving them a responsibility to support the education systems where those investments are made. Yet World Bank figures show that only 3 per cent of funding for education budgets in developing countries comes from international sources.

486. We call for international action in this area to be reinforced. The "Education for All" Fast Track initiative must be moved up the priority agenda. The goal is to deliver on the global commitment made at the World Education Forum in Dakar in April 2000 to ensure that by 2015 all children have access to, and complete, free and compulsory primary education of good quality, and that gender discrimination is eliminated. In order to meet this objective, international financial support to education must be increased substantially. However, bilateral aid flows for education fell to US$ 3.5 billion in 2000, a 30 per cent decline in real terms from 1990.

487. We also support calls for more ambitious proposals aimed at helping low-income countries to rapidly raise technological capability. One important means is

to engage education institutions from the North in distance learning. [93] Online distance learning could become a powerful tool for developing countries – reducing the need for expensive physical infrastructure for tertiary and vocational educational facilities and enabling investments to be made instead in communications equipment, with curricula and teaching provided through regional initiatives. The Global Distance Learning Network (GDLN) is one such initiative which deserves support. It is a worldwide network of institutions which are developing and applying distance learning technologies and methods with a focus on development and poverty reduction. Such networks are likely to play an important role in building technological capabilities.

Adjustment, security and social protection

488. In a competitive international economy, there is greater vulnerability to sudden change than in protected national markets. Globalization triggers the need for frequent adjustments to national production processes, and hence to jobs and the life strategies of women and men. Adjustment takes time and requires public policy interventions to support the restructuring of production systems and the creation of new opportunities.

489. This calls for a focused set of domestic policies, which we discussed in section III.1. As a minimum, systems of social protection are required which can stabilize incomes, distribute some of the gains of globalization to groups which would otherwise be excluded, and support the development of new capabilities. Yet the reality is that 80 per cent of the world's families have little or no social protection. The wave of globalization a century ago was associated with a strengthening of social protection systems, notably in Europe and the United States. By contrast, the tendency today is just the opposite. In many societies, both industrialized and developing, social protection systems are under financial strain, due to structural adjustment programmes, slow growth or national budgetary restrictions, often compounded by demographic changes. Where there is pressure on public expenditure, social transfers are among the prime targets.

Need for better social protection supported by international action and solidarity

490. International action is now essential. There is a need for donors and international and regional financial institutions to contribute to the development of national social protection systems in developing countries, and to invest in the retraining and economic restructuring which can promote more equitable adjustment and a fairer distribution of the gains from globalization. Private solidarity initiatives can also contribute. At the very least, technical assistance in this field should be strengthened.

491. Achieving progress in this area will clearly require an increase in international solidarity. This is a key issue for the global community, as it is for any community. Basic security is a recognized human right, and a global responsibility. [94] All industrialized countries devote substantial resources to social protection and

---

[93] See, for example, Manuel Castells: "Information and communications technologies and global development", keynote address at the Economic and Social Council of the United Nations, New York, 12 May 2000.

[94] The Commission on Human Security argues that this extends beyond basic economic security to encompass a minimum of "vital freedoms", including basic health, education, shelter, physical safety, clear air and water, and gender equality. The Universal Declaration of Human Rights recognizes the rights to both personal security and social protection. The ILO's current global campaign for universal social protection aims to mobilize opinion around these issues.

social transfers but such policies are extremely limited at the global level. Yet the gaps in income and security between countries are vastly greater than would be tolerated within them. A certain minimum level of social protection needs to be accepted and undisputed as part of the socio-economic floor of the global economy. As long as countries – however poor – are able to collect some taxes and contributions, they can afford some levels of social protection. If they do so, they deserve international support as well. A global commitment to deal with insecurity is critical to provide legitimacy to globalization. We believe that steps should be taken now to strengthen a sense of common responsibility and to reinforce mutual support across borders.

Making decent work a global goal

International economic policies should promote decent work

492. As argued in earlier sections, there is a strong need to reform international policies to make them more supportive of growth, enterprise development, poverty reduction and the creation of decent work for all. At present these policies emphasize market-opening measures and give low priority to goals such as full employment and social protection. We believe that it is imperative to redress this imbalance and to build a global strategy for sustainable growth aimed at achieving decent work for all. Decent work, identified in section III.1 as an important goal for national action, encompasses full employment, social protection, fundamental rights at work and social dialogue – all key ingredients for achieving global social justice.

493. The performance of the global economy has major implications for the creation of employment and its quality within each country. Today, countries cannot achieve employment goals on their own. Patterns of international investment, the growth of trade and the cross-border movement of workers all affect jobs, incomes, security and the rights of workers. We believe that more coordinated international policies are essential to improve the prospects for achieving decent work for all in the global economy. We discuss in turn the coordination of macroeconomic policies, the promotion of decent work in global production systems, and the broader question of establishing coherence between economic and social goals.

Coordinated macroeconomic policies for full employment

494. One of the most obvious effects of globalization has been to increase the interdependence between countries in macroeconomic policies. For example, countries which aim to increase employment levels through more expansionary macroeconomic policies have little space to do so on their own without generating adverse reactions in international capital markets. Enhanced coordination of macroeconomic policy among countries is therefore important to attain the global goal of full employment and decent work.

495. More specifically, market liberalization needs to be accompanied by effective policies for global macroeconomic management, in order to ensure that global growth is higher and more stable. There is a need for a better mechanism to achieve orderly adjustment to persistent balance of payments deficits and surpluses, and a balanced distribution of the responsibilities for maintaining effective demand in the global economy, so that no single country is seen as the consumer of last resort. All countries, developing and industrialized, have a strong obligation to adopt fair and responsible trading policies, and domestic policies which are fiscally responsible, provide adequate social protection and adjustment assistance, and take into account the impact on other countries.

496. An improved framework for international coordination must be developed. This coordination should include both fiscal and monetary policy and their timing. It should also include more determined efforts to prevent contagion effects, as pointed out in section III.2.2 above. It should take account of the particular needs and vulnerabilities of countries at different levels of development. In particular, means are required to ensure that middle-income countries have greater space to apply countercyclical macroeconomic policies. At present they are much more constrained in this respect than industrialized countries. Coordination should involve not only governments, but also central banks, given their critical role in determining output growth and employment levels. The latter are already mandated goals for some central banks, such as the US Federal Reserve.

497. We recommend that these issues be treated as a high priority for action at the global level. Just as employment must be a priority in macroeconomic policy decisions at national level, so it must be made a priority in international economic coordination. Macroeconomic policies must take into account not only financial targets but also their social impact. A political momentum must be built around this issue.

Promoting decent work in global production systems

498. Global production systems are now a significant source of employment growth for those developing countries that have managed to become part of them. Although MNEs alone account for only a fraction of employment in most countries, outsourcing to domestic producers implies that these global systems have a considerable impact on the labour market in many parts of the world. Regulation is weak in these new production systems, and there is widespread debate about whether there is a "race to the bottom" in labour and other standards. At the same time, for many countries, participation in these systems is an important way to attract investment and increase technological capability.

499. The system of Export Processing Zones has become a prominent issue. Over 50 million workers are now employed in such zones worldwide. Persistent concerns have been expressed that EPZs are sometimes given exemptions from national labour laws, or that there are obstacles to exercising rights in practice,[95] and that they engage countries in a competition for foreign investment which leads to damaging tax and subsidy policies. By their nature, EPZs are linked closely to the global economy. However, they often have few linkages back to national economies, thereby creating international enclaves. Outside such zones, similar concerns are expressed about employment and working conditions in a variety of smaller enterprises in international subcontracting chains, both formal and informal.

Rights at work and employment quality in EPZs

500. At the same time, EPZs are widely seen to make important contributions to development strategy. Wages and working conditions, and opportunities for employment for women, are often observed to be better than the national average. There are possibilities which have not been fully used to ensure that EPZs, and participation in global production systems more generally, contribute to both development and decent work. This applies not only to manufacturing, but increasingly to services. Trade in services is the fastest growing component of world trade, and

---

[95] International Confederation of Free Trade Unions: *Export Processing Zones: Symbols of Exploitation and a Development Dead-End* (Brussels, September 2003).

increasingly service activities such as data processing, call centres and software services are undertaken in developing and transition countries as part of global production and distribution networks.

501. Improved competition policy and a development framework for FDI, as discussed in section III.2.2 above, are important elements of any policy framework for global production systems. But promoting decent work will require a broader range of integrated economic and social policies. We cannot accept a policy based on lowering labour or environmental standards or excessive tax competition. We recommend that the main international organizations and other actors concerned work together to develop proposals for effective international policies to promote decent work, investment and trade both in EPZs and more generally in global production systems. Such proposals should address issues of labour standards, backward linkages to the domestic economy, and the ways that enterprises can move up the "value chain" through investment and technological upgrading. The primary beneficiaries of such an approach would be the countries, enterprises – both domestic and multinational – and workers concerned. We also believe that social dialogue among workers and employers is an important means by which this can be achieved, an issue to which we return in the next section.

Policy coherence for decent work

502. Action in the above areas will make a significant contribution to achieving the goal of decent work for all. However, it will have a much larger impact if there is greater consistency and coherence within the multilateral system. A key step towards this policy coherence is to ensure that the goal of decent work is adequately recognized by all the organizations concerned. This includes not only the promotion of full, productive employment but also a range of other key elements of decent work such as conditions of work, gender equality, social security, safety at work and social dialogue. International labour standards have been developed which cover all of these issues, in addition to the core standards discussed earlier.

Full employment should be a major international goal

503. This approach has deep roots in the international system as a whole. From the outset, the United Nations was mandated to promote "higher standards of living, full employment, and conditions of economic and social progress and development".[96]

504. The international community renewed this commitment in 1995 at the World Summit for Social Development and agreed "to promote the goal of full employment as a basic priority of our economic and social policies, and to enable all men and women to attain secure and sustainable livelihoods through freely chosen productive employment and work."[97] Gender equality was an important aspect of this goal.

505. The importance of the employment goal is also recognized by the key economic organizations of the international system. The purposes of the IMF, for instance, include "to facilitate the expansion and balanced growth of international trade, and to contribute thereby to the promotion and maintenance of high levels of employment and real income…". As recently as 1994, the Marrakech Agreement which gave birth to the WTO recognized that "relations in the field of trade and

---

[96] Charter of the United Nations, Article 55.

[97] United Nations, 1995, Declaration and Programme of Action agreed at the World Summit for Social Development.

economic endeavour should be conducted with a view to raising standards of living, ensuring full employment and a large and steadily growing volume of real income and effective demand ...".

506. In practice, however, the international economic organizations have tended to regard employment as derivative from their main mandates, rather than as an objective in its own right. The WTO promotes the expansion of trade, and this is seen as the way to create employment: "Trade liberalization increases national income and fosters growth and employment".[98] The IMF promotes sound financial policies as a basis for growth and employment creation. The World Bank tends to assume that what is needed is growth, and that growth creates jobs and incomes. As a result, employment and enterprise are not seen as major policy goals in their own right. This was evident in the lack of emphasis on employment in the design of the PRSP process.

507. The need for better coordination in international economic policy was reflected in the conclusions of the Special Session of the United Nations General Assembly held in 2000 to review progress made towards the Social Summit commitments. The representatives of 189 countries unanimously invited the ILO to "elaborate a coherent and coordinated international strategy on employment".[99] In response, the ILO has developed the Global Employment Agenda, which aims to place employment at the heart of economic and social policy, on the basis of a tripartite strategy which engages government, business and workers' organizations in a wide range of actions. It includes proposals for strategic alliances with the Bretton Woods institutions and others, including the United Nations Educational, Scientific and Cultural Organization (UNESCO), the United Nations Environment Programme (UNEP) and the WTO, in pursuit of employment objectives.

Need for better coordination in international economic policy

508. In practical terms, this means ensuring the consistency between the goals of decent work and full employment, on the one hand, and the financial, trade and production goals of the economic system, on the other. The ILO already has an explicit constitutional mandate to oversee the social implications of international economic policy. In the 1944 Declaration of Philadelphia, the ILO was given a special responsibility to "examine and consider all international economic and financial policies and measures" in order to ensure that they were compatible with the right of all human beings "to pursue both their material well-being and their spiritual development in conditions of freedom and dignity, of economic security and equal opportunity".[100]

509. In practice, responsibility at the international level for finance, development, trade and social policy was assigned to different institutions, and adequate coordination mechanisms were never created. There were also fundamental power asymmetries between institutions dealing with finance and trade, and those dealing with normative and social matters.

510. We believe that the organizations of the multilateral system should deal with international economic and labour policies in a more integrated and consistent way. There are some positive recent trends at this level that should be expanded.

---

[98] ILO: "Trade liberalization and employment", paper presented to the ILO Working Party on the Social Dimension of Globalization, November 2001.

[99] United Nations, Report of the Ad Hoc Committee of the Whole of the Twenty-Fourth Session of the General Assembly, 2000, para. 36, p. 24.

[100] Constitution of the ILO, Annex, Declaration Concerning the Aims and Purposes of the International Labour Organization (Philadelphia Declaration), sec. II, p. 23.

In the major international conferences of the past decade the international community moved towards consensus on the need for a concerted and coordinated effort to reduce poverty and make globalization more inclusive. Collaboration between the World Bank and the ILO has started to give employment growth a more prominent place in some national PRSPs. At the IMF, there is growing recognition of the importance of the social dimension of globalization. [101] In addition, fundamental rights at work are increasingly being accepted as an essential foundation for international economic policies.

Integrating economic and social goals

Achieving social goals requires an integrated approach

511. The principle of a more coherent approach, which we have developed with reference to decent work, applies more generally. Education, health, human rights and environmental goals also need to be addressed in a more consistent and integrated way, because they interact with each other and with economic goals and relationships. Policies at international, national and local levels are likewise interdependent and need to be developed in integrated ways.

512. Correctives are required, not only in the international agenda, but also in the actions of the international system at the country level. A better coordinated effort by the United Nations system as a whole is required to ensure that a coherent approach to economic and social goals is adopted in international advice and support to PRSPs and other country-level frameworks. These should adequately reflect decent work, education, health, human rights, gender equality and other key aspects of social development.

513. New initiatives are required to promote coherence at these different levels and more effective collaboration among the international institutions concerned. We invite the ILO, taking advantage of its wide-ranging Constitution and its constituency of workers' and employers' organizations as well as governments, to develop new instruments and methods which can promote coherence between economic and social goals in the global economy, in coordination with other organizations of the multilateral system. In Part IV we make a number of concrete proposals on how to take forward a more integrated agenda.

514. At the political level, we see a need for a regular meeting between finance and trade ministers, and ministers responsible for key labour and social policies, in order to review policy coherence among them, preferably with the participation of representatives of labour and business and, when appropriate, civil society. This might be organized initially at a regional or subregional level. At global level, advantage could be taken of the High Level Segment of ECOSOC, a point to which we return below.

---

[101] See, for example: "Toward a Better Globalization" by Horst Köhler, Managing Director of the IMF, Inaugural Lecture on the Occasion of the Honorary Professorship Award at the Eberhard Karls University in Tübingen, 16 October 2003.

III.2.4 More accountable institutions

515. Globalization has empowered public opinion through better communications and new technologies. As a result, both national and international institutions face greater pressure for more participatory and democratic governance.

516. The key issue in global governance is better accountability to people, both in terms of setting the global agenda and assessing the results of global policies. Greater representativeness, participation, transparency, efficacy and subsidiarity are essential principles to achieve better accountability and legitimacy of authority.

517. While most international actors are quick to express their support for such principles, in practice there are very different understandings of what these are. Accountability can be interpreted in many different ways, from the narrower sense of simply making information publicly available, to a broader conception which holds international organizations directly accountable for the impact of their policies.

518. In some cases the principles will come into direct conflict with each other. For example, inclusiveness and maximum participation may not be wholly consistent with effective and politically relevant decision-making. Again, the principle of efficacy must be reconciled with the principle of subsidiarity. Less formal, "networked" governance may be the best way of fulfilling some global purposes.

519. In this section we examine some ways that democratic governance can be strengthened, as an essential precondition for the implementation of reforms in international economic and social policies proposed in preceding sections. We build on the work of several previous commissions and many scholars who have examined the global governance system and made recommendations for its reform and renewal.[102] We first indicate a number of reforms that would enhance the strength and effectiveness of multilateral institutions, before turning to recommendations on the tasks and responsibilities of States, parliaments, business, organized labour, civil society and the media.

Strengthening the multilateral system

520. The UN multilateral system constitutes the core of the existing system of global governance. Armed with experience, knowledge and competence acquired over more than 50 years and a legitimacy endowed by its near universal membership of States and its mandate, it is uniquely equipped to spearhead the process of reform in economic and social policies. At the same time, as the world moves to ever greater interdependence in a widening range of activities, the need for new international agreements and new areas and forms of cooperation will become even more urgent. For the multilateral system to cope with the current and emerg-

Effectiveness of UN multilateral system needs to be enhanced

---

[102] See, for example: Commission on Global Governance: *Our Global Neighbourhood* (Oxford University Press, 1995); Meltzer Commission: *Report of the International Financial Institutions Advisory Commission* (Washington DC, 2000); United Nations: *International Monetary and Financial Issues for the 1990s* (New York and Geneva, 1997); Erskine Childers and Brian Urquart: *Renewing the United Nations System* (Uppsala, Sweden, Dag Hammarskjöld Foundation, 1994); Mahbub Ul-Haq et al (eds.): *The United Nations and the Bretton Woods Institutions: New Challenges for the 21st Century* (New York, St. Martin's Press, 1995); Global Governance Reform Project: *Reimagining the Future: Towards Democratic Governance* (2000); Deepak Nayyar (ed.), op. cit; Joseph Stiglitz, op. cit.

ing challenges of global integration, it will need to enhance its effectiveness through constant upgrading of its technical services, knowledge base and management systems. Its effectiveness also depends on the quality of its governance. Three areas are of particular concern: democratic representation and decision-making, accountability to all stakeholders, and coherence in economic and social policy. In addition, there is a critical need to ensure the adequacy of resources for multilateral agencies to enable them to strengthen the social dimension of globalization.

Democratic representation in governing councils

Reconciling power with democratic participation

521. In a world comprising nation States with vastly unequal power and wealth, it is inevitable that countries will have unequal influence in international organizations. The challenge lies in reconciling the reality of power with equality and democratic participation. There is widespread dissatisfaction with the present decision-making systems in the Bretton Woods institutions, the WTO and the United Nations. For example, membership of the Security Council is based on the situation in the period after the Second World War and does not take into account the present day realities. Reform of the membership and decision-making procedures of the Security Council has become more urgent than ever.

522. There have been many calls to increase the representation and voting strength of developing countries in the IFIs. According to one estimate, the developed countries, with around 15 per cent of the world's population, account for 17 per cent of voting strength in the UN, 34 per cent in the International Fund for Agricultural Development (IFAD), and over 60 per cent in the World Bank and the IMF. [103]

523. The voting formula in the Bretton Woods institutions is based on a calculation of various economic indices together with a discretionary element. This has given rise to various anomalies. Even when measured in terms of GDP in US dollars, and more so in terms of GDP in purchasing power parity, the developing countries, especially Asia and to a lesser extent Latin America and sub-Saharan Africa, are under-represented in voting power.

524. The situation is somewhat improved by the constituency system of representation in the Bretton Woods institutions. While eight countries appoint their own representatives to the Board of Executive Directors, all the remaining countries are grouped into 16 constituencies, each represented by an Executive Director. Furthermore, it is open to countries to move to different groupings and be represented by other directors, thus giving them some room for manoeuvre.

525. Despite these qualifications, it remains true that the industrialized countries, which are the main shareholders, exercise decisive influence on important policy decisions, as compared with stakeholders. We recommend the establishment of a fairer system of voting rights. This should result in increased representation for developing countries, with a significant proportion of voting rights still vested in the industrialized countries. As a first step we recommend that the size of the Board be increased to include one more representative from sub-Saharan Africa.

---

[103] G. Helleiner: "Markets, Politics and Globalization" in *Journal of Human Development*, Vol. 2, No. 1, 2001.

Increasing accountability

526. All international institutions, by virtue of their enhanced responsibilities in the era of globalization, need to be accountable to the public at large as well as to their own governing bodies. While it is for each public or private institution to examine how it can make its activities more transparent and more accountable to people, globalization requires that they now explicitly recognize this responsibility.

527. The international institutions responsible for finance, development and trade have been subjected to considerable public criticism in recent years. Many critiques and protests have focused on their lack of transparency and their failure to engage in consultations with civil society and interest groups on their policies and programmes. Some institutions, like the World Bank, have responded positively to these criticisms and are starting to devote valuable time and energy to dialogue with representatives of trade unions, business and CSOs. Recently, these groups have also become increasingly involved in WTO issues. The WTO has responded by establishing a more systematic dialogue with them. But the problem remains that the procedures adopted for negotiations have resulted in the WTO agenda and agreements being dominated by the interests of major trading groups and countries. It is essential to reform the working methods and negotiation procedures to ensure full and effective participation in agenda setting and negotiations by all member States. The outcome of the Cancun Conference has only reinforced the need for such reforms.

528. On the issue of public accountability, there has been an improvement in the performance of multilateral agencies, but more needs to be done. For instance, the World Bank and the IMF now publish a range of previously confidential information on their policies, operations, decisions and evaluations. However, Executive Directors still do not publish the minutes of their Board meetings. We recommend that members of the Executive Boards of the Bretton Woods institutions be accountable to the national parliaments of their respective constituencies.

529. The World Bank and the IMF have also developed more elaborate evaluation methods. The World Bank's Operation and Evaluation Department has four evaluation units, whose reports are available to the public. The IMF has established an Independent Evaluation Office which also publishes its reports. The evaluation offices are independent from the management structure and report directly to the Boards of Executive Directors. Accountability in the UN has traditionally been exercised through external oversight bodies such as external auditors and the Joint Inspection Unit, or by internal oversight mechanisms such as the UN's Office for Internal Oversight Services. Most UN organizations also have well established evaluation units, some of which report directly to the executive management. Member States have repeatedly called for strengthening of these evaluation capacities, as well as increased transparency through publication of their reports. CSOs have also called for the implementation of recommendations that emerged from these evaluation processes. While some UN bodies have taken steps to publish the findings and recommendations of their evaluations, we recommend that all UN agencies strengthen their evaluation units, adopt clear disclosure policies with regard to the results of internal and external evaluations of their programmes, policies and projects, and publish these findings accordingly. There should be regular reporting on the follow-up to recommendations arising from such evaluation processes. We also welcome independent evaluations by stakeholders and others. [104]

530. As pointed out in section III.2.3, policy coordination and coherence is a critical issue for the multilateral system. Proposals have been made for the establishment of a more representative and politically effective body that can provide leadership on harmonizing and balancing social and economic policy to achieve agreed objectives. Among the most important of these is the establishment of an economic and social security council with similar status to the UN Security Council but without the authority to make legally binding decisions. This is an important idea that should be considered. However, there has been no serious consideration of this proposal owing to lack of interest from a number of key States and the hurdle of amending the UN Charter in order to establish such a body.

531. Another proposal to improve global coherence of policy and action was advanced recently by the UN Secretary-General's High-Level Panel on Financing for Development chaired by Ernesto Zedillo, the former President of Mexico. In their Report, the panel wrote that "Despite recent worthy efforts, the world has no fully satisfactory mechanism to anticipate and counter global economic shocks". Further: "... global economic decision-making has become increasingly concentrated in a few countries. Tensions have worsened as a result. For a range of common problems, the world has no formal institutional mechanism to ensure that voices representing all relevant parts are heard in the discussion". The Panel proposed the creation of a global council "at the highest political level to provide leadership on issues of global governance ... through its political leadership, it would provide a long-term strategic policy framework to promote development, secure consistency in the policy goals of the major international organizations and promote consensus building among governments on possible solutions for issues of global economic and social governance". [105]

532. In view of the critical importance of achieving greater coherence in international socio-economic policy, we recommend that this issue be placed on the agenda of gatherings of world political leaders such as the biennial high-level dialogues of the regular sessions of the UN General Assembly, the regional and subregional summits, and enlarged meetings of the Group of 8 (G8). Adequate technical work has been done both on the need for reform and on a range of feasible institutional arrangements. At the international level, the time has come for Heads of State and Government, acting collectively, to give clear mandates to the relevant international organizations to ensure greater coherence of international social and economic policies.

533. Under the UN Charter, ECOSOC has the major responsibility for promoting global policy coordination in the economic and social fields. However, ECOSOC's mandate has always been far larger than the actual exercise of it. The political and functional separation of the Bretton Woods institutions from the United Nations, and the failure to set up an International Trade Organization at an early stage of the UN system, has inevitably resulted in ECOSOC's limited capacity to influence the dynamics of globalization in the areas of trade, finance, investment and technology.

534. Although ECOSOC was never given the authority to fully exercise its mandate, this has lost none of its original significance and legitimacy. There is much that could be done within the present mandate of ECOSOC by changing the political attitude towards the UN's role in economic and social issues. It would re-

---

[104] For example, the Global Accountability Project, developed by One World Trust. See www.oneworldtrust.org

[105] High-Level Panel on Financing for Development, op. cit.

quire new forms of functioning, upgrading its level of representation and a clear will on the part of the main actors in the economic, trade and financial spheres to use it as a high level policy-making body. Pending a major political decision on its role, some reforms could be undertaken immediately within the existing structure to strengthen ECOSOC and improve policy coherence. The High Level Segment of its annual session could promote interaction on specific aspects of global macro-economic, social and environmental management among the ministers concerned – finance, labour, social affairs, environment or others, as appropriate to the subject. ECOSOC could also use its capacity to hold short, focused sessions during the year to discuss high priority or emergency issues with the participation of relevant ministers. ECOSOC could also be serviced by a multi-agency Secretariat, headed by the Under-Secretary-General for Economic and Social Affairs. An Executive Committee of ECOSOC, at the ministerial level, could help provide the necessary leadership to achieve such reforms.

Increasing resources

535. Contrary to popular perceptions, the UN system disposes of pitifully small resources in relation to its huge responsibilities for maintaining peace and security, promoting human rights and the rule of law, undertaking humanitarian work and assisting countries to meet the essential development needs of their population. The regular budget of the UN Secretariat, some US$ 1.3 billion per year, has remained constant in nominal terms (so declining in real terms) for the last eight years. The entire UN system, including its Funds, Programmes, Specialized Agencies and peacekeeping operations, spends about US$ 12 billion per year – less than the annual budget of the New York City Board of Education.

Increase UN resources and effectiveness to meet responsibilities

536. In view of this, the position of some developed countries of maintaining zero nominal growth in their mandated contributions to the UN system is deplorable. In order to discharge its enhanced responsibilities in an effective manner, it is essential that the international community agree to increase financial contributions to multilateral institutions and reverse the trend toward raising voluntary contributions at the expense of mandatory contributions. This must go hand in hand with increased effectiveness and efficiency in the management of these institutions.

Nation States

537. Although globalization has reduced the power and autonomy of States in various ways, States – particularly the powerful ones – continue to exercise important influence on global governance through their own policies and behaviour and their decisions in intergovernmental agencies. It is therefore surprising that so few States subject the decisions taken by their representatives in those fora, to parliamentary or other public scrutiny. Even the principle of collective cabinet responsibility does not seem to work well in many countries with regard, for instance, to positions taken by their representatives on issues such as trade, agricultural, environmental or financial matters. There are several reasons for this: the overloading of parliamentary agendas; the increasingly technical nature of the issues involved; and a lack of adequate and balanced information for an informed public debate. It is important that governments and parliaments address this problem through normal channels of collective cabinet responsibility and deliberate parliamentary and public debate.

Greater accountability of governments for positions in global fora

538. National governments can thus contribute significantly to improved accountability of international organizations. Just ensuring that governments report publicly on what they do in the national name at international gatherings, and a

rigorous review of their decisions by parliaments and interested and expert groups, could have an immensely beneficial impact on the role played by their national representatives operating internationally. Public interactions with ministers, parliamentarians and public servants in capitals can have significant impact.

Global policy coherence has national roots

539. Equally important is the contribution that States can make to achieving greater coherence in global social and economic policy. It should be noted that, fundamentally, the roots of the problem of global policy coherence lie at the national level. The United Nations system is based on the principle of decentralized functional coordination. Intergovernmental organizations are sectoral in nature and their governance is the responsibility of different ministries of national governments. These organizations, additionally, have their own constitutional mandates. As a result, the solution has to be primarily sought at the national level, where there is often no consensus among different sectors and ministries within governments as to what a coherent global policy should be. Global coherence, like good governance, begins at home. We call on Heads of State and Government to adopt the necessary measures, at the national level, to ensure that the positions taken by their representatives in international fora promote a coherent integration of economic and social policies which focus on the well-being and quality of life of people.

540. Unless action is taken at the national level to achieve policy coherence through cabinet, parliamentary and public discussions of global economic and social issues, there is little hope of major improvements in global policy coordination. National Economic and Social Councils, which exist in many countries, with membership drawn from governments, business, labour and civil society, can play a particularly valuable role in this process.

541. States must also act consistently and responsibly by adhering strictly to international laws, regulations and norms that are the foundations of global governance. As underlined in section III.1 above, they should carefully consider the consequences of their actions and policies on the rest of the world, especially the LDCs and the poor. As in other domains, the richer and stronger countries carry a heavier burden of responsibility to ensure that domestic decisions do not harm the interests of people in other parts of the world.

542. A global community can only be nurtured if States extend their concerns to the plight of others beyond their borders, especially the poor. Although people in industrialized countries are generally concerned about development issues, there are few votes in these issues at national level. However, the number of people concerned, and their influence, are increasing in most countries. While the strongest voice is that of civil society organizations and movements, and voluntary advocacy and development agencies, sections of other influential groups, such as parliamentarians, religious groups, foundations, organized labour, professional associations and multinational enterprises are increasingly aware of their global responsibilities and committed to working towards a more just and stable world order.

Parliaments

National and global parliamentary oversight

543. Parliaments are the focus for accountability at the national level. They are the most important national fora for public debate about global issues and for reviewing action by governments at the international level. Parliamentary committee hearings can be influential ways of publicizing issues and engaging public opinion. We urge national parliaments to strengthen their role and capacity to provide adequate checks and balances over their governments' positions at international fora.

544. Parliaments can also play an important role in promoting accountability and coherence of public policy at the global level. Global parliamentary associations such as the Inter-Parliamentary Union (IPU), Parliamentarians for Global Action, World Women Parliamentarians for Peace and regional parliamentary assemblies such as the European Parliament, Latin American Parliament and African Union Parliamentary Assembly, can encourage better performance and accountability on the part of international agencies. Several inter-parliamentary groups have already been established to promote action and monitor developments with reference to specific areas of global social and economic policy. These include parliamentary networks involving the World Bank and WTO. We call for a progressive expansion of accountability for global policies and actions to such parliamentary groupings. We call in particular for the creation of a Global Parliamentary Group concerned with coherence and consistency between global economic and social policies, which should develop an integrated oversight of major international organizations of the UN system, the Bretton Woods Institutions and the WTO.

545. The annual meeting of the IPU at the United Nations is a useful means of increasing cooperation between members of national legislatures on international issues. Parliamentary groups in different areas can coordinate their positions on reform of global governance, using electronic means of communication. We invite the IPU and other parliamentary fora to explore ways of mobilizing public opinion on the social dimension of globalization, and ask the international agencies to facilitate such action.

Business

546. Companies, both national and transnational, make an important contribution to the social dimension of globalization. They shape the world of work and influence the social and economic environment in which people live. Enterprises are the primary source of employment and income creation and their values, practices and behaviour have a major impact on the attainment of social goals.

Contribution of companies

547. It is important to distinguish between corporate governance and corporate social responsibility.

Corporate governance

548. Corporate governance is essentially concerned with issues of ownership and control of enterprises and the rules governing financial procedures, disclosure and transparency. It includes both legal standards and internal company procedures. Good corporate governance is at the heart of both a market economy and a democratic society. As stated in the OECD Principles of Corporate Governance (1999), an influential benchmark, "good corporate governance helps to ensure that corporations take into account the interests of a wide range of constituencies, as well as of the communities within which they operate ... . This, in turn, helps to assure that corporations operate for the benefit of society as a whole".

549. Corporate governance has become a major issue in an increasingly globalized economy where different national systems need to adapt to new market pressures. The recent spate of scandals concerning corporate behaviour, including corruption, and non-compliance has increased the need for change and greater accountability.

Corporate Social Responsibility (CSR)

550. CSR concerns the voluntary initiatives enterprises undertake over and above their legal obligations. It is a way by which any enterprise can consider its impact on all relevant stakeholders. CSR is a complement to, not a substitute for, government regulation or social policy.

551. An increasing number of global corporations make social responsibility an inherent part of doing business. Initiatives range from the adoption of codes of conduct to partnerships in social initiatives at community level. They are prompted by business's own ethical concerns as well as by pressure from NGOs, trade unions, ethical investors and socially conscious consumers.

552. Many companies develop their own approaches to CSR, which vary with the type of business and the economic and social environment. Important benchmarks and reference points include the ILO Tripartite Declaration of Principles concerning Multinational Enterprises and Social Policy (1977, revised 2000), the ILO Declaration on Fundamental Principles and Rights at Work (1998) and the OECD Guidelines for Multinational Enterprises (1976, revised 2000). The issue is under intensive debate in many fora. A recent contribution includes a Green Paper and a Communication on corporate social responsibility from the European Commission. [106]

UN Global Compact

553. A particularly influential initiative is the UN Global Compact initiated by the UN Secretary-General. The Compact calls on companies to embrace and promote nine core principles derived from universally accepted agreements on human rights, labour and the environment, in collaboration with the UN, ILO, Office of the High Commissioner for Human Rights (OHCHR), UNEP, the United Nations Industrial Development Organization (UNIDO) and other actors. The Compact has already made progress, for example in facilitating compliance with relevant national legislation, promoting dialogue and addressing the obstacles to realizing universal principles in global supply chains. It is important for the ILO to monitor its involvement with the Compact and to assess its future potential and further increase its effectiveness.

Strengthening voluntary initiatives

554. Voluntary initiatives such as the Global Compact can help to build public trust and confidence in enterprises and contribute to the sustainability of their business. But there remains scepticism among some actors about their real impact. The view was expressed, in Commission dialogues and elsewhere, that for voluntary initiatives to be credible, there is a need for transparency and accountability, requiring good systems of measurement, reporting and monitoring.

555. The contribution of voluntary initiatives can be strengthened in a number of ways:

- Supporting companies in their efforts to develop credible reporting mechanisms and performance measures both for global business and domestic suppliers, in line with internationally accepted principles and standards.
- Improving methods of monitoring and verification, taking into account diverse situations and needs. Independent accreditation and certification is growing, because some firms find this is a source of credibility.
- Developing more broad-based industry level partnerships, such as the recent agreement in the cocoa sector aimed at eliminating abusive labour practices,

---

[106] For a review of recent initiatives, see "Information note on corporate social responsibility and international labour standards", GB.288/WP/SDG/3, ILO, Geneva, November 2003.

notably child labour.[107] These can engage enterprises, employers' organizations, unions, cooperatives, governments, and CSOs, in programmes which combine promotional policies with monitoring and certification.

- Undertaking more research into the application and impact of codes of conduct, and developing guides to good practice.

556. The international representatives of business have an important role to play. The International Organisation of Employers (IOE) could expand its current efforts in this field as a privileged actor engaged in promoting both corporate governance and corporate social responsibility, and it could help improve business participation in managing globalization through dissemination, training and discussion on these important issues. The IOE could reinforce its leading role in initiatives like the Global Compact, to act as a worldwide centre for initiatives that help sponsor and harmonize economic growth and social development and promote social dialogue.

557. With its tripartite composition, the ILO offers a unique place for research, dialogue and policy development on these issues. It should convene a Forum to develop a practical agenda around the contribution of business to the social dimension of globalization.

558. Beyond the issues of corporate governance and social responsibility, the relationship between the private sector and international organizations has strengthened in recent years. In some important new instances of multisectoral collaboration, the private sector is now playing a pivotal role. For example, the Global Alliance for Vaccines and Immunization (GAVI) is now the key player in efforts to immunize children in low-income countries. Representatives of the Gates Foundation – the primary funder – and industry sit on its board alongside international organizations, governments and civil society.

Expanding partnerships between private sector and international organizations

559. The private sector's deeper involvement in international public policy has great potential as a source of additional finance for global programmes and as a provider of expertise and access to business networks. We believe that such involvement should be encouraged and promoted. There is a need to address concerns for the protection of the public interest, through arrangements which ensure that policy choices are not distorted by conflicts of interest. We look to the Secretary-General's Commission on the Private Sector and Development to propose ways of strengthening such partnerships and possibilities.

Organized labour

560. In 2000, the international trade union movement made "globalizing social justice" its prime objective for the new millennium.[108] In reality this objective is not new but one that trade unions have been pursuing for more than a decade. Over this period the trade union movement has adopted several different strategies to influence the process of globalization. These have included: pressuring key governments at regular meetings of the G8 and similar economic summits; an intensive effort to introduce labour and social issues onto the agenda of regional economic

Trade union strategies to influence globalization

---

[107] The "International Cocoa Initiative – Working towards Responsible Labour Standards for Cocoa Growing" Foundation was established in 2002. It involves the global chocolate and cocoa industry, trade unions and NGOs, with the ILO providing advisory services. See www.bccca.org.uk

[108] International Confederation of Free Trade Unions: *Globalizing Social Justice: Trade Unionism in the 21st Century*, World Congress Report (Durban, April 2000).

and trade meetings; and an effort to engage directly with multinational companies through the negotiation of framework agreements covering fundamental issues like child labour, bonded labour, discrimination and freedom of association.

561. In addition, for the last decade or so the international trade union movement has sought to influence globalization through attempts to reorient some of the activities and policies of international agencies such as the World Bank, IMF, WTO, the UN Conference on Trade and Development (UNCTAD) and the OECD. At the same time, trade unions have devoted considerable resources to promoting greater consistency and cooperation between the multilateral organizations responsible for economic development, trade and social policy. In particular, they have encouraged the international institutions with an economic mandate to broaden their perspective and put more emphasis on equity, human rights and social considerations.

Need for formal consultation structures in the World Bank, IMF and WTO

562. The impact of the trade union movement on globalization and the policies of the key international institutions depend partly on their influence on the decision-making process. For instance, within the ILO trade unions are a key part of the governance structure and exercise considerable influence over the policies of the organization. In other international organizations, such as the OECD, there exists a formal structure for consultations with both the labour movement and the business community that enables the social partners to engage in regular policy discussions with OECD staff and government representatives. We recommend that formal consultation structures similar to the OECD type should be established at the World Bank, the IMF and the WTO, while fully respecting the constitutional provisions and governance structures of these organizations. This would provide the social partners with structural entry points into the workings of the international organizations exercising a profound influence over globalization. This would enhance the external transparency, accountability and credibility of the international organizations with an economic mandate. Similar arrangements should be made in the burgeoning number of inter-regional and bilateral trade, investment and economic cooperation arrangements.

Social dialogue in global production systems

New forms of global social dialogue are developing

563. The development of industrial democracy and collective bargaining at national level has historically provided an important mechanism to promote productivity and equitable outcomes at work, and to give workers and trade unions an important voice in the production process. Given the growth of global production systems, new institutions of social dialogue between workers and employers seem likely to develop around them and may well play an increasingly important role in the global economy.

564. At present there is a great deal of experimentation taking place and some interesting voluntary approaches are emerging. For example, there are now more than 25 Framework Agreements between Global Union Federations and multinational companies. While the content of these agreements differs, most cover the core international labour standards and some also cover issues such as a "living wage" and health and safety matters. Regional and global works councils are also being increasingly used to foster social dialogue.

565. A comprehensive form of global social dialogue has emerged in the shipping industry, which is by its nature a highly global business. A pioneering international collective agreement between the International Transport Workers Federation and

the International Maritime Employers' Committee covers wages, minimum standards and other terms and conditions of work, including maternity protection.

566. Such forms of global social dialogue are developing on a voluntary basis among the global players concerned. They warrant further research by ILO and other bodies to determine their potential to promote productive relations between workers and managers, and facilitate the resolution of disputes between them. The ILO should closely monitor all such developments and provide the parties concerned with advice and assistance when required.

Civil society

567. A striking feature of globalization has been the rapid emergence of a community of civil society actors, who network globally to tackle issues of concern to citizens throughout the world. They have grown from some 1,500 in the mid-1950s to about 25,000 in 2001. While the nature and frequency of contact and mode of interaction between international agencies and CSOs vary, the trend towards increased collaboration has been across the board.

568. CSOs make a major contribution to raising and debating the issue of a fairer globalization. They raise public awareness, undertake research, document the impact of globalization on people, communities and the environment, mobilize public opinion and ensure democratic accountability. They also provide development assistance and humanitarian services, promote human rights, supply expertise and spearhead new initiatives, such as the treaty banning the use of landmines and the establishment of the International Criminal Court. Prominent examples – among many others – include Oxfam's work to promote fair trade, the Jubilee 2000 debt cancellation campaign, the World and regional Social Forums, and many others. Their contribution to inclusive globalization can be further enhanced by a more active engagement in mobilizing national support for global reform measures. In recent years there has been a notable increase in CSO interactions with other groups such as the trade unions and parliaments and with governments, especially over WTO negotiations.

Contribution of civil society

569. CSOs, like all other actors in globalization, should be transparent and accountable to stakeholders. We recognize that there is a wide diversity of organizations in civil society, including NGOs organized by governments or supported by corporations, people's movements, non-profit organizations providing services and those representing civic groups. It is important to recognize these differences when addressing issues of representativeness and accountability. Steps to address the accountability of CSOs should not impede the legitimate rights of citizens to organize and voice opinions and concerns in the public interest. The starting point might be to encourage voluntary initiatives of self-regulation within the CSO sector, in accordance with the values that they espouse and pursue. The civil society community could lead the way in promoting peer review.

570. There is currently a lack of balanced representation within the global civil society community. CSOs from developing countries and organizations of the underprivileged and marginalized communities are inadequately represented. It is important to address this problem so that their concerns and interests can be adequately articulated in national and global discussions and negotiations. The global civil society community as well as governments and the international community should make special efforts to promote and strengthen CSOs in the poorest countries, and especially associations of marginal or deprived groups such as poor

Ensuring balanced representation

women, slum dwellers, indigenous peoples, rural workers and small traders and artisans.

Interactions
between civil
society,
governments and
international
agencies

571. Inevitably tensions exist in the relationship between civil society, governments and multilateral agencies. Some multilateral agencies feel their capacity to deal with the rapid expansion of NGOs is severely limited. Some States feel that NGOs are encroaching on their territory and thus complicating the task of negotiating agreements. NGOs themselves often become impatient at the bureaucratic and political constraints of working with governments and UN agencies. Many feel their independence and integrity are impaired by the inevitable compromises necessary to achieve consensus.

572. The involvement of CSOs in international organizations also raises the complex issue of reconciling participatory democracy with representative democracy. Various mechanisms have evolved in different multilateral processes and in different intergovernmental organizations.[109] Lessons should be learned from the strengths and weaknesses of these, especially in terms of ensuring the representation of marginalized sectors from developing countries. System-wide and structured dialogues between the CSOs and intergovernmental organizations, which fully respect each others' constitutional provisions and governance structures, should be sustained. These could tap the strengths of CSO self-organization processes and use these to inform the further development of effective mechanisms for enhanced interaction between the United Nations system and CSOs. The Secretary-General of the United Nations has established a high-level panel of experts, under the leadership of Fernando Henrique Cardoso, former President of Brazil, to formulate recommendations for enhancing the interaction between the United Nations and civil society, including parliamentarians and the private sector. We encourage the panel to explore innovative methods of civil society participation in and interaction with the multilateral system, building on good experience and best practices, and to examine how to better address the representativeness and accountability of CSOs seeking greater interaction with the UN.

Communications and media

Access to
information
through global
media essential
for democratic
decision-making

573. Access to information is essential to democratic decision-making. The media are the main means of disseminating information and providing a forum for public debate.

574. Technological developments such as the Internet and low-cost delivery systems for TV and radio have increased the quantity and range of information available, often even to people in remote areas of developing countries. Governments that wish to interrupt the free flow of information now have a harder task. Diversity of programming has been a spur to cultural development, helping linguistic and other minorities.

575. However, some aspects of communications-driven technology are cause for concern. The dominant role of English as a medium has led to a preponderant role for Anglo-American news sources. This may be changing as other major languages such as French, Spanish and Arabic develop global programming capability, and English speakers from Asia and Africa play a larger part in international English-language media. Buyers of television news feeds, wire services and syndicated print

---

[109] For an overview, see "The UN system and civil society: an inventory and analysis of practices" at http://www.un.org/reform/panel.htm

journalism need to press harder to ensure that vendors provide ever more balanced views of cultures, realities and interests at play.

576. Much of the developing world has been seeing greater diversity as new commercial channels have ended what were once State broadcasting monopolies, and as increased consumer power has supported new newspapers and magazines. But the largest, Western-owned media have seen multiple amalgamations which can reduce the scope of diversity of news and views.

577. Policies everywhere need to emphasize the importance of diversity in information and communication flows. Responsible media can play a central role in facilitating a movement towards a fairer and more inclusive globalization. A well informed public opinion on the issues raised in this Report will be essential to underpin change.

Networked governance

578. In recent years there has been a rapid expansion of global issues networks and other informal arrangements for global social policy development, with the participation of both public and private actors. Such forms of "networked governance" help to address specific inadequacies and gaps in existing institutions and arrangements.[110] They are often multisectoral, in that they involve the participation of some combination of national governments, multilateral agencies, CSOs and the private sector. They also tend to have informal governance arrangements and light organizational structures, often drawing on new technologies.[111]

Global networks on specific issues bring public and private actors together in informal governance

579. Global networks, projects and partnerships take many forms and may carry out a number of functions, such as setting international practice, disseminating information or mobilizing resources. We have referred above to examples of such networks, such as the UN Global Compact and the new Global Fund to Fight AIDS, Tuberculosis and Malaria. Another example is the Medicines for Malaria Venture, a global partnership designed to create incentives for pharmaceutical companies to develop a new antimalarial vaccine. International organizations can play an important role, as in the case of the Global Environment Facility or the Youth Employment Network convened by the UN, the World Bank and the ILO.

580. Numerous other networks have been established for exchange of information and advocacy relating to social, humanitarian, development and gender issues. Many civil society campaigns and movements have used the possibilities of global networks very effectively.[112] The Internet is enabling decentralized networks of responsibility and solidarity to develop around different projects for social change. In order for these networks to operate and exchange information in open and democratic societies, the governance of the Internet itself needs to remain open and democratic.

---

[110] See Ngaire Woods: "Global Governance and the Role of Institutions", in D. Held and A. McGrew (eds.): *Governing Globalization* (Cambridge, UK, Polity Press, 2002); and Bob Deacon, Eeva Ollila, Meri Koivusalo and Paul Stubbs: *Global Social Governance: Themes and Prospects*, Elements for Discussion Series, Ministry for Foreign Affairs of Finland, Department for International Development Co-operation (Helsinki, 2003).

[111] See Jeremy Heimans: *Reforming Global Economic and Social Governance: A Critical Review of Recent Programmatic Thinking*, background paper prepared for the World Commission, Geneva, 2003.

[112] For example, Third World Network, which is an important contributor to debate and information on the reform of the global trading system. See www.twnside.org.sg

581. Several advantages have been claimed for these new mechanisms: the benefits of rapid and non-bureaucratic action; the ability to mobilize diverse actors and skills; and a results-based approach because they focus on specific issues. On the other hand, in many cases this approach restricts participation to a select number of actors, raises questions of accountability and representation of all interested parties, and runs the risk of being technocratic. To help reduce these problems there should be better coordination between these global networks and partnerships and international organizations, while maintaining their spirit of entrepreneurship and experimentation.

* * *

582. Experience suggests that the creation of major new institutions within the UN system, or even the comprehensive reform and upgrading of existing institutions such as ECOSOC and the voting systems of the Bretton Woods institutions, is difficult and may take time. On the other hand, global networks are likely to multiply as a result of globalization itself, and we need to look to these for new and promising forms of governance. It is however, important to continue to pursue politically viable possibilities for institutional reform. Major progress is possible, as the creation of the International Criminal Court has recently demonstrated.

IV. MOBILIZING ACTION FOR CHANGE

Introduction

583. A variety of voices are pressing the case for change in the current process of globalization. The wide-ranging recommendations in previous sections are a response to that demand. But there is no guarantee of consistent action without systematic follow-up to the recommendations we make. We propose action to engage the commitment and sustained involvement of both State and non-State actors. In all cases we envisage a central role for the multilateral system of the United Nations in animating and supporting the follow-up process as a whole.

584. Follow-up has to be national as well as international. Much can be done by national governments and national non-State actors. Based on our experience of national dialogues, we make a specific proposal below to expand exchange and interaction between the many groups within countries which are concerned with globalization issues.

New actors and forces needed to help find solutions

585. The nature of globalization requires us to look beyond inter-governmental processes and nation States, to involve new actors and forces that can help find solutions. We need the energy, creativity and reach of the many networks of non-State actors which are already active, involving both business and civil society. [113] We need to adapt international institutions to the realities of the new era. This means forming coalitions for change, often with partners well beyond the precincts of officialdom.

586. We invite governments, parliaments, international organizations and other relevant actors, such as the International Confederation of Free Trade Unions (ICFTU),

---

[113] Many aspects of globalization are already being examined in different fora such as the World Economic Forum and the World Social Forum. In addition, many innovative projects are under way, such as the International Forum on Globalization, the Ethical Globalization Initiative, the Global Stakeholder Panel Initiative on Globalization and Global Governance and the State of the World Forum's Commission on Globalization.

the World Confederation of Labour (WCL), the International Organisation of Employers (IOE), the International Chamber of Commerce (ICC) and relevant NGOs, to examine and, where appropriate, to act upon our recommendations for improving national and global governance and ensuring greater coherence in policies relating to globalization. We welcome the Helsinki Process on Globalization and Democracy, and look to it to deepen dialogue on some of our key recommendations.

587. We have made many recommendations, but commitment is central. The guiding values and principles for globalization, which we have highlighted in our vision, provide the basis for a widespread commitment to a fair and inclusive process of globalization. We invite all stakeholders mentioned in this Report to be guided by those values and principles in their own conduct and activities, and in the relationships and rules that govern the process of globalization.

588. At the international level, we envisage follow-up action to be undertaken in two phases. The first phase would aim to publicize and build widespread awareness of and support for the proposals and objectives. The second phase would initiate action to change the current process of globalization in line with the policy recommendations in this Report.

Phase one: building awareness and support

589. As part of the first phase of action we encourage all actors within the global community to use this Report as a basis for discussion and analysis; to consider its policy proposals; to take up recommendations; and to develop plans for advocacy and action. In our work we have attempted to move from confrontation to dialogue. We hope that this Report will provide a platform where consensus can be built to take the necessary corrective action.

590. In the first instance, our Report will be submitted to the Governing Body of the ILO which established the Commission. At the same time, in view of the wide-ranging scope of the Report, it will be submitted to the Secretary-General of the United Nations, and presented to all Heads of State and Government on the occasion of the 59th session of the United Nations General Assembly. The Report will also be presented to other intergovernmental bodies and groupings, including ECOSOC, the Executive Boards of the IFIs, the WTO, the Regional Economic Commissions of the UN, the EU, the AU, the Arab League, the Organization of American States, the Association of South-East Asian Nations, the South Asian Association for Regional Cooperation, the Group of 77 (G77) and G8. We also intend to present the Report to major actors of the global community, such as workers' and employers' organizations, business associations, parliamentarians and local authorities, relevant NGOs, academic institutions and foundations, professional and consumers' associations, religious groups, economic and social councils, political parties and social movements. We urge all these fora to debate our recommendations and consider appropriate follow-up action in their own spheres of responsibility.

591. Clearly, the implementation of the commitments taken in the United Nations Conferences of the 1990s, and in the Millennium Summit Declaration, would go a long way towards meeting the goals laid out in this Report. But it is important to reiterate that achieving a fair globalization depends on the political decisions of the most powerful actors to move forward. Those with the authority to decide in government, parliaments, business, society and international organizations will have to assume their responsibilities.

592. A significant number of our recommendations can be implemented through reaching fair and balanced outcomes in ongoing negotiations within existing multilateral frameworks. Others, however, will involve the more complicated task of developing new frameworks and policy initiatives. We concentrate on this latter group of recommendations in what follows.

593. The second phase of the follow-up action will be based on a strategy for greater policy coherence and for better policy development. This will consist of several elements. First, we urge that action be initiated at the national level to review and follow up our recommendations on local, national, and regional policies. Second, we also urge that immediate steps be taken to launch initiatives for achieving greater policy coherence within the multilateral system, and we make a specific proposal on this. Third, we propose a process to develop specific policies to implement the key recommendations, with the involvement of all concerned stakeholders. Fourth, we recommend that a Globalization Policy Forum be established among interested international organizations. Fifth, we propose more systematic research to provide essential technical inputs to support this process and, more generally, to strengthen the knowledge base on the social dimension of globalization.

Follow-up at the national level

594. A key part of the follow-up to our recommendations should take place at the national level. We invite all governments and non-State actors to review the broad set of recommendations we made in section III.1 of the Report on national, local and regional policies to enable countries to benefit more from globalization, and to ensure that these benefits extend to all people. We draw special attention to the importance of strengthening national governance, of achieving greater coherence in national policies on issues of global governance, of adopting the goal of decent work for all as a central policy objective, and of social dialogue in the policy formulation process.

595. The national dialogues organized by the Commission created new opportunities for exchange and interaction between many different groups concerned with globalization. They showed the value of analysing and deepening exchanges between different actors at the national level. Broad-based dialogue aimed at reconciling differences in perspectives and interests is a fundamental step towards achieving the social cohesion that is essential for upgrading the capacity of countries to defend their legitimate national interests.

596. We therefore invite governments and other actors to take forward this dialogue, in the light of the recommendations of our Report. We call on governments to consider appropriate mechanisms for this purpose, by utilizing existing facilities or by creating new public platforms, such as national commissions on the social dimension of globalization. This would bring together diverse stakeholders to raise issues of concern, and help broaden understanding of the impact of globalization on people and communities. They would aim to identify problems, disseminate information, share good practices and consider alternative policy responses. The outcomes of these exchanges should feed into the work of the multilateral agencies at the country level that is proposed below. It will be essential to support these national dialogues through strengthening national research programmes and networks on the social dimension of globalization. It will also be useful to support networking among these national commissions as a means of learning from different experiences with policy responses to globalization.

The multilateral system

597. The multilateral system of the United Nations system, the World Bank, the IMF and the WTO have a clear responsibility to take forward the call of the Millennium Declaration to "make globalization a positive force for the world's people". That is no less than the abiding challenge of the 21st century. It must be the unifying theme for their activities.

598. The purpose of any reform of the multilateral system should be to make it more democratic, participatory, transparent and accountable. Such reform is essential for realizing our vision of a fairer and more inclusive process of globalization.

Reform of the multilateral system to make it more democratic, participatory, transparent and accountable

599. While we do not envisage that action on all recommendations in this Report should be confined to the organizations of the multilateral system, we do believe that many should be centred there. Major projects on globalization already exist in the United Nations, its Funds, Programmes and Specialized Agencies. [114]

600. Beyond their direct support to the follow-up of this Report, we invite the governing bodies of the relevant international organizations concerned, to consider how to take account of our recommendations in the development of their own programmes. This would help to provide the underpinning necessary to change the rules and shift policies towards a fairer and more democratically governed globalization.

601. However, in order to discharge this pivotal role effectively the multilateral system needs to be strengthened. A key requirement is a renewed political commitment to multilateralism. All countries must acknowledge their common interest in, and obligation to, a strong, effective multilateral system that can support a fair, productive and sustainable global economy.

602. Moving towards a values-based globalization requires coherence of action on values between different international organizations within the multilateral system. It also requires more effective international promotion and realization of universal values. As a first step, all international organizations should apply their mandates in ways that respect human rights consistent with their obligations under international law. Second, we invite each organization of the multilateral system, particularly the UN Commission on Human Rights and the ILO, to examine their existing procedures and current systems for the promotion and protection of universally accepted principles and human rights, in order to better implement them in practice, and to improve the international dialogue on shared values.

Achieving policy coherence

603. In principle, there is congruence between the founding principles and aims of the main international organizations, and they therefore share many objectives. International law requires them also to interpret their mandates, as far as possible, in harmony with the mandates of other international organizations, and in line with the ultimate goals they have in common. They should all, irrespective of differences in economic power and influence, apply their mandates in practice in ways that do not place their members in contradiction with obligations which they have also undertaken in other international instruments and treaties.

---

[114] Such as those of FAO, ILO, IFAD, UNCTAD, UNDP, UNEP, UNESCO, UNIDO and WHO.

604. In practice, the multilateral system is under-performing in terms of ensuring coherence among economic, financial, trade, environmental and social policies to promote human development and social progress. As argued earlier, international rules and policies have favoured measures for market expansion over economic and social policies to achieve a pattern of globalization that benefits all countries and all people. This has been a reflection of the greater economic power and influence of organizations dealing with trade and finance compared to those dealing with development and social policy. A key aspect of ensuring greater coherence for a fair and inclusive globalization is thus the redressing of these unbalanced outcomes.

605. Ensuring greater coherence among policies is the responsibility not only of the organizations of the multilateral system but also of the governments and parliaments which oversee their work. In particular, the international organizations need to be given a clear political mandate to achieve greater policy coherence.

Regular national reviews of the social implications of economic policies

606. An important means of achieving greater policy coherence so as to redress the imbalance between social goals and economic policies, and hence to shift the focus from markets to people, lies at the national level. We recommend that there should be regular national reviews of the social implications of economic, financial and trade policies. The IMF and the WTO conduct regular reviews of these latter policies but they focus on issues within their respective mandates. There is a clear need for reviews that examine the implications of these policies for decent work, gender inequality, education, health and social development. They should aim to expand the space for national policies to promote social development. These reviews should be undertaken by the ILO[115] and other relevant organizations of the international system with a mandate on social issues such as the UNDP and the Specialized Agencies of the UN. National ownership of the entire process is indispensable. As far as employment is concerned, the ILO's Employment Policy Convention provides a framework which could be used as the basis for a global approach.

607. At the international level we propose that a new operational tool be systematically developed to upgrade the quality of policy coordination between international organizations on issues in which the implementation of their mandates intersects and their policies interact. This would correct the imbalance between economic and social policies, eliminate the harm inflicted by policies working at cross-purposes, and harness the synergy from complementary policies.

Policy Coherence Initiatives needed to address key issues

608. We recommend that Policy Coherence Initiatives (PCI) be undertaken by the relevant organizations on key issues addressing the social dimension of globalization. The objective would be to progressively develop integrated policy proposals that appropriately balance economic, social and developmental concerns on specific issues.[116]

609. We invite all Executive Heads of the multilateral system to consider issues for Policy Coherence Initiatives with other agencies in which they consider that, by working together, they can make a contribution to a more fair and inclusive globalization. A number of priority issues that are cross-cutting in nature could be

---

[115] As pointed out in paragraph 508 above, the ILO already has an explicit constitutional mandate to oversee the social implications of international economic policy.

[116] Some efforts to develop integrated policy approaches are already under way, involving UNAIDS, system-wide follow-up of the MDGs and the recently created Geneva Migration Group.

immediately considered. These include employment creation and the reduction of poverty, gender inequality and the empowerment of women, the integration of the informal economy into the economic mainstream, the protection of core labour rights, education, health, food security and human settlements.

610. Executive Heads of the Agencies could decide to move forward with other organizations on issues they consider appropriate for Policy Coherence Initiatives and define in each case the best method of joint work. The understandings reached on balanced policies for achieving more equitable outcomes would be brought to the attention of their respective boards or governing bodies for consideration and action. The Chief Executives Board of the United Nations, headed by the Secretary-General, and the Economic and Social Council would be kept informed of the evolution of these initiatives. This approach would significantly enhance the quality of policy-making while using a methodology which is flexible and can be applied in a pragmatic manner.

611. In the first instance, we invite the Executive Heads of the relevant UN bodies, the World Bank, the IMF, the WTO and the ILO to address the question of global growth, investment and employment creation, through a Policy Coherence Initiative. Given the questions dealt with in the Report, we consider this subject to be of the highest priority. The institutions involved could make a significant contribution by addressing this major concern of government, business, workers, civil society and people everywhere. Such an initiative would respond to a major political demand in all countries, and would demonstrate the capacity of the institutions concerned to pioneer new cooperative ways to find solutions in this critical field.

Global growth, investment and employment creation

Better policy development

612. Follow-up also requires a process to further develop specific recommendations into operational policies, in the light of the views and interests of those most directly affected by them.

613. We suggest that our proposals be further considered and developed through a series of Policy Development Dialogues. The dialogues would create space for communication and exchange between all actors concerned. They should be designed to bring about agreement on and concrete implementation of specific policy proposals in the medium to long term. They can also serve to initiate or deepen discussions on important policy issues that have received relatively little attention to date.

Policy Development Dialogues

614. Such dialogues would engage administrators, politicians, parliamentarians, business, labour, civil society, and other groups under-represented in formal governance structures. They would thus bring into the process those who have important expertise in relevant fields, those whose interests are at stake, and those with responsibilities in the implementation of change.

615. The nature of each dialogue, its agenda and the participants could vary, depending on the stage of the debate and the subject involved.

616. These policy dialogues could include the following areas:

- Building a multilateral framework for the cross-border movement of people. A process is laid out in paras. 440–44. The United Nations Secretariat, ILO, IOM, OHCHR, UNHCR, UNCTAD, and the United Nations Office on Drugs and Crime (UNODC) should all be engaged.

- Corporate social responsibility for a fairer globalization. It is proposed in para. 557 that the ILO convene a forum on this issue. The IOE and the ICFTU should play a major role.

- A development framework for FDI, which balances the rights and responsibilities of investors (domestic and international), host and home countries, taking into account the social impact (para. 399). This would involve all relevant international organizations and ensure that all interests are represented.

- Globalization, adjustment and social protection (paras. 490-91). This dialogue would build a policy agenda aimed at strengthening social protection in the global economy. It would engage UNDP, the World Bank, WTO, IMF and ILO among others.

- Global capacity building on education and skills for information technology to widen the benefits from globalization (para. 487). Building on the existing Education for All initiative and the outcome of the World Summit on the Information Society, this should be led by UNESCO and the World Bank, and engage the International Telecommunications Union (ITU), UNDP and others.

- The contribution of regional and sub-regional integration to a fairer globalization (paras. 333-34). This would engage the secretariats of the regional organizations concerned, along with the UN Regional Economic Commissions, regional parliamentary assemblies, regional development banks and other regional bodies, along with relevant international organizations.

- Gender equality as an instrument for a more inclusive globalization bringing together the United Nations, UNDP, the United Nations Development Fund for Women (UNIFEM) and other relevant actors.

617. We call on international organizations to promote and contribute to these dialogues on subjects that are within their respective mandates.

618. Beyond these focused policy dialogues, we believe that there is a need for a broader platform for exchange of ideas among people with different perspectives on globalization. Our experience as a Commission has convinced us that this exchange is fruitful. As individual members of the Commission we reflect views from different parts of the world, from business and labour, as policy-makers and parliamentarians, from civil society and the academic world. We have found that bringing our views into dialogue enriches our understanding, even when – as is sometimes inevitable – we differ. It is an essential step towards finding common cause and ways forward. Our national and regional consultations have likewise shown the value of dialogue in promoting broader exchange and mutual understanding, and in identifying possible actions by different social actors in the common interest.

Proposal for a Globalization Policy Forum involving interested international organizations

619. For this reason, we recommend that a Globalization Policy Forum be established among interested international organizations, as part of a sustained effort to make dialogue between different points of view the foundation of a fairer globalization. It would examine the key issues relevant to the social dimension of globalization.

620. The role of the Forum will be to mobilize the collective effort of the multilateral system to create a platform for multi-stakeholder dialogues and to build public support for proposals emerging from them. Such a Forum would be a space which could bring together the agencies of the multilateral system, and in particular the UN and its specialized agencies, with other organizations, groups and individuals who are concerned with the social dimension of globalization. It would

assess the social impact of developments and policies in the global economy on a regular basis. It would tap the knowledge, resources and perspectives of all participating organizations in monitoring trends on the social impact of globalization and analysing key policy issues.

621. We believe that, in the light of the experience of the World Commission on the Social Dimension of Globalization, the ILO should take the initiative to follow up this recommendation in cooperation with interested international organizations.

622. Participating institutions could also make an important contribution by preparing a regular "State of Globalization Report" reflecting the experience and perspectives of their wide-ranging constituencies.

Research support

623. The actions proposed above on the social dimension of globalization need to be grounded in better information on trends in globalization and its impact on people and communities, and in-depth analysis of international policies on key issues. We need to draw on multiple sources and expertise from all regions of the world. Knowledge development is essential to make globalization a positive force for people throughout the world, and to support the specific proposals we have made to this end. Better and more gender-sensitive monitoring and measurement, research, policy reviews, and systematic reporting are all necessary to mobilize public opinion and guide action.

Better monitoring and measurement

624. What is measured is acted upon. We badly need a stronger, up-to-date knowledge base on globalization. While aggregate information already exists on many economic dimensions of globalization such as trade, movement of people and capital flows, these data are incomplete. They need to be extended and reinforced with better information on subjects which are poorly covered at present, such as global production systems and their networks of suppliers, the spread of and access to technology, and the growing international networks of people and organizations. Reliable and regular information, disaggregated by gender, is also required on the social impact of globalization and the distribution of its benefits. This work should build on and connect with a wide variety of existing attempts to improve measurement of progress. We also need better, more reliable and more systematic information on the attitudes and reactions of people to key globalization-related issues. The aim would be to provide new survey instruments which could help answer the question: how can globalization respond to people's needs and aspirations?

Need for a stronger, up-to-date knowledge base on globalization

625. On all of these areas there is a need to bring together the work of statistical offices and observatories around the world which are collecting and collating information on these topics, and promoting networking and exchange.

More systematic research programmes

626. The work of the World Commission has revealed the need for more information and better analysis of the social dimension of globalization. In-depth reviews of key policy issues are also badly needed.

... and for in-depth reviews of key policy issues

627. In almost all countries, one or more research institutions are engaged in research into various aspects of globalization. [117] Instead of replicating existing efforts, we encourage all such institutions and networks to collaborate and invest in a broad-based common research effort on the social dimension of globalization, engaging the multilateral system as well as NGOs. We believe that networks of national, regional and global institutions could build the capacity needed to address different aspects of the social dimension of globalization in a coherent and multidisciplinary way. For example, a key aspect is the development of a basic socio-economic floor at the national level in the context of the global economy.

Multilateral organizations should develop joint research programmes

628. The main multilateral organizations should also develop joint research programmes on the key issues. UNCTAD, WTO and ILO should establish a joint research programme to objectively examine the impact of trade developments on the quantity and quality of employment, and the gender implications of this impact. Similar inter-organizational programmes should be developed to examine significant changes in finance and development policy, and to find ways to reinforce positive linkages between rights, employment and development.

629. Apart from the Policy Development Dialogues, we also call for general support to existing multidisciplinary task forces and policy forums which bring together researchers, policy-makers and civil society networks to identify viable options in these and other domains. This can contribute to the goal of policy coherence. A number of existing initiatives can provide the foundation for such an effort. In addition, a regular academic conference and journal on the social dimension of globalization would also help to maintain open intellectual debate and provide a route for the regular publication of empirical research. There is a strong case for developing this on a regional basis, so as to ensure that all regions of the world can engage with such initiatives.

Institutional support

630. We invite the ILO and other interested organizations to give operational assistance to the overall follow-up of this Report. There will clearly be a need for the institutions involved to mobilize extra-budgetary resources to implement many of these initiatives. In view of the substantial stake the international community has in realizing a fairer globalization, we look to donor countries and other funding institutions to support this endeavour.

631. We recognize that an active follow-up by members of the Commission is necessary to help achieve tangible results. We will monitor reactions to the Report, support campaigns and debates, and promote policy action in different fora. We shall remain engaged to carry forward our recommendations.

* * *

---

[117] Many are specialized in the subject, such as the Yale Center for the Study of Globalization and the London School of Economics Centre for the Study of Global Governance. Many institutions are members of regional networks such as the Council for the Development of Social Science Research in Africa (CODESRIA) in Dakar, the Economic Research Forum for the Arab Countries in Cairo, CLACSO in Buenos Aires and similar networks in other regions. Others form part of global networks such as the Global Development Network or participate in global projects such as those of the United Nations University World Institute for Development Economics and Research (UNU-WIDER) in Helsinki, the International Institute for Labour Studies, UNRISD, and the South Centre in Geneva.

632. As we stated at the beginning, ours is a critical but positive message. We have sought to reflect the values and aspirations of people everywhere for a fair globalization: one which respects the diversity of needs and perspectives, and where there is greater opportunity for all.

633. The task ahead is to generate the political will which can turn commitment into action. Progress demands a more open exchange and an improved quality of dialogue between all concerned. We suggest new initiatives which respond to current needs for the better governance of globalization, both between countries and within them. They are based on the awareness of growing interaction and interdependence and guided by a sense of solidarity.

Turning commitment into action

634. Our proposals call for a wider participation of people and countries in the making of policies which affect them. They require those with the capacity and power to decide – in governments, parliaments, business, labour, civil society and international organizations – to assume their common responsibility to promote a free, equitable and productive global community.

ANNEXES

Annex 1: Guide to proposals and recommendations

This annex summarizes the main policy proposals and recommendations of the report, indicating the relevant paragraph numbers.

To achieve a fair globalization improved governance is needed at all levels: local, national, regional and global.

National governance

Policies, institutions and actions within nations are fundamental determinants of whether countries, and all people within them, benefit from globalization. Our proposals are therefore anchored at national and local levels. Recognizing that policies must respond to the needs and specific conditions in each country, the key priorities include:

1. Good national governance, built on a democratic political system, respect for human rights and gender equality, social equity and the rule of law. There should be institutions for the representation of all interests and for social dialogue. (238-245)

2. An effective role of the State in providing essential public goods and adequate social protection, in raising the capabilities and opportunities of all people and in enhancing economic competitiveness. (249-251, 255-259, 269-277)

3. Sound institutions to support and supervise markets; prudent management of the process of integration into the global economy; and macroeconomic policies for achieving high and stable growth. (247-248, 251-254)

4. Policies and institutional reforms to integrate the informal economy into the economic mainstream, through policies to raise productivity, incomes and protection and ensure a legal and institutional framework for property and labour rights and enterprise development. (261-268)

5. Making decent work a key goal of economic policy, by giving priority to employment creation, protecting fundamental rights at work, strengthening social protection, and promoting social dialogue. Policies should be gender-sensitive and based on a new social contract which reflects the interests of both employers and workers. (278-289)

6. Laying the groundwork for sustainable development by encouraging the adoption of the right technologies by enterprises and sustainable natural resource management by local communities. (290-292)

7. Empowering local communities through the devolution of authority and resources in line with the principle of subsidiarity; strengthening local economic capabilities; and recognizing the need to respect culture and identity, as well as the rights of indigenous and tribal peoples. (293-312)

8. Taking advantage of all potential benefits from cooperative action at the regional level, including the contribution of regional institutions to global governance, and ensuring that social goals are adequately reflected in the process of regional economic and political integration. (313-334)

9. Coherence between national policies and global interests. All States have to be responsible actors within global governance, taking into account the cross-border impact of national policies. (243, 260, 541)

Global governance

At the global level, the present system of governance is based on rules and policies that generate unbalanced and often unfair outcomes. Global governance needs to be reformed in the following key areas:

Fair rules

The rules of the global economy should be aimed at improving the rights, livelihoods, security and opportunities of people, families and communities around the world. That includes fair rules for trade, finance and investment, measures to strengthen respect for core labour standards, and a coherent framework for the cross-border movement of people.

The multilateral trading system and the international financial system should allow more space for policy autonomy in developing countries to enable them to accelerate their development in an open economic environment. (361-367)

(i) Trade

1. Unfair barriers to market access must be substantially reduced, especially for goods in which developing countries have a strong comparative advantage. In agriculture, new export credits and subsidies, and trade-distorting domestic measures should be prohibited and existing measures rapidly phased out. Trade barriers in textiles and garments also need to be addressed. At the same time, governments have the responsibility to put in place policies for the security of workers and industrial restructuring in both developed and developing countries. (369-379)

2. Technical standards for traded goods should be set in an objective and participatory way and developing countries should be provided with increased assistance to upgrade product standards. It is also important to prevent abuse of anti-dumping measures and to ensure that developing countries have technical support to assist them in procedural matters. (380-382)

3. Greater market access is not a panacea. A more balanced strategy for sustainable global growth and full employment is essential, based on an equitable sharing among countries of the responsibility for maintaining high levels of effective demand in the global economy. (372)

4. Fair rules for intellectual property must balance the interests of technology producers and technology users, particularly those in low-income countries for whom access to knowledge and technology is limited. (383)

5. Global rules also need to better recognize the need for affirmative action in favour of countries which do not have the same capabilities as those who developed earlier, and to this end the WTO provisions on Special and Differential Treatment need to be significantly strengthened. (369, 385-386)

(ii) Global production systems

There is a need for a more consistent and coherent framework for FDI and competition policy, which balances all interests, rights and responsibilities.

1. Dialogue and cooperation on cross-border competition policy needs to be enhanced to make global markets more transparent and competitive. Among other benefits, this will make it easier for firms from developing countries to enter global production systems. (390-393)

2. A more transparent, coherent, and balanced framework for FDI is required, which reflects all interests, reduces problems of incentive competition and strengthens the contribution of FDI to equitable development. Efforts should be stepped up to find a generally agreed multilateral forum to work out such a framework. (394-399)

(iii) International financial system

Gains in the spheres of trade and FDI cannot be fully reaped unless the functioning of the international financial system is significantly improved. It should support sustainable global growth and improve the terms of integration of poor countries into the global economy.

1. A determined effort is required to ensure that there is greater participation of developing countries in the process of reforming the international financial system. (405-407)

2. It is imperative to accelerate progress towards reducing the problem of financial volatility and contagion in emerging markets. Rapid steps should be taken to ensure that the supply of emergency financing is increased in times of crisis and that this is available to countries facing financial contagion. (411)

3. Global financial rules and policies should permit developing countries with underdeveloped and poorly regulated financial systems to adopt a cautious and gradual approach to capital account liberalization and to have greater scope for adjustment policies which minimize social costs. (408-409, 413)

4. Efforts to devise more effective mechanisms that provide for a fair allocation of responsibilities and burdens between debtors and lenders should be intensified. (412)

(iv) Labour in the global economy

Fairer economic rules of the game need to be complemented by stronger respect for core labour standards and fair rules for the cross-border movement of people.

1. The capacity of the ILO to promote respect for core labour standards should be reinforced. All relevant international organizations should assume their responsibility to promote these standards and ensure that their policies and programmes do not impede their realization. (426)

2. Steps should be taken to build a multilateral framework that provides fair and transparent rules for the cross-border movement of people. We recommend a systematic approach which (a) extends and revitalizes existing multilateral commitments on issues such as the rights and protection of migrant workers and trafficking, especially of women; (b) develops common approaches to major policy issues through dialogue between countries of origin and destination (c) and seeks to build a global framework for an orderly and managed process in the common interest. (433-444)

3. A global forum for exchange of views and information on the cross-border movement of people is needed, and multilateral organizations dealing with this issue should be strengthened. (445-446)

Better international policies

Action to achieve fairer rules must be supplemented by more coherent and equitable international policies.

1. A greater effort of resource mobilization at the international level is a basic requirement. The commitment to the target of 0.7 per cent of GDP for ODA must at long last be respected. The effectiveness of aid delivery must be improved. (453-458)

2. Debt relief should be accelerated and deepened. (459-462)

3. A wide range of options for additional sources of funding should also be actively considered. These must be additional, and not seen as a substitute for commitments to achieve the 0.7 per cent ODA target. (463-470)

4. The potential of voluntary private contributions and philanthropic endeavours for global solidarity should be more fully tapped. (471-472)

5. There should be more support for socially responsible investment initiatives to channel resources to low-income countries. (474-475)

6. International action is essential to raise educational investment and technological capability in developing countries. (482-487)

7. International action is likewise needed to support national social protection systems, in order to ensure that there is a minimum level of social protection in the global economy. (488-491)

8. There is a need for a more effective mechanism for global macroeconomic management. Beyond the need to manage financial flows and exchange rates in the short term, macroeconomic policy coordination should also aim to achieve full employment over the longer term. (410, 494-497)

9. There should be stronger action and wider social dialogue to promote decent work in EPZs and more generally in global production systems, and the ILO should provide advice and assistance to those engaged in such dialogue when required. (498-501, 563-566)

10. Decent work for all should be made a global goal and pursued through more coherent policies within the multilateral system. All organizations in the multilateral system should deal with international economic and labour policies in a more integrated and consistent way. (502-510)

11. Education, health, human rights, the environment and gender equality should all be addressed through an integrated approach to economic and social goals. (511-514)

More accountable institutions

(i) The multilateral system and State actors

A critical requirement for better global governance is the reform of the multilateral system to make it more democratic, transparent, accountable and coherent.

1. The Bretton Woods institutions should establish a fairer system of voting rights giving increased representation to developing countries. (521-525)

2. The working methods and negotiation procedures in the WTO need to ensure the full and effective participation of all member States. (527)

3. All UN system bodies should strengthen their evaluation units, adopt clear policies on disclosure and publish results accordingly. External evaluations should be encouraged and there should be regular reporting on follow up. (529)

4. We call on Heads of State and Government to promote coherent policies in international fora which focus on the well-being and quality of life of people. The issue of achieving greater international socio-economic policy coherence should also be placed on the agenda of gatherings of world political leaders. (532)

5. There should be serious consideration of existing proposals to create an economic and social security council, and a global council on global governance. (530-531)

6. ECOSOC's capacity to coordinate global polices in the economic and social fields should be strengthened by upgrading its level of representation, including an executive committee at ministerial level and inter-ministerial interaction on key global policy issues, and the adoption of new forms of functioning. (533-534)

7. Financial contributions to the multilateral institutions must be increased so that they can discharge enhanced responsibilities, and this should be combined with increased efficiency and effectiveness. (536)

8. All organizations, including the UN organizations, need to be more accountable to the public at large for the policies they pursue. National governments and parliaments should contribute to this process by reviewing decisions taken by their representatives to these organizations. (528, 539-540, 543)

9. We also call for the progressive expansion of parliamentary oversight of the multilateral system at the global level and for the creation of a Global Parliamentary Group concerned with coherence and consistency between global economic and social policies. (544-545)

(ii) Non-State actors

Beyond the multilateral system, business, organized labour, CSOs, and global networks all make an important contribution to global governance.

1. The voluntary initiatives of companies, both national and transnational, could be strengthened to enhance their contribution to the social dimension of globalization. The ILO should convene a forum on this issue. (555-557)

2. Formal structures for consultation with the international labour movement and the business community should be established in the Bretton Woods institutions and the WTO. (562)

3. Greater support should be given to strengthening civil society organizations and movements, and respect for the rights and freedom of individuals to form associations should be enhanced. The representation of CSOs from developing countries in global civil society networks should be increased. Greater interaction with the multilateral system should be promoted. (568, 570-572)

4. CSOs should be transparent and accountable, without impeding the rights of citizens to organization and voice. Self-regulation initiatives could be encouraged. (569)

5. Responsible media can play a central role in facilitating a movement towards a fairer and more inclusive globalization. Policies everywhere need to emphasize the importance of diversity in information and communications flows. (577)

6. There should be better coordination between international organizations and global networks and partnerships engaged in exchange of information, advocacy and resource mobilization in the economic and social field. (581)

Mobilizing action for change

Action to achieve these reforms will require the mobilization of many actors. Beyond the current negotiations and debates in existing national and multilateral fora, we propose the following actions and initiatives:

1. At the national level, we invite governments and non-State actors to engage in broad-based dialogues to review and formulate follow-up action at local, national and regional level. (594–596)

2. The organizations of the multilateral system should examine their own procedures to ensure that there is coherence of action with respect to universal values and human rights to better implement them in practice, and to improve international dialogue. (513, 602)

3. International organizations should launch Policy Coherence Initiatives in which they work together on the design of more balanced and complementary policies for achieving a fair and inclusive globalization. The first of these should address the question of growth, investment and employment in the global economy. (608–611)

4. National reviews of the social implications of economic, financial and trade policies should be undertaken by the organizations of the international system with a mandate on social issues. National ownership is indispensable. (606)

5. A series of multi-stakeholder Policy Development Dialogues should be organized by the international organizations most concerned to further consider and develop key policy proposals in this Report. (613–617)

6. A Globalization Policy Forum should be established by interested international organizations. The Forum will be a platform for regular dialogue between different points of view on the social impact of developments and policies in the global economy. Participating institutions could produce a regular "State of Globalization Report". (618–622)

7. Research programmes and data collection on the social dimension of globalization should be strengthened. (623–629)

Annex 2: The World Commission: Background and composition

The World Commission on the Social Dimension of Globalization was created by decision of the ILO Governing Body in November 2001. The Commission was to prepare a major authoritative report on the social dimension of globalization, including the interaction between the global economy and the world of work.*

The ILO's Director-General was invited to consult widely in order to appoint Commissioners with recognized eminence and authority, with due regard to gender, regional balance, tripartite perspectives, and reflecting the principal views and policy concerns in globalization debates.

In February 2002, H.E. Ms. Tarja Halonen, President of the Republic of Finland, and H.E. Mr. Benjamin Mkapa, President of the United Republic of Tanzania, accepted the Director-General's invitation to act as Co-Chairs of the Commission. Nineteen other members were appointed from across the world's regions, with a diversity of backgrounds and expertise. Five ex-officio members, including the Director-General and the Officers of the Governing Body, provided linkage between the Commission and the ILO.

The Commission has functioned as an independent body and takes full and independent responsibility for this Report and its methods of work. All its members served in their individual capacities. The Commission has thus been free to address any issues, solicit any advice, and formulate any proposals and recommendations that it considered pertinent to its task.

Members of the Commission

Co-Chairs

H.E. Ms. Tarja Halonen, President of Finland

Tarja Halonen was elected President of Finland in February 2000 and is Finland's first female Head of State. She graduated from the University of Helsinki with a Master

---

* See ILO Governing Body documents: "Enhancing the action of the Working Party on the Social Dimension of Globalization: Next steps" (GB.282/WP/SDG/1), Geneva, November 2001; and "Report of the Working Party on the Social Dimension of Globalization (GB.282/12), Geneva, November 2001.

of Law degree. President Halonen became a lawyer with the Central Organisation of Finnish Trade Unions in 1970, a position which she held during her political career as MP and Cabinet Minister. She was a Member of Parliament from 1979 until she assumed the office of the President of Finland. Her cabinet appointments have included Minister of Justice (1990-91), Minister for Foreign Affairs (1995-2000) and Minister responsible for Nordic cooperation (1989-91). President Halonen has been active in the Council of Europe, acting as a Member of the Committee of Wise Persons of the Council of Europe (1998-99). She has paid close attention to issues of human rights, democracy, the rule of law and civil society throughout her political career.

H.E. Mr. Benjamin William Mkapa, President of the United Republic of Tanzania

Benjamin William Mkapa was elected President of the United Republic of Tanzania in November 1995. He studied at Makere University College in Uganda, obtaining a Bachelor of Arts in English in 1962. In 1966, he embarked upon a long career in journalism, serving as Managing Editor of two of Tanzania's leading newspapers, *The Nationalist Uhuru* and *The Daily News*. He was appointed, in 1974, as Press Secretary to the President of the United Republic of Tanzania, H.E. Mr. Mwalimu Julius Nyerere. His career in international diplomacy included serving as High Commissioner to Nigeria (1976), Minister for Foreign Affairs (1977-80), High Commissioner to Canada (1982), and Ambassador to the United States (1983). In 1984 he was again appointed Minister for Foreign Affairs. In the early 1990s he became Minister for Information and Broadcasting and, in 1992, he served as Minister for Science, Technology and Higher Education, prior to being elected President in 1995. Throughout his political career, President Mkapa has worked to strengthen Tanzanian democracy, while increasing the country's openness to international trade and investment.

Members

Giuliano Amato – Dr. Amato has served twice as Prime Minister of Italy, 1992-93 and 2000-01. More recently, he was Vice-President of the Constitutional Convention of the European Union. A Member of the Italian Senate, Dr. Amato has held several major Government positions, including those of Deputy Prime Minister, Treasury Minister, Minister of Institutional Reforms and President of the Italian Antitrust Authority. Dr. Amato is a lawyer by training. From 1975 to 1997, he was Professor of Italian and Comparative Constitutional Law at the University of Rome, School of Political Science.

Ruth Cardoso – President of the *Programa Capacitação Solidaria*, an organization that promotes partnerships in the fight against poverty and social exclusion. Dr. Cardoso, who was First Lady of Brazil from 1995 to 2002, was previously Senior Researcher at the Brazilian Centre of Analysis and Planning and Professor of Anthropology at the University of São Paulo. She is a member of the Board of the United Nations Foundation and the High-level Panel on Youth Employment. Dr. Cardoso is the author of several books on youth, social movements, civil society and new social actors.

Heba Handoussa – Professor Handoussa is a member of the Shura Council, Egypt's Upper House of Parliament, and a member of the Board of the Central Bank of Egypt. An economist by training, Professor Handoussa was Managing Director of the Economic Research Forum for the Arab countries, Iran and Turkey until 2003. She taught at the American University in Cairo and was subsequently appointed as Vice Provost. She has served as an adviser to the Egyptian Government and consultant to the World Bank. Her numerous research publications cover the areas of structural adjustment, industrial policy and foreign aid, institutional reform and comparative development models.

Eveline Herfkens – Executive Coordinator for the Millennium Development Goals Campaign and former Minister for Development Co-operation of the Netherlands (1998–2002). From 1996 to 1998, Ms. Herfkens served as Ambassador to the United Nations and the WTO, and was a member of the Board of the UN Research Institute for Social Development (UNRISD) and Chair of the Bureau of the Economic Commission for Europe. From 1990 to 1996, she was Executive Director of the World Bank Group. Before that, she was a Member of Parliament for the Labour Party of the Netherlands for nine years. Trained as a lawyer, Ms. Herfkens has also been active in several non-governmental organizations.

Ann McLaughlin Korologos – Vice Chairman of the Rand Corporation, Senior Advisor to Benedetto, Gartland and Company, an investment banking firm in New York, and a member of the Boards of several corporations including Microsoft Corporation, AMR Corporation and its subsidiary American Airlines, Fannie Mae, Harman International Industries, Kellogg Company, Vulcan Materials and Host Marriott Corporation. Ms. Korologos, who served as US Secretary of Labor from 1987 to 1989, also served as Under-Secretary of the Department of the Interior and as an Assistant Secretary of the Department of the Treasury. From 1996 to 2000, she was the Chairman of the Aspen Institute.

Lu Mai – Secretary-General of the China Development Research Foundation since 1998. Mr. Lu has also been Senior Research Fellow of the Development Research Center of the State Council since 1995. Mr. Lu has extensive experience in rural reform in China, and was Director of the Experimental Area office for Rural Reform, Research Centre for Rural Development of the State Council in the late 1980s. He is the author of numerous publications on economic reform, and served as a consultant for the World Bank, the Asian Development Bank and other international organizations.

Valentina Matvienko – Governor of St. Petersburg since 2003. Before that, Ms. Matvienko served as Deputy Prime Minister of the Russian Federation with responsibility for social issues, education and culture. She was also responsible for relations between the Government and trade unions, social movements and associations, religious organizations and the mass media. Ms. Matvienko first served as Deputy Prime Minister in charge of social issues in 1998. Prior to that, she was a diplomat and long-serving Government official. From 1991 to 1995, she served as Russian Ambassador to Malta, and from 1997 to 1998 as Russian Ambassador to Greece.

Deepak Nayyar – Vice Chancellor of the University of Delhi. Professor Nayyar is a distinguished economist. He taught at the University of Oxford, the University of Sussex, the Indian Institute of Management, Calcutta and Jawaharlal Nehru University, New Delhi. He served as Chief Economic Adviser to the Government of India and was Permanent Secretary in the Ministry of Finance. The author of several books and numerous articles, Professor Nayyar is Chairman of the Board of Governors of the World Institute of Development Economics Research, Helsinki, Chairman of the Advisory Council for the International Development Centre at the University of Oxford and Member of the Board of Directors of the Social Science Research Council in the United States.

Taizo Nishimuro – Chairman of the Board of Toshiba Corporation. A career business executive with Toshiba, Mr. Nishimuro has worked in international sales and marketing of electronic components and consumer electronics. He is currently Vice Chairman of the Japan Business Federation which was established in May 2002 through the merging of Japan's two main employers' organizations, Keidanren and Nikkeiren.

François Perigot – President of the International Organisation of Employers since June 2001. Mr. Perigot has had an extensive career in French industry, having served as Chairman and CEO of Thibaud, Gibbs et Cie (1968–1970) and then held the position of Chairman and CEO of Unilever France (1971–1986.) From 1986 to 1994, Mr. Perigot served as President of the National Council of French Employers. Since 1997, he has been President of the Mouvement des Entreprises de France (MEDEF) International, the main employer organization in France.

Surin Pitsuwan – Member of Parliament and former Minister of Foreign Affairs of Thailand. Dr. Surin has had a long career in Government and foreign affairs. He served as Minister of Foreign Affairs from 1997 to 2001, and before that was Deputy Minister of Foreign Affairs from 1992 to 1995. He has served as a Member of Parliament for six consecutive terms since first being elected in 1986. A graduate in political science, Dr. Surin holds a Ph.D. from Harvard University. He was a member of the Commission on Human Security and is a regular columnist for major newspapers in Thailand and the region.

Julio Maria Sanguinetti – President of the *Circulo de Montevideo*, a forum which aims to open up new forms of governance and achieve sustainable development in Latin America. Mr. Sanguinetti was elected as President of the Republic of Uruguay for two terms, from 1985 to 1990, and 1990 to 1995. He has had a long and distinguished career in politics, culture and journalism. His many accomplishments were recognized in the award of the UNESCO Simón Bolívar prize in 2000, and of several honorary degrees from universities around the world.

Hernando de Soto – President of the Institute for Liberty and Democracy in Lima, Peru, according to *The Economist* one of the world's most important think-tanks on development issues. An influential author of best-selling books on economic policy, in 1999 Mr. de Soto was chosen by *Time* magazine as one of the five leading Latin American innovators of the century. Regarded as one of the most influential thinkers on the informal sector, he has worked as an adviser to the Peruvian Government, notably on the development and implementation of strategies for bringing informal enterprises and property ownership into the economic mainstream.

Joseph Stiglitz – Professor of Economics, Business and International Affairs at Columbia University. A renowned scholar and teacher, Professor Stiglitz is one of the founders of modern development economics. He has held professorships at Yale, Princeton, Oxford and Stanford and was Chief Economist of the World Bank. He was Chairman of the U.S. Council of Economic Advisors from 1993 to 1997. Joseph Stiglitz received the Nobel Prize for Economics in 2001.

John J. Sweeney – President of the American Federation of Labor and Congress of Industrial Organizations (AFL-CIO). A native of Bronx, New York, Mr. Sweeney has been President of the AFL-CIO since 1995. His trade union career began as a research assistant with the Ladies' Garment Workers. In 1960, he joined the Service Employees International Union (SEIO) as a contract director for New York City, and went on to become President of the International Union in 1980, an office which he held for four terms before being elected as the President of the AFL-CIO.

Victoria Tauli-Corpuz – Executive Director of Tebtebba Foundation (Indigenous Peoples' International Center for Policy Research and Education). An indigenous activist from the Cordillera region in the Philippines, Ms. Tauli-Corpuz founded and managed various NGOs involved in social awareness-raising, community organizing, research and development work. She is a member and the chairperson-rapporteur of the Board of Trustees of the United Nations Voluntary Fund for Indigenous Populations since l994. She was recently appointed a Commissioner of the National Commission on the Role of Filipino Women, representing indigenous peoples.

Aminata D. Traoré – Author and Director of Centre Amadou Hanyrat Ba (CAHBA), one of the organizations of the African Social Forum. Dr. Traoré previously served as Minister of Culture and Tourism of the Republic of Mali. She has worked and published on development issues, including North-South relations, bilateral and multilateral cooperation, democratic, local and international governance and globalization. She is one of the organizers of the first African Social Forum, held in Bamako in January 2002.

Zwelinzima Vavi – General Secretary of Congress of South African Trade Union (COSATU). Mr. Vavi worked in a gold-mining territory of Klerksdrop and Orkney, and joined the National Union of Mineworkers (NUM) as an organizer in 1987. In 1988, he became COSATU's regional secretary for the Western Transvaal. Four years later, he took up the position of National Organizing Secretary. Before taking his current position as General Secretary, he served as COSATU's Deputy General Secretary from 1993 to 1999.

Ernst Ulrich von Weizsaecker – Scientist and Parliamentarian. A member of the German Bundestag since 1998, Dr von Weizsaecker served as Chairman of the Bundestag commission on "Globalization of the World Economy: Challenges and Answers". A distinguished scientist in the fields of biology and physics, Dr. von Weizsaecker has served as Director of the United Nations Centre on Science and Technology and of the Institute for European Environmental Policy. He has been a member of the Club of Rome since 1991 and has written and published widely on public policy, environmental and energy-related topics.

Ex officio members

Bill Brett – Chairperson of the ILO Governing Body for 2002–2003. Lord Brett served as a member of the Workers' Group of the Governing Body of the ILO for ten years and Worker Vice-Chairperson of the Governing Body for nine years. He has had a long and committed career with trade unions. He was appointed a member of the House of Lords of the United Kingdom in June 1999.

Eui-yong Chung – Chairperson of the ILO Governing Body for 2003-04. Permanent Representative of the Republic of Korea to the United Nations and other international organizations in Geneva, 2001-04. Ambassador Chung was Chairman of the WTO's Special Session of the TRIPs Council for the Doha Development Agenda for 2002-04.

Daniel Funes de Rioja – Vice-Chairperson of the ILO Governing Body and Chairperson of the Employers' group. Mr. Funes is Vice President of the International Organisation of Employers, Chairman of the Business Technical Committee in Labor Affairs of the Organization of American States, and Director of Social Policy in the Union of Industry of Argentina.

Juan Somavia – Director-General of the ILO since 1998 and former Permanent Representative of Chile to the United Nations. Mr. Somavia has had a long and distinguished career in civil and international affairs. He served twice as the President of the United Nations Economic and Social Council (ECOSOC), and was Chairman of the Preparatory Committee of the World Social Summit for Social Development, Copenhagen.

Alain Ludovic Tou – Chairperson of the ILO Governing Body (2001-2002) and Minister of Employment, Labour and Social Security of Burkina Faso since November 2000. Mr. Tou has occupied a number of senior Government positions, including Minister of Housing and Urbanization and Minister of Health.

The Secretariat

A Secretariat was established by the ILO to support the work of the Commission. The World Bank also seconded a senior staff member to the Secretariat. The Secretariat worked in close coordination with the Advisers to the Co-Chairs: Jarmo Viinanen and Heikki Pohja (Advisers to President Halonen), and Fulgence Kazaura, Ombeni Sefue, and Tuvako Manongi (Advisers to President Mkapa).

The members of the core Secretariat were Padmanabha Gopinath (Executive Secretary), Gerry Rodgers (Technical Director), Eddy Lee (Economic Adviser), Dharam Ghai, Arna Hartmann (World Bank), Susan Hayter, Michael Henriques (Manager, Operations), Rolph van der Hoeven (Manager, Technical Secretariat), Ruth McCoy and Aurelio Parisotto. Zohreh Tabatabai served as Communications Adviser.

Substantial contributions to the Secretariat's work were also made by Manolo Abella, José-Guilherme Almeida dos Reis, Rashid Amjad, Philip Bowring, Susan Davis, Janelle Diller, Tayo Fashoyin, Deborah France, Ajit Ghose, K.P. Kannan, Richard Kozul-Wright (UNCTAD), Bob Kyloh, John Langmore, Virgilio Levaggi, Francis Maupain, Steven Oates, Nana Oishi, Stephen Pursey and Hamid Tabatabai.

Annette Schut served as documentalist, and editorial support was provided by Rosemarie Beattie, Sheila Davey and Geraldeen Fitzgerald. Administrative, financial, information systems and secretarial support were organized by Barbara Collins and Clare Schenker, and provided by Rowena Ferranco, Zydre Pember, Judy Rafferty, Véronique Arthaud, Mila Cueni, Sharon Dubois, Catherine Harada, Zohreh Mobasser, and Meral Stagoll. Additional web development support was provided by Michiko Miyamoto and Roberto Zachmann. Research assistance was provided by Renato Johnsson, Andrew Lang, Malte Luebker and Muriel Meunier.

Annex 3: Commission meetings, consultations, and research

Commission meetings

Six meetings of the Commission were held in Geneva on 24–26 March, 2002; 20–21 May, 2002; 12–15 October, 2002; 16–18 February, 2003; 17–20 May, 2003; and 10–12 August, 2003. An open-ended exchange was also held in Geneva from 4–6 October 2003.

In addition to its meetings, the Commission held extensive consultations and dialogues, and drew upon a programme of substantive technical work, organized by the Secretariat.

Consultations

The Commission benefited from an exchange of views with Horst Köhler, Managing Director of the IMF on 12 October 2002, Supachai Panitchpakdi, Director-General of the WTO on 14 October 2002 and James Wolfensohn, President of the World Bank on 18 February 2003.

The Commission also held a series of dialogues around the world, in order to hear a wide range of views and perspectives on globalization. Individual Commissioners and members of the Secretariat participated in 19 national dialogues, seven regional dialogues and nine consultations with key actors, which were held during the course of its work. These engaged a large cross-section of global public opinion involving over 2,000 leaders and opinion makers from governments, business, trade unions and civil society from all regions. Full reports of these dialogues are posted on the Commission website (www.ilo.org/wcsdg).

National dialogues

•	Tanzania	Dar es Salaam, 19–20 August 2002
•	Senegal	Dakar, 26 August 2002
•	Uganda	Kampala, 4 October 2002

• Philippines	Manila, 12 September 2002
• Russia	Moscow, 25 September 2002
• Mexico	Mexico City, 8 October 2002
• Costa Rica	San José, 28 October 2002
• Chile	Santiago, 4 November 2002
• South Africa	Johannesburg, 9 November 2002
• Finland	Helsinki, 13 November 2002
• China	Beijing, 26 November 2002
• Argentina-Uruguay	Carrasco, 2 December 2002
• India	New Delhi, 11 December 2002
• Egypt	Cairo, 21–22 December 2002
• Brazil	Brasilia, 20–21 January 2003
• Poland	Warsaw, 6 February 2003
• United States	Focus groups in Indianapolis, IN, 22 April 2003 Washington, DC, 24 April 2003
• Germany	Berlin, 28 April 2003

Regional and sub-regional dialogues

• Latin America	Lima, 7 December 2002 Santiago de Chile, 1 July 2003
• Asia	Bangkok, 16–17 December 2002
• Europe	Brussels, 3–4 February 2003
• Africa	Arusha, 6–7 February 2003
• Caribbean	Barbados, 9 April 2003
• Arab States	Beirut, 8–9 May 2003

Other dialogues

- Side event at the World Summit on Sustainable Development, Johannesburg, 30 August 2002
- Informal session with civil society organizations at the World Summit on Sustainable Development, Johannesburg, 2 September 2002
- High-level Business Delegation meeting with the World Commission, IOE, Geneva, 16 October 2002
- Dialogue with the International Trade Union Movement, ICFTU and WCL, Brussels, 26 November 2002
- Informal session at the State of the World Forum, Commission on Globalization, Mexico City, 4 December 2002
- Dialogue on "The Social Dimension of Globalization – A Critical Assessment by Civil Society", Thammasat University and Friedrich-EbertStiftung, Bangkok, 17–18 December 2002
- Side event at the World Social Forum, Porto Alegre, 24 January 2003
- Side event "The Values of Globalization" at the World Economic Forum, 25 January 2003
- Roundtable with leaders of non-governmental organizations, Geneva, 6 June 2004

Technical support

An extensive knowledge base was developed by the Secretariat to support the Commission's work. This included a review of the work of previous Commissions, surveys of relevant literature and research, a compilation of policy ideas and experiences, the preparation of a number of substantive papers and gathering of data on trends in the social dimension of globalization. There were also technical consultations with other international organizations, including the United Nations Department of Economic and Social Affairs (DESA), UNDP, UNCTAD, the World Bank, the WTO, and the IMF.

Knowledge Networks, involving policy practitioners, technical experts, academics and other actors, were established to tap expertise on the following subjects:

- Values and goals in the context of globalization
- Local markets and policies in the global context
- Policies for inclusion at the national level: making the benefits of globalization reach more people
- Cross-border networks of production and technology: promoting development and decent work
- International migration: labour mobility as part of the global policy agenda.
- International governance for inclusive globalization
- Globalization and culture.

Gender and employment were addressed as cross-cutting themes.

A series of meetings was organized by the Secretariat to draw on the expertise of these Knowledge Networks; a list is given below. These helped to identify the issues that needed to be addressed, reviewed different policy approaches that could be taken and highlighted options for consideration by the Commission.

Reports of Knowledge Network meetings, a statistical database, an electronic "ideas bank" of policy proposals relevant to the social dimension of globalization, an annotated bibliography and a series of technical papers are being made available on the Commission website (www.ilo.org/wcsdg). Separate arrangements are being made for publication of this material.

Meetings of the Knowledge Networks

•	Globalization and Exclusion	Geneva, 16–17 September, 2002
•	International Migration	Geneva, 18–19 September, 2002
•	Cross-border Networks of Production and Technology	Geneva, 19–20 September, 2002
•	Values and Globalization	Electronic conference, 24–30 September, 2002
•	Local Markets and Policies in Global Context	Geneva, 7–8 November, 2002
•	Regulatory Frameworks in the Global Economy	Geneva, 21–22 November, 2002
•	Governance for Better Globalization	New York, 22 November, 2002
•	Making Globalization work: Expanding the benefits to working families and the poor	Washington, 2–3 December, 2002 (in cooperation with The Brookings Institution and the Carnegie Endowment for International Peace)
•	Trading for Fairer Globalization	Geneva, 6 December, 2002
•	International Migration	Geneva, 16–17 December, 2002

- Globalization, Culture and   Geneva, 30–31 January, 2003
  Social Change   (in cooperation with UNRISD)
- Corporate Social Responsibility   Geneva, 14–15 February, 2003
- Globalization and Labour Market   London, 8 April, 2003
  Adjustment in Developing Countries   (in cooperation with DFID)

Acknowledgements

Many individuals and institutions contributed to the Commission's work. Their contributions are gratefully acknowledged.

Financial contributions

The ILO supported the bulk of the Commission's activities. In addition, funding for specific aspects of the Commission's work was received from the Governments of Denmark, Norway, Switzerland and the United Kingdom.

Support to dialogues and consultations

Many organizations assisted in organizing dialogues and consultations. They included: Al-Ahram Center for Political and Strategic Studies, Cairo; Andean Community; China Development Research Foundation (CDRF), Beijing; Colegio de Mexico, Mexico City; Council for the Development of Social Science Research in Africa (CODESRIA), Dakar; Economic Commission for Africa (ECA); Economic Commission for Latin America and the Caribbean (ECLAC); Economic and Social Research Foundation (ESRF), Dar es Salaam; European Commission, DG Employment and Social Affairs; Federal Ministry of Economy and Labour of Germany; Flemish Ministry for Home Affairs, the Civil Service and Foreign Policy; Friedrich-Ebert-Stiftung, Bangkok; Government of Barbados; Hart Research Associates, Washington DC; International Confederation of Free Trade Unions (ICFTU); International Organisation of Employers (IOE); Institute of Research on International Relations (IPRI) of the Ministry of Foreign Affairs of Brazil; Institute for Studies on Labour and Society (IETS), Rio de Janeiro; Ministry of Economy, Labour and Social Policy of Poland; Ministry of Gender, Labour and Social Development of Uganda; Ministry of Labour and Employment of Brazil; National Economic Development and Labour Council of South Africa (NEDLAC); Office of the President of the Republic of Finland; Office of the President of the United Republic of Tanzania; Public Opinion Strategies, Washington DC; Research on Poverty Alleviation (REPOA), Dar es Salaam; Thammasat University, Bangkok; State of the World Forum, Commission on Globalization; United Nations Non-Governmental Liaison Service (NGLS); World Confederation of Labour; World Economic Forum; World Social Forum.

Significant support was also provided by the ILO field offices. Particular mention should be made of support provided by the Directors and staff of the ILO Regional Offices in Abidjan, Bangkok, Beirut, Geneva and Lima; the Directors and staff of the ILO Subregional Offices in Budapest, Cairo, Dakar, Manila, Moscow, New Delhi, Lima, Port of Spain, Santiago and San José; the Directors and staff of the ILO Offices in Beijing, Bonn, Brasilia, Brussels, Buenos Aires, Dar es Salaam, Mexico City, New York, Pretoria, and Washington.

Contributions to knowledge networks

Many experts participated in substantive discussions or knowledge network meetings, provided written comments, or contributed background papers. They included: Nermin Abadan-Unat, Aderanti Adepoju, Yilmaz Akyuz, Yoginder Alagh, Alice Amsden, Catherine Aniagolu, Abdullahi An-Na'im, Edna Armendariz, Tony Atkinson, Farooq Azam, Jim Baker, Stephanie Barrientos, Graziano Battistella, Noureddine Benfreha, Raj Bhala, Arne Bigsten, Mark Bogan, Jan Breman, Nilüfer Çağatay, Wendy Caird, Marilyn Carr, Manuel Castells, Stephen Castles, Gopal Krishan Chadha, Dan Chiribuca, Martha Chen, Anthony Clunies Ross, Barry Coates, Jeff Crisp, Dan Cunniah, Sriyan de Silva, Simon Deakin, Nitin Desai, Alisa DiCaprio, Zdenek Drabek, Asbjorn Eide, Kimberly Ann Elliott, Korkut Ertürk, John Evans, Richard Falk, Gary Fields, Michael Finger, Augustin Fosu, Torbjörn Fredriksson, Alvaro Garcia Hurtado, Charles Gore, Duncan Green, David Greenaway, Rebecca Grynspan, Basudeb Guha-Khasnobis, Bernhard Gunter, Sanjeev Gupta, Cees J Hamelink, Ulf Hannerz, John Harriss, Pamela Hartigan, Jeremy Heimans, Hazel Henderson, Fred Higgs, Michael Hopkins, Edwin Horlings, Renate Hornung-Draus, Naomi Hossain, James Howard, John Humphrey, Didier Jacobs, Elizabeth Jelin, Richard K Johanson, Emmanuel Julien, Dwight Justice, Naila Kabeer, Evance Kalula, Rashid Kaukab, Neil Kearney, George Kell, Martin Khor Kok Peng, Mwangi Kimenyi, Evans Kituyi, Michelle Klein Solomon, David Kostzer, Zeljka Kozul-Wright, Viktor Kuvaldin, Brian Langille, Frédéric Lapeyre, Ernst Ligteringen, Sachinkonye Llyod, Robert Lucas, Archie Mafeje, Philip Martin, Susan Martin, Joerg Mayer, Sharon McClenaghan, Allister McGregor, Malini Mehra, Claire Melamed, Ronald Mendoza, Jörg Meyer-Stamer, Thandika Mkandawire, Branko Milanovic, William Milberg, John Morley, Oliver Morrissey, Lamiya Morshed, Jill Murray, Sali Nasr, Sopiee Noordin, Anita Normark, Martha Nussbaum, Kingsley Ofei-Nkansah, Rene Ofreneo, Irena Omelaniuk, Banji Oyeyinka, Florence Palpacuer, T S Papola, Ebrahim Patel, Roberta Piermartini, Roger Poole, Carolina Quinteros, Dan Rees, Steve Richards, Lesley Roberts, Virginia Rodríguez, Bruno Roelants, Jorge Saba Arbache, Lloyd Sachikonye, Ignacy Sachs, Ashwani Saith, Saskia Sassen, Rene Scharer, Elliot J Schrage, Kunal Sen, Iddi Simba, Andrés Solimano, Lina Song, Simon Steyne, Seán Siochrú, Alain Supiot, Hiromi Suzumura, Michelle Swenarchuk, Kaarin Taipale, Dirk Willem te Velde, Elizabeth Thomas-Hope, Anthony Tsekpo, Andras Uthoff, Valpy Fitzgerald, Gijsbert van Liemt, Anthony Venables, Anil Verma, Anna Walker, Simon Walker, Kevin Watkins, Jonas Widgren, Meredith Woo-Cumings, Adrian Wood, Ngaire Woods, Zhang Xiao Shan, Gisèle Yitamben.

We also acknowledge the contributions of many ILO staff members, over and above those who participated directly in the work of the Secretariat, for the ideas, suggestions and information they have provided to the Commission's work.

The United Nations Research Institute for Social Development (UNRISD), the Department for International Development of the Government of the United Kingdom (DFID), the Brookings Institution and the Carnegie Endowment for International Peace co-sponsored and helped to organize and manage several of the technical meetings. The Government of Norway hosted a special consultative meeting to support the Commission's work.

Index

Note: Arabic numbers refer to paragraphs; Roman numerals refer to page numbers in the Synopsis; superscript numbers refer to footnotes.

Central Europe 245
charitable donations 471-72
child labour 274, 423, 426, 455, 555
Chile 99, 180, 409
China 92, 181, 341, 409
    economic growth 177, 178
    FDI in 94
    poverty reduction in 91, 201
    unemployment 173
Chirac, Jacques 468
civil liberties 240, 288
civil society organizations xii, 27, 310,
    567-72
    accountability of 569
    global civil society 343, 570
    influence of 343, 568-72
    and international institutions 527, 529, 572
    in national governance 240, 241, 542
    view of globalization 124-29
CLACSO, Buenos Aires 627[117]
cocoa 375, 555
CODESRIA, Dakar 627[117]
collective bargaining 289
Commission on Global Governance 519[102]
Commission on Human Security 491[94]
Commitment to Development Index 456
communications, 10, 310, 573-77, Fig. 9
communism, collapse of 154
comparative advantage 146, 150, 369, 377
competition policy 156, 359, 363, 392-93, 501
conditionality 125, 153, 365, 458
conflicts 25
    civil strife 23, 239
cooperatives 307
corporate governance 122, 242, 244, 548-49,
    556
corporate social responsibility (CSR) 550-59
corruption 244
Costa Rica 67, 100
cotton 375, 376
Council of Europe 319
credit
    and property rights 265
    see also micro-finance
crime
    multinational 223-24
    see also trafficking
cross-border investments 187, 473-74
cross-border movement of people 134, 319, 360,
    428-46
    and multilateral rules xii, 354, 416, 616
    see also international migration
cultural heritages, local 299, 301, 309-12

culture 310
    diversity of 41, 50
    impact of globalization on 68, 107, 222, 574
currencies, common regional 316

David and Lucile Packard Foundation 472
debt crisis 127, 151
debt relief 127, 412, 459-62
decent work 100, 280-84, 288, 492-93
    full employment 494-97, 502
    in global production systems 498-501
    as policy goal 502-10, 594
    see also labour standards
decentralization 294, 300, 539
decision-making
    in multilateral system 520, 521
    role of developing countries in 27, 347, 349
democracy 238, 358
    basis for good governance 240, 519, 521-25
    participatory 15, 293, 329, 572
    representative 15, 572
    spread of 220, 342
democratic accountability 14, 350
developing countries 151, 158, 258, 425
    comparative advantage 89, 105, 369, 377
    economic performance 175, Fig. 3, Fig. 11,
        Tab. 1
    FDI inflows, 168, 180, Fig. 4
    and financial standards 405-6
    marginalization 169, 173, 323, 570, 572
    poverty 69, 182, 256, 274, 295, 461
    role in global institutions 27, 347-49, 522
    skills migration from 207, 432-33, 437-38
    social protection systems 287, 490
    and trade rules 158, 353-56, 381
dialogue x, 618
    and consultations (World Commission) 62-64, 595
    international 49, 55-60
    migration 442-43
    national 584
    trade unions 120-23
    see also Policy Development Dialogues; social
        dialogue
discrimination, labour 423

East Asia 10, 180, 248, 362, 432
    unemployment 195, Fig.13
Eastern Europe 104-7, 180, 245, 248
economic growth
    global macroeconomic policies for 495, 611
    impact of globalization 174-82, Figs. 10 and 11
economic policies
    multilateral agreements 354

global governance x, xi, 225-32, 515
    analytical framework 335-39
    fair rules 359-60
    imbalances in xi, 353-58
    major deficiencies 340-52
    role of nation States xi, 340-41, 348-52, 537-42
    role of non-State actors xiv, 53-59, 342-46, 542,
        545, 559, 586
    see also global policies; international
        institutions
global networks 53, 306, 487, 579
global policies 24, 447-49
    achieving coherence 33, 352, 496, 603-11
    better development of 612-22
    for decent work 502-10
    economic environment 151-55
    economic and social integration 511-14
    institutional support for 630-31
    research support for 623-29
    resources for 450-75
global production systems 140, 159-62, 258
    decent work in 498-501
    and FDI 162
    rules for 387-99
    social dialogue in 563-66
global rules *see* rules
Global Social Trust, concept of 471
Global Stakeholder Panel initiative on Globalization
    and Global Governance 585[113]
Global Union Federations 564
Globalization Policy Forum, proposed xiv, 593,
    619-21
governance 21, 34, 58
    local 293-301
    national 233-37, 238-45
    networked 578-82
    and ODA 458
    see also corporate governance;
        global governance
Grameen initiative 308
Group of 7 (G7) 348
Group of 8 (G8) 532, 560
Group of 10 (G10) 348
Group of 20 (G20) 406[56]

health 249, 479, 609
Helsinki Process on Globalization and
    Democracy 586
HIV/AIDS 85, 273, 319, 455, 479
human dignity 16, 18, 41
human rights 6, 21, 34, 37, 127, 238, 358
    centrality of 478
    social protection as 491

ICFTU 586, 616
IFIs 15, 120, 344, 352
    and conditionality 125, 153, 365
illicit activities 223, 224
ILO 52, 121, 426, 611, 616
    collaboration with World Bank 510
    Committee on Freedom of Association 423[68]
    Convention on Indigenous and Tribal
        Peoples 478[90]
    and corporate social responsibility 557
    Declaration on Fundamental Principles and Rights
        at Work 40, 373, 418, 421, 552
    Declaration of Philadelphia (1944) 508
    Global Employment Agenda 507
    International Programme for the Elimination of
        Child Labour (IPEC) 426[69]
    Migrant Workers (Supplementary Provisions)
        Convention, 1975 428[70]
    and migration 446
    Migration for Employment Convention,
        1949 428[70]
    and policy coherence 606
    role of 420, 423 (box), 602, 621, 628, 630
    and social dialogue 566
    trade unions and 562
    Tripartite Declaration of Principles concerning
        Multinational Enterprises and Social Policy
        (1977, 2000) 552
    Worst Forms of Child Labour Convention,
        1999 419[61]
IMF 84, 348, 522, 611, 616
    accountability 528-29
    Debt Initiative for HIPCs 460
    and employment 505, 506, 510
    Fourth Amendment to Articles of Agreement 466
    International Tax Dialogue 465
    trade union movement and 561
import-substitution policies 151
income inequality, 198-200, Figs. 16, 17 and 18
India 93, 181, 341, 409, 432
    economic performance 177, 178
    poverty reduction in 91, 201
    Self-employed Women's Association (SEWA) 308
indigenous peoples 124, 211, 286
    rights of 311-12
industrial development 362
industrialized countries
    dominance of 401, 525
    economic performance 175, Table 1
    education and skills in 259, 271
    employment 197
    immigration controls 429
    policy instruments 362, 362[39]

self-employment 196, 261-62, Fig. 15

Senegal 80-81

services, growth in trade in 156, 160, 207, 500

SICA (Central American Integration System) 322[35], 326

Singapore 187

skills 275-77, 482-87

    circulation 437

SMEs (small and medium-sized enterprises), policies for growth 282, 306

social dialogue 242, 566

    and employment policies 283-89, 501

    global production systems 563-66

    in regional integration 329-30

social dimension 13, 21

    impact of globalization on 172, 206-17

    of regional integration 327-31

social equity 34, 238

social protection xiii, 478, 488-91, 616

    and decent work 287

    for self-employed and informal
        workers 264

    State provision 249

Socially Responsible Investment (SRI) 427

socio-economic floor xiii, 287, 476, 491, 627

socio-economic security 171, 357

solidarity x, 41, 127, 335, 580

    globalization with x, 28, 221, 358, 471-72, 633

    local 293, 299

    private initiatives 490

    regional 103

South Africa 308, 342

South Centre, Geneva 627[117]

South East Asia, unemployment 195, Fig.13

Special Drawing Rights (SDRs) 466

standards

    international 380-81

    see also labour standards

State

    effect of globalization on role of ix, 101, 105, 149, 249-51

    provision of public goods 249, 255, 269

    see also nation States

State of the World Forum, Commission on Globalization 585[112]

structural adjustment 13, 234

    policies 152, 413, 461

    and social protection 488-91

sub-Saharan Africa 138, 169

    and Bretton Woods institutions 523, 525

    and debt 169, 182

    HIV/AIDS in 273

ODA for 458

poverty 13, 182, 201

subsidiarity, principle of 302, 518

subsidies 364

sustainable development ix, 21, 290-92, 475, 480

Tanzania 70, 83

tariffs 83, 374, Fig. 2

    escalating 379, 387

tax cooperation 464-65

tax evasion 223

tax havens 354, 464

tax systems

    effect of globalization on 193

    and informal economy 253

    local 303

taxes, global 468-69

technology x, 133, 282, 482-87

    access of developing countries to 147-48, 186, 264, 364, 383, 624

    development of 356

    and globalization 146-48

    TRIPS 380, 479

technology transfer 116

territorial pacts 304, 304[30]

terrorism, global 11, 23, 43

textiles and clothing 377

    and market access xiii, 377-79

Third World Network 580[112]

Tobin tax 468

tourism, global 299

trade 137-38, 149-50

    multilateral rules 368-86

    multilateral trading system 156-58

    and net FDI inflows Fig. 1

    special and differential provisions 367, 369

trade barriers 355, 369, 380

    private cartels 391

    see also tariffs

trade liberalization 137, 183-85, 370-72

    effect on employment and wages 184-85, 506, 627

trade unions

    dialogues with 120-23

    influence of 346, 562

    and international institutions 560-62

    rights violations 423

    see also labour organizations

trafficking in people 96, 223, 319, 428[70], 433

training, investment in 275-76

transparency 350, 390, 392, 398, 527

Uganda 82, 272

UN Commission on Human Rights 602